Twenty Years in E

A Consul-General's Memories of Noted People,
With Letters From General W. T. Sherman

S. H. M. Byers

Alpha Editions

This edition published in 2024

ISBN : 9789362519429

Design and Setting By
Alpha Editions
www.alphaedis.com
Email - info@alphaedis.com

As per information held with us this book is in Public Domain. This book is a reproduction of an important historical work. Alpha Editions uses the best technology to reproduce historical work in the same manner it was first published to preserve its original nature. Any marks or number seen are left intentionally to preserve its true form.

Contents

NOTE FROM THE AUTHOR. ....- 1 -
CHAPTER I 1869 ....- 2 -
CHAPTER II 1869 ....- 6 -
CHAPTER III 1870 ....- 14 -
CHAPTER IV 1871 ....- 20 -
CHAPTER V 1872 ....- 27 -
CHAPTER VI 1872 ....- 32 -
CHAPTER VII 1872 ....- 36 -
CHAPTER VIII 1872 ....- 44 -
CHAPTER IX 1873 ....- 59 -
CHAPTER X 1873 ....- 68 -
CHAPTER XI 1874 ....- 75 -
CHAPTER XII 1875 ....- 84 -
CHAPTER XIII 1876 ....- 98 -
CHAPTER XIV 1877 ....- 107 -
CHAPTER XV 1877 ....- 112 -
CHAPTER XVI 1877 ....- 117 -
CHAPTER XVII 1878 ....- 122 -
CHAPTER XVIII 1878 ....- 128 -
CHAPTER XIX 1879 ....- 131 -
CHAPTER XX 1879 ....- 138 -
CHAPTER XXI 1879 ....- 142 -
CHAPTER XXII 1880–1881 ....- 158 -
CHAPTER XXIII 1881 ....- 173 -
CHAPTER XXIV 1882–1883 ....- 182 -
CHAPTER XXV 1884 ....- 199 -

CHAPTER XXVI 1884 .... - 207 -
CHAPTER XXVII 1885 .... - 223 -
CHAPTER XXVIII 1886... - 237 -
CHAPTER XXIX 1887–90 .... - 248 -
CHAPTER XXX 1891.. - 263 -
FOOTNOTES .... - 275 -

NOTE FROM THE AUTHOR.

While staying in Switzerland and Italy as a consular officer, during a period of well on to twenty years, I kept a diary of my life. Without being a copy of the diary, this book is made up from its pages and from my own recollections of men, scenes, and events. It was during an interesting period, too. There were stirring times in Europe. Two great wars took place; one great empire was born; another became a republic; and the country of Victor Emmanuel changed from a lot of petty dukedoms to a free Italy. It seemed a great period everywhere, and everything of men and events jotted down at such a time would of necessity have its interest. This book is not a history--only some recollections and some letters.

Among the letters are some fifty from General Sherman, whose intimate friendship I enjoyed from the war times till the day of his death. They are printed with permission of those now interested, and they may be regarded as in a way supplementary to the series of more public letters of General Sherman printed by me in the North American Review during his lifetime. They possess the added interest that must attach to the intimate letters of friendship coming from a brilliant mind. Their publication can only help to lift the veil a little from a life that was as true and good in private as it was noble in public.

S. H. M. BYERS.

ST. HELENS, DES MOINES.

CHAPTER I
1869

A LITTLE WHITE CARD WITH PRESIDENT GRANT'S NAME ON IT--A VOYAGE TO EUROPE--AN ENGLISH INN--HEAR GLADSTONE SPEAK--JOHN BRIGHT AND DISRAELI.

In the State Department at Washington, there is on file a plain little visiting card, signed by President U. S. Grant. That card was the Secretary's authority for commissioning me Consul to Zurich. "I would much like to have that little card," I said to an Assistant Secretary, long years afterward. "Most anybody would," replied the official, smiling. "You may copy it, but it can not be taken from the files."

That card, in its time, had been of consequence to me. It took me from a quiet little Western town to a beautiful Swiss city, where I was to spend many years of my life, and where I was to meet people, look on scenes and experience incidents worth telling about. And now it has led to my writing down the recollections of them in a book.

I had served four years, that were full of incident, in the Civil War. At its close the opportunity was mine to enter the regular army with a promotion; but many months in Southern prisons had nearly ruined my health and I declined the proffered commission.

"You did well," wrote General Sherman to me, "to prefer civil to military pursuits; and I hope you will prosper in whatever you undertake. You now know that all things resulted quite as well as we had reason to expect" (referring to the Carolina campaign), "and now, all prisoners are free--the war over."

The years immediately following the war were spent in efforts to get well, and now when this offer to go to Switzerland, with its glorious scenery and salubrious climate, came, I was overjoyed.

On the 23d of July, 1869, my newly wedded wife and I were standing on the deck of an ocean steamer in the harbor of New York. It was the "City of London."

As the sun went down in the sea that night, many stood on the deck there with us, straining their eyes at a long, low strip of land bordering the horizon, now far behind them. It was America. Some were looking at it for the last time. My wife and I were not to see it again, except on flying visits, for sixteen years. The gentle breeze, the summer twilight, the vast and quiet ocean, the limitless expanse, the silence, save the panting of the engines, the white sails and the evening light of distant ships passing, gave us a feeling of far-offness from all that belonged to home.

Shortly the great broad moon, apparently twice its usual size, quietly slipped up out of the sea. At first we scarcely realized what it was, it was so great, so splendid, so unexpected. Moonlight everywhere is calming and impressive to the senses, but at sea, spread out over the limitless deep--with the great starlit tent of the heavens reaching all around and down to the waters, it touches the heart to its very depths. We scarcely slept that night--the sea and the moonlight were too beautiful. We walked the deck and built air castles.

August 3, 1869.--Yesterday our ship entered the Mersey and turned in among a wilderness of masts in front of Liverpool. We walked about some in the city of Gladstone's birth, and that night had our first experience of the quiet comforts of a little English inn. The gentility, the welcome, the home snugness, the open fireplace, the teakettle, the high-posted, curtained beds, all contrasted strongly with a noisy, American tavern, with its loud talk and dirty tobacco-spitting accompaniments. The enormous feet of the Liverpool cart-horses also impressed us.

This morning we called at the American Consulate. The clerk said the Consul was away at the bank. Possibly like Hawthorne, one of his predecessors, he found nothing to do here but look after his salary. Anyway this Consulate is one of the best things in the gift of the President. In Hawthorne's time, the pay was four times that of a Cabinet officer. Some years, the fees equaled the President's own salary.

August 10.--The sights we had most wanted to see in London were the Tower, the Abbey, the Fish Market, the docks, and the fogs; these and Mr. Gladstone. The fogs we did not need to see; we could *feel* them in our very bones. It was fog everywhere. Three people were reported killed the very day we got here--run over by wagons and omnibuses, plowing through the murky thickness. Street lamps are burning in the middle of the afternoon.

Billingsgate Fish Market was not half so wicked as I had heard. It is said to be two hundred years old. It smells as if it were a thousand. There is possibly nothing so interesting to an American elsewhere on English earth, as the "Poets' Corner" in Westminster Abbey, and, next to that, the Tower of London.

The opulence of the London docks also simply amazed us. Imagine an underground wine vault, seven acres in extent. The total vaults of the Eastern Dock Co. measure 890,000 square feet. The St. Catherine Docks cost nine millions of pounds.

John Lothrop Motley, the historian, is American Minister at London. We called. Found him a tall, aristocratic, consumptive-looking man, apparently not over glad to see traveling Americans. He had in his youth been a fellow student of Bismarck. Later, his daughters married Englishmen. Mr. Motley, like some other Americans sent to high office in London, is not extremely popular among his own countrymen. Neither did Grant approve him; but removed him later, spite of his backing by Charles Sumner.

The Secretary of Legation kindly got me a ticket to the gallery of the House of Parliament. It seemed extraordinary good luck, for whom else should I hear speak, that very afternoon, but John Bright, Mr. Gladstone and the future Lord Disraeli. I looked for oratory in Mr. Gladstone and saw none, either of voice, manner or word. The subject possibly required none. It was the Scotch Education Bill. The tall, grave, spare-looking man stood there with papers in his hand, talking in the most commonplace manner. Often he turned to some colleague and looked and waited as if expecting an explanation. At last he sat down suddenly, as if he had got up out of time. Mr. Disraeli had been sitting there, writing something on the top of his hat, which he had just taken off for the purpose. There seemed to be no desks. When I first noticed numbers of the members with their hats on, I wondered if the session had begun. What I noticed about Mr. Disraeli was the long legs he stretched out before him, the dark, intellectual face, the large features, the yellow skin, the long black hair, the Jewish expression. He followed Mr. Gladstone, but in a voice so subdued that I, in the gallery, did not understand a word he said. Burly John

Bright, with his noble face and sturdy mien, followed. He looked like the typical Englishman. He spoke to the bill in an earnest voice and loud enough, but said nothing that I remember. A Scotch member then rose in confusion, mumbled a few words, got scared, mixed up, turned red and sat down. And this is English oratory, I meditated, and called to mind the names of Douglas and Webster and Lincoln and Blaine. I suppose I was simply there on the wrong day.

Sunday.--We spent a rainy Sunday in London, walking about the deserted streets. Every blind was down--there was silence everywhere. We seemed the only people alive in great London town. Our melancholy was added to by having, through misunderstanding, missed a train that was to take us to a friend in the country, where a hot dinner and English hospitality had awaited us.

At the Channel.--Up to this time there had been nothing so interesting and romantic to me in English scenery as the big castle above the white cliffs of Dover. There was the high, sloping, green plateau and the grey old Castle a thousand feet above us--below it was the sea--across the Channel, only thirty miles away, lay sunny France.

CHAPTER II
1869

IN SWITZERLAND--THE ALPS--EMBARRASSMENT IN NOT KNOWING THE LANGUAGE--CELEBRATED EXILES MEET IN A CERTAIN CAFE--BRENTANO--WAGNER--KINKEL--SCHERR--KELLER--AND OTHERS.

We stayed in Paris for a week. Then, one night, we crossed the plains of France, and at daylight saw with beating hearts the Jura Mountains. They were as a high wall of cliff and forest, green, deep valleys and running rivers, between France and the land of William Tell. The afternoon of that day saw us at our journey's end. We were in beautiful Zurich. "Next to Damascus," said Dixon, the English traveler, "I adore Zurich."

That day the Glarus Alps, that usually shine so gloriously in front of the city, were obscured with clouds. But the beautiful lake was there, and old walls, and ivy-covered towers, and all the story of a thousand years.

Zurich.

Zurich was half a mediæval city in 1869. Years have since changed it; its walls and towers have been torn down, and granite blocks and fashionable modern streets take the place, in part, of its picturesqueness, as we saw it at that time.

Pretty soon I was, in a way, representing my country in a republic five times as old as our own. My predecessor recognized that he had been "rotated" out of office. He knew American party customs and turned over to me a few chairs, a desk, some maps, a flag, some books, some accounts and an enormous shield that hung over the door with a terrible-looking eagle on it, holding a handful of arrows. This was the coat of arms.

Living was cheap in Switzerland in the seventies. For one whole year we stayed in the "Pension Neptune," a first-class place in every sense. Our apartment included a finely furnished salon, a bedroom, and a large room for the consulate. For these rooms, with board for two persons, we paid only $3.00 per day. Just outside the pension, workmen were laying street pavements of stone. They worked from daylight till dark, for forty cents a day. The servants in the pension were getting ninety cents a week and board. The clerk in the consulate was working for $300 a year, without board. Good wine, and we had it always at dinner, was a franc a bottle. Things have changed since then. Switzerland is a dear country to live in now.

In the "Neptune" we found the interesting family of Healy, the American artist. He had painted half the famous men of Europe, even then. There, too, was the family of Commander Crowninshield, distinguished of late days as an adviser of the President in the Spanish War.

What we were to do now, was to learn the French and German languages. Good teachers received but two francs, or forty cents, a lesson, and the necessity of the situation impelled us to hard study.

One evening, shortly after our arrival at Zurich, we were out boating with some friends, on the beautiful lake. There were myriads of pretty water-craft, filled with joyous people, circling all about. On a floating raft near by, a band of music was playing airs from Wagner. Zurich was a Wagner town. It was nearing sunset, when suddenly I happened to cast my eyes away from the people and the boats toward the upper end of the lake. "Look at the beautiful clouds," I exclaimed. My companion smiled. "They are not clouds," said he. "They are the Glarus Alps." It was the fairest sight I ever beheld in my life. Some clouds on the horizon had suddenly floated away, and the almost horizontal rays of a setting summer sun were shining on the white snowfields and ice walls of the mountains, turning them into jasper and gold. "That is what we call the 'Alpine glow,'" continued my friend. "It is like looking at the walls of Paradise," I exclaimed. Pretty soon the sun went down behind the Zurich hills, the jasper and the gold faded from the ice and the rocks of the distant mountains, a cold gray-white, striving to keep off the coming darkness, fell upon the scene. It was the mountains putting on their robes of night. These were the scenes that I was now to live among. Music, they say, takes up the train of thought, where common words leave off. That night, by the waters of Lake Zurich, the soft strains of well-tuned instruments expressed a delight for me that tongue could not utter or pen describe.

Switzerland is full of scenes as glorious as this Glarus range, but this scene here, we were to have from our dining-room window always.

September 5.--The consul of the French Empire called to-day to pay his respects to the consul of the great republic. My consular experiences were about to commence. I was in a dilemma. My Swiss clerk, who spoke six languages for twenty-five dollars a month, had stepped out. I, a plain American, spoke no language except my own.

"Bonjour, Monsieur," cheerily chirped the Frenchman. I advanced, and, seizing his neatly gloved hand, said "Good morning" in the plainest American. "What! Monsieur, you no parlez Francais? Ah! certainlee. Monsieur he parle Allemand. Monsieur speak a leetle Dutch?" he continued, bowing and smiling. "I am sorry," I interrupted in embarrassment. "No Dutch--no Francais." "Oh! Monsieur no understand. No, no. Ah, si, Monsieur, he speak Spanish, certainlee--Spanish better--Spanish better--very fine--Americans all speak Spanish--veree." Again I shook my head, and again the consul bowed, and I bowed, and we both bowed together; and, after a few more genuflections and great embarrassment, he smiled and went backward out of the room. The situation was absurd. Then the Italian consul called, and then the Austrian consul, and similar scenes occurred. The same nonsense, without understanding a word.

I saw at once what was necessary for me to do. Solid months, years, day and night almost, were to be spent learning the language of the people among whom I was to live. Of course, Americans are not born with a knowledge of international law and an ability to speak half a dozen foreign languages.

The routine work of legalizing invoices, attending to passports, getting foolish fellow-countrymen out of jail, and helping others who were "strapped" to get to the nearest seaport, went on. Then there was the doing the polite thing generally by American travelers who called at the office to pay their respects to the consul.

There were many Americans abroad even then. The Swiss hotels reaped great harvests from the rich American and English nabobs who traveled about, displaying themselves and throwing away money.

"I have special charges for all these fine fellows," said the landlord of the Bellevue to me. "Indeed, I have three rates, one for the Swiss, a higher one for foreigners, and a still higher one for the Americans and English. The rooms are the same, the dinners are the same, the wines the same; but the bills--ah, well, I am very glad they come."

Soon I commenced writing reports for our Government. They were asked for on every conceivable subject, from sewer building to political economy. Every American who has a hobby, writes to his Congressman to know what they do about such things in Europe. The Congressman asks the State Department and the State Department asks the consul. *He* must answer in some way.

In this way, and in guarding against frauds on the customs, the time passed.

In the meantime my official position secured me the entrée into Swiss society. It enabled me at last to know Swiss life and to meet men and women worth the knowing. Many of them living in Zurich, or passing there, had European reputations, for the city, like Geneva, had that about it that attracted people of intellect. Zurich is called the Swiss Athens. Novelists, poets, historians, statesmen and renowned professors occupied chairs in the great University, or whiled away pleasant summers among the glorious scenery of the Alps near by.

Lorenzo Brentano.

August 10, 1870.--On this day I made the acquaintance of a remarkable man. It was Lorenzo Brentano of Chicago. He called at the consulate, and, after first greetings, I found out who he was. It was that Brentano who had been condemned to death after the Revolution of 1848 in South Germany. He had been more than a leader; he had been elected provisional president of the so-called German Republic. When the cause failed on the battlefield, he fled to America, and there, for many years, struggled with voice and pen for the freedom of the slaves, just as he had struggled in Germany for the freedom of his countrymen. The seed he helped to sow in Germany, at last bore fruit there, and he also lived to see American slavery perish. He was a hero in two continents. He had made a fortune in Chicago and was now educating his children in Zurich. His son is now an honored judge of the Superior Court of Chicago, a city Brentano's life honored. He was also at this time writing virile letters for European journals, moulding public opinion in our favor as to the Alabama claims. We needed his patriotism. Americans will never know the great help Brentano was to us, at a time when nine-tenths of the foreign press was bitterly against us. I once heard a judge on the bench ask Brentano officially if he wrote the letters regarding America. "Yes," said Brentano, who was trying a case of his own, and was a witness, "I wrote them." "Then that should be reckoned against you," said the judge, so bitter and unjust was the feeling abroad concerning our country, especially among Englishmen traveling or living on the Continent at this time. A kind word for America or Americans was rare.

Through Brentano's friendship, I secured many notable acquaintances. The Revolution of 1848 in Germany was led by the brightest spirits of the country. Its failure led to death or flight. Many had crossed into the Republic of Switzerland and formed here in Zurich a circle of intellectual exiles. They were authors, musicians, statesmen, distinguished university professors. Brentano naturally stood high among them all.

Johannes Scherr.

The Orsini Cafe.--Around a corner, and not a block away from our home, stood a dingy, old building, known as the Cafe Orsini. Every afternoon at five, a certain number of exiles, and their friends, among them men of culture and European fame, met and drank beer at an old oak table in a dark corner of the east room. It was the room to the right of the entrance hall.

Many people frequented the Orsini, for it was celebrated for its best Munich beer, and they could catch there glimpses sometimes of certain famous men. Johannes Scherr, the essayist and historian, called the "Carlyle of Germany," came there, and Brentano, the patriot. So did Gottfried Keller, possibly the greatest novelist writing the German language, though a Swiss. There was Gottfried Kinkel, the beloved German poet, whom our own Carl Schurz had rescued from death in a German prison, now a great art lecturer at the University. Beust, the head of the best school without textbooks in the world; Fick, the great lawyer and lecturer, and sometimes Conrad Meyer, the first poet of Switzerland. Earlier, Richard Wagner was also among these exiles at the Orsini, for he, too, had been driven from his country. That was in the days when the celebrated Lubke, the art writer, was lecturing at the Zurich University, together with Semper, the architect. Often the guests around the little table were noted exiles, who, even if pardoned, seldom put a foot in the German fatherland. The lamp above the table was always lighted at just five in the evening, and the landlord's daughter, in a pretty costume, served the beer. It was my good fortune, through Mr. Brentano, to join this little German Round Table often, to listen to conversations, that, could they be reported now, would make a volume worth the reading.

Gottfried Kinkel.

- 12 -

Richard Wagner.-

Almost nightly, in the winter, at least, the little circle came together, shook hands, and sat around that table. Each paid for his own beer. To offer to "treat" would have been an offense. "How many glasses, gentlemen?" the pretty waitress would ask. Each told what he had drunk and how much cheese or how many hard-boiled eggs he had added; the pretzels were free. "Gute Nacht, meine Herren, und baldiges Wiedersehen," called out the little waitress, as they would again shake hands and go out into the fog and darkness. For years that little waiting-girl lighted the lamp over the table, served us the beer, and found a half-franc piece under one of the empty glasses. She knew what it was for. Had she been a shorthand reporter, she could have stopped passing beer long ago, and the Orsini Café might have been her own.

CHAPTER III
1870

IN THE ORSINI CAFE--GREAT NEWS FROM FRANCE --WHAT THE EXILES THINK--LETTER FROM GENERAL SHERMAN--I GET PERMISSION TO GO AND LOOK AT THE WAR--IN THE SNOW OF THE JURAS--ARRESTED--THE SURRENDER OF THE 80,000 --ZURICH IN THE HANDS OF A MOB--A FRIENDLY HINT.

August 15, 1870.--At six in the evening of this day I was sitting with these other friends in the little corner of the Orsini, when a boy called out:

"Great news from France!"

Yesterday (August 14, 1870) was a day to be forever remembered in history, the day that was to begin the foundation of the German Empire. Louis Napoleon had declared war against Prussia. The news came into our little corner of the Orsini like a clap of thunder--but the exiles around that table went right on drinking beer. Pretty soon, grave Johannes Scherr, the historian, spoke: "It is good-by to Napoleon's crown, that." "They don't know Bismarck in Paris yet," said Beust. Beust did not like Bismarck very much either. "And what can we do?" said another. "Nothing," replied Brentano. "Look on. We are exiles." They all loved Germany.

Twenty years they had been waiting in Switzerland, to see what would happen. A new war tocsin was now really sounding. One empire was dying--great, new Germany was about at its birth. Almost that very night the strongest-souled, most dangerous man in modern times was playing his cards for empire. Even then, in a little German town, Bismarck was manipulating telegrams, deceiving the people, "firing the German heart," deceiving his own Emperor, even. That was diplomacy. A hundred thousand men were about to die! What of it? Get ready, said the man of blood, dig their graves. The hour for Prussian vengeance on the name of Napoleon had arrived. "We are ready for war, to the last shoe-buckle," wrote the French war minister to Louis Napoleon. Bismarck knew that to be a lie. His spies and ambassadors in Paris had not spent their time simply sipping wine on the boulevards. They had been seeing things, and he knew ten times more about the shoe-buckles of the French army than the French themselves did.

The next morning (August 16) things sounded strange enough to American ears in Zurich. A trumpeter rode through every street, blowing his bugle blasts between his cries for every German in Zurich to go home and fight for fatherland. But the exiles were not included and the little meetings in the Orsini went on. Then came a note from Napoleon to the Swiss government: "Can you defend your neutrality?" If not, he would instantly surprise Bismarck and Von Moltke by overrunning Switzerland and suddenly pour his armies all over South Germany. Then the Rhine would be behind him, not in front.

Switzerland saw her own danger. Permit this once, and her name would be wiped from the map of Europe. She knew that. A few days' hesitancy and, for her, all would have been lost. That night at midnight the Swiss drums beat in every valley of the Alps. Twenty-three thousand men, with a hundred cannon, were thrown into the fastnesses and passes of the Jura Mountains, on the French frontier, inside of three days. That was the answer to Napoleon's note, and it changed the destinies of the war. That prompt deed of the Swiss *made the German Empire*. Had the French army got possession of the Alpine passes once, and the Rhine, they would have taken Berlin. The backbone of the German minister at London was what brought on the war at last. England had proposed to join France in requesting the King of Prussia to promise that no German prince should aspire to the Spanish throne. The German minister at St. James indignantly declined to even report the British suggestion to his government. Had he reported England's wishes, Bismarck, possibly, fearing two against him now instead of one, would have given that one little promise, and then the war would not have taken place.

The Americans had the war news by cable almost as soon as the Swiss, who were in sound of the guns.

Shortly I received a little note from General Sherman:

"WASHINGTON, D. C., Aug. 19, 1870.

"DEAR BYERS: Consul H. did not hand me your letter of May 1 st until to-day, else it should have been answered earlier. I was very glad to see that your health was improved by the change of climate and country, and that you had entered on your new career with zeal and interest. So interesting a country as Switzerland, topographically and historically, cannot but prove of inestimable value to you, in whatever after career you may engage, and I feel certain that you will profit by the opportunity.

"At this moment we are all on tiptoe of expectation to hear of the first events of the war begun between France and Prussia. The cause assigned for this war seems to us in this distance so trivial that we take it to be a mere pretext, and that the real cause must lie in the deeper feelings of the two countries. You are so near and so deeply concerned in the lines of traffic that must cross the paths of the contending armies that you cannot escape the consequences. Many Americans will go abroad to see these armies, and as much of the war as will be permitted them, and it may be that you will see at Zurich some of our soldiers. General Sheridan proposes to start at once, and one of my aids, Colonel Audenreid, begs to go along. If Sheridan wishes it I will let Audenreid go, and I will remind him that you are at Zurich, and he may drop in on you, and you can talk over events. You will remember him as one of my aids at Columbia, S. C.

"Always wishing you honor and success, I am truly your friend,

W. T. SHERMAN."

With almost unbroken success for the Prussians, the dreadful war went on all that autumn. The Swiss were neutral and their sympathies were divided, or, if one-sided, they were with the Germans; at least, until that terrible Sedan day, when the Emperor himself fell a prisoner. Then Bismarck wanted more. It was Paris, and French humiliation, he wanted. He had tasted blood, and was he never to have enough? The war went on into the cold and storm of winter. Troops were nearly freezing to death in both armies in the east of France, and half the Swiss people were changing their minds. France was down, and Bismarck must not play the monster.

December, 1870.--I had been a soldier four years in our own great war, and was anxious to see European armies on a battlefield. The commander of the Swiss troops gave me a letter to the leader of the German army next the frontier, and got me passes. It was midwinter, and fearfully cold, and the snow was two feet to three feet deep when I went into the camp of the Swiss, away up in the Jura Mountains. None but well-clad, well-fed men could stand guarding the passes in such weather. What must the French army be doing, not far away, in their worn-out shoes and ragged overcoats? The German army lay not far from Montbeliard, when one cold evening I passed the frontier, and on foot, in the snow, wended my way to a deserted French hamlet. The village just beyond was occupied by a squadron of German Uhlans. Now all was new to me. Not far away that evening I heard the constant thundering of the cannon at Belfort. At the place where I stayed, an attack by the French could be expected any moment in the night. Shortly I saw captains of Uhlans ride to every house in the village and put a chalk-mark on the door, designating what companies were to take it for quarters. There was no room left anywhere, and one could freeze out of doors, unless hugging a camp-fire. An officer of Uhlans took me in and shared his bed on the floor of a cabin. We had a cup of coffee, a glass of brandy and some rations. Nobody knew that night what would happen out in the snow before morning. Next day I could get no horse; but if I could get to General Manteuffel at the next village, I would be all right. On I trudged afoot, but the advanced pickets outside the village could not read my French papers. They fearing me to be a French spy, I was arrested and jogged about very unceremoniously. The General was out somewhere with the troops, and it was hours before I was released. All this time I was kept in a little café that was full of Uhlans carousing and drinking, and acting as if they would like to make short work of me. On the General's return, I was marched up to headquarters, followed by a number of idle soldiers, who anticipated a drumhead court-martial and a little shooting. Of course, I was promptly released with an apology. But there I was, on foot, in the snow, and not a horse to be had, had the King himself wanted it; for the French army, 80,000 strong, was making for a battle, or else for the Swiss frontier. It was the frontier. That very night, Bourbaki, the French commander, shot himself, and the whole army, 80,000 strong, tumbled, pell-mell, into Switzerland, and surrendered. That was January 31st.

It was a sad-looking army that gave itself up to Switzerland. Their red trousers were worn, dirty and black, their shoes were almost gone. Some wore wooden sabots, some had their feet wrapped in rags. Their faces and hands were black as Africans', from close huddling over scanty camp-fires, to keep from freezing. All were discouraged, disgraced, many boiling over with wrath at their incompetent leaders. And these leaders, hundreds of them, were followed by courtesans of Paris, in closed carriages. That was a spectacle for the gods; this host of poor, ragged, freezing privates, wading through the snow of the Alps, followed by a procession of gilded carriages, filled with debauched women, drunken officers and costly wines.

The surrender there in the snow included the whole army of 80,000 men, 284 cannon, 11,000 horses and 8,000 officers' swords.

In a week's time the Swiss had this great army of Frenchmen quartered at the different cities. Zurich had 11,000 of them. They were a happy lot of men, to be out of a dreadful war, and in the hands of a people who bestowed on them every kindness. Many never left Switzerland, but settled among their sympathizers and benefactors for the remainder of their lives.

The war went on. Paris, for months, lay besieged and starving. Then the end came.

Tower in Old Zurich.

At Zurich, the friends of Germany now undertook to celebrate the close of hostilities. Speeches and a banquet were to be had one night at the great Music Hall on the lake. Some consuls were invited to take a part, myself among the number. I was to be asked to send a telegram to our President. At four o'clock of the afternoon a man called at my office and whispered in my ear, "Stay away from that banquet; something is to happen." I remained at home. That night, just as the toast to the new German Emperor was being read, and at a preconcerted signal, every window in the vast hall was smashed in. Stones and clubs were hurled at the banqueters. A large and excited mob of French sympathizers and French prisoners, with side-arms, surrounded the building. Many dashed into the galleries, waved French flags, struck people down with sabers and fired revolvers. The banqueters were in terror till, led by the courageous among them, they broke their five hundred chairs into clubs and drove the rioters from the hall. A few had been killed, a number injured. All the night the mob stayed outside and howled. The police fled for their lives. The militia, called out, stood in line, but when the order to fire on the mob was given, threw down their arms.

Inside the hall, the banqueters stood with clubs in their hands till the grey of morning, waiting the attack. The women, alarmed and terrified, were hidden under the tables, or in corners.

Zurich seemed in the throes of a revolution. The bad elements of every kind joined in the mob, and the Socialists and Anarchists cried out: "This is the people, striking for their rights."

Ten thousand troops were hurried into Zurich from other cantons. Cannon bristled at the street corners, and placards warned the people to stay in their houses. A battery was posted in the street in front of our door. Climbing up on to the terrace by the minster, I saw a terrible mob below, and watched a cavalry squadron ride through it with drawn sabers. The mob gave way, and the alarm was at an end. Murders had been committed, and many men were arrested and punished. The man who had kindly whispered to me to keep away from the banquet, fled. He was afterward condemned, and is to this day a fugitive in England.

CHAPTER IV
1871

THE PARIS HORRORS--SOME EXCURSIONS WITH LITERARY PEOPLE--BEER GARDENS--A CHARACTERISTIC FUNERAL--FUNERAL OF A POET'S CHILD--CAROLINE BAUER, THE ACTRESS--A POLISH PATRIOT--CELEBRATING THE FOURTH OF JULY AT CASTLE RAPPERSCHWYL--THE ST. BERNARD--THE MULES AND DOGS--ON A SWISS FARM--FOR BURNING CHICAGO.

June, 1871.--Horrible news continues to come of the atrocities of the "Communists" in Paris. The most beautiful city of the world is half burned up by its own children. Hundreds of innocent people have been slaughtered. Nobody here understands wholly what it is these Paris murderers want. It looks as if all the criminals and their ten thousand abettors were simply avenging themselves on civilization.

Europe looks on with horror. The world did not know that it contained a whole army of such wretches in one single city. Yet New York has just as many, if they were let loose. There are men right here in Switzerland, the kindliest governed state in the world, who are walking around the streets, quietly thanking God for all the indescribable things at Paris. There was a man in France once (Madame Roland's husband), who killed himself, rather than live longer in a land so given over to dastards. The Paris anarchists will again, and soon enough, have made suicide sweeter than living there. That is what they want. Anarchists would rejoice if all the decent people in the world would kill themselves and get out of it.

This summer of 1871 we made many little foot excursions with the Brentanos, the Kinkels, or the Scherrs. The whole party was always more or less literary. Even Mrs. Scherr had written her book, much liked by German housewives. These afternoon walks have been to points along the beautiful lake or to some near valley, and often to the Uetliberg or to Rüssnacht. We always turned up at some simple country beer garden, with its quiet tables under shady bowers, where the beer and the pretzels were good, and the view fine of lake and mountain.

What delightful times we have had with our cheap lunches of black bread, beer and cheese and much talking! We walked home by dusk, always stopping at many a vantage point, to look in wonder at the sunset and the gorgeous glow on the Alps. I never saw these sunsets in the Alps without thinking of another world. They seemed to belong to something more beautiful, more lasting than our mere lives. If I spoke of it, however, Scherr would shrug his shoulders and say, "Ich glaub' es nicht. Wir werden es nur hoffen," and once he added: "The whole world is but a graveyard. Above the door is written *The End.*" Mrs. Scherr always smiled and said, "No, it is not so, what he says. What is all that grandeur that you see over there in the mountains for? Surely not only for a little party like us to gaze on, of an afternoon, and then say good-by to, forever. No, it is not true. I expect to see the beautiful mountains, and with these friends, too, a thousand years from now."

Alas! sooner than we knew, she was to look beyond these Alps. A heart trouble, aggravated by the *deeper* heart trouble of a mother, through a wayward son, suddenly terminated her life. Just after leaving our home, one day, where she had been calling, she fell dead upon the steps of St. Peter's church.

I was present at this friend's funeral, conducted in accordance with German Swiss custom.

An old woman had carried the funeral notices to the friends. They were printed on large, full sheets of paper, with black edges an inch wide. The woman, in delivering these messages, was in full black, and carried with her an enormous bunch of flowers, apparently a symbol of her office. At the appointed hour I found all our male friends at the house of mourning. It was designated by a broad, black cloth stretched across the front of the building and running up the stairway. Here, in a room denuded of all carpet and furniture, I found Prof. Scherr, waiting to receive the condolence of the invited friends.

"To the left," said the old messenger woman, who had brought the death notices. She stood in the hall, beside an urn, into which friends put their black-edged cards. Again she held a bunch of flowers. All, as they entered the room, turned to "the left," where they silently grasped the Professor's hand a moment, and then took their places, standing in a line along the four walls of the room. No one spoke. There was utter silence. All had tall hats and wore black gloves. Those who had not been invited by card, remained in the street, to join the procession as it left the house. There was not a woman in sight anywhere, save the old messenger. Just as the church bells were ringing the hour, the messenger called in at the open door: "Gentlemen, it is three o'clock," and the little procession of friends followed the Professor down to the rear of the hearse. There had been no ceremony. The body, during the waiting, lay in a plain coffin in the lower hall. The day before, we had called to have a last look at our friend. To us, accustomed to American ostentation over the dead, the extreme simplicity seemed shocking. She was in a plain, white cotton robe. The coffin, or pine box, was not even painted. But it was not indifference nor littleness, this simplicity. It was a custom. A hundred years ago in Switzerland, people were buried in sheets, and without any coffins. Our friend was borne to the chapel in the graveyard, followed by many people, all on foot. There was no carriage, save the hearse. There was a short address in the chapel, no singing or prayers; then the body was carried out to the grave. Each of us threw a spray of evergreen, or a bit of earth, into the grave. When the friends had mostly gone, the Professor looked long and sadly into the grave, lifted his hat to her who had been his helpmeet, and silently and alone walked away. The funeral had been characteristic of the country; plain, and simple, and impressive. To the Swiss, the ostentation and the gorgeous casket at American funerals are not only unbecoming, but a sacrilege and sin. "What good can we do the poor dead bodies?" said Kinkel to me one night at the Round Table in the Orsini. "If you have something to do for a man, do it for him while he lives, and not to his poor, senseless dust."

Kinkel carried out his theory when his beloved daughter died. They came first to my wife, to have her select them a little black crepe--that was all--and a plain board coffin, and some flowers. All her schoolmates must be invited to come and stand by her grave. When the coffin containing his most loved of earth was lowered, the good, gray-haired poet bared his head, stepped to the side of the grave, and, with eyes full of tears, made a touching speech. It was about the child's goodness in life, its sweetness and sunshine, and its father's and mother's loss. Deep emotion filled all present. The children sang a song, and then strewed many flowers upon the grave.

"I will never see her again," he said to me long days afterward. "Like all beautiful, changing things, she has become a part of the beautiful universe. I know her breath will be in the perfume of the flowers, and she will linger in the summer wind." He spoke in sincerity, but the beauty and poetry of his belief had little comfort for us, who also had lost, but with an absolute faith that we should find our buried one again.

In one of our little excursions, Professor Kinkel took us to see the celebrated actress, Caroline Bauer, now the Countess Plater. She and her husband, a rich Pole, who has good claims on the throne of Poland, live on an estate overlooking Lake Zurich. They received us all with great courtesy, and insisted on our having lunch with them on the terrace. The whole estate, not large, is surrounded by a high stone wall, and inside of that a line of trees and hedges higher still. The Countess is seventy, white haired, good looking, genial and happy as a girl. She played several airy things on the piano for us, and would have danced a jig, I think, had Professor Kinkel but said the word. In her heyday of beauty and fame she was the morganatic wife of the King of Belgium. But little was thought of that, for she showed us his picture hanging in the drawing-room, with pride. She and Kinkel talked and laughed much about things that were Greek to us. When we were leaving, the white-haired old beauty followed the white-haired old poet out to the garden gate, and gave him a good-by kiss. It was, in fact, a pretty and touching scene. The Count owns the great Castle of Rapperschwyl at the end of the lake. It contains a Polish museum. One Fourth of July, later, he invited all the Americans to celebrate the day there, and sent a steamer, with music and flags, to carry us up to his banquet. The flags of lost Poland were intertwined with the flags of the United States.

August, 1871.--Next to Westminster Abbey, in London, I have always wanted to see the St. Bernard pass, with its hospice and its dogs. At Martigny, the other day, my wife and I hired a man and a mule to help us up the pass that gave Bonaparte so much trouble. The man's name was "Christ." He often addressed the mule as "you diable." We walked, rode and climbed past the most poverty-stricken villages in the Dranse valley I ever saw in my life. This should be called the valley of human wretchedness. We reached the famous stone hospice on the top of the pass late at night, in a storm of sleet, and tired to death. We had overtaken a German student on the way, and our poor mule had to drag or carry four of us up the worst part of the pass. The thunderstorm also made us overdo ourselves. My wife sat on the saddle; the student hung to the mule's tail; I hung to one stirrup, and Christ to the other. I am glad it was dark, for the scene was not heroic, like that of Napoleon leading his army over the mountains.

The monks met us at the hospice entrance, and gave us places to rest for an hour. To me, who was utterly exhausted and used up, they gave drams of good, hot whisky.

An hour later they took us down to the Refectory, where we had a substantial supper of hot soup, bread, potatoes, omelets, prunes, and also wine. A fire blazed in the immense fireplace, for it is chilly and cold up here even in August. A wind was now blowing outside, and it was very dark. We were glad to sit around the fire with some of the monks and tell them strange things about the country we came from. One of them spoke English, a few of them German.

These zealous monks live up in this inhospitable pass solely to rescue and aid lost travelers. Thousands of poor men, seeking labor in better climates, walk over this pass to Italy every season. Many lose their way and are hunted up by the noble St. Bernard dogs; many freeze to death, and the monks have piled their unidentified bodies up out there in the stone dead-house. There is not enough soil on this rocky height for a grave. And the air is so rarefied that graves are not needed; the dead simply dry away at last, or, in their half-frozen condition, remain like unembalmed mummies. The high air is ruinous to health, and the monks after a few short years go down into the Rhone valley to die, while others for another little space take their places.

The next morning I climbed through an open window into the dead-house. The dead found on the pass during twenty years either lay on the floor or stood against the wall. It was a hideous spectacle, and yet numerous of the bodies were lifelike in every feature. They were placed in there just as they were found. All have the clothes on they wore when they were lost. Many are in the same attitude of despair and agony they had when the storm closed them in its icy embrace. I saw a man with form bent and arms extended as if groping to find his way. A dead woman sat in the corner with her frozen child in her arms. She has been there these dozen years. Some of the faces could yet be recognized had any friend in the world come to look at them.

After breakfast we had a play with a number of the noble dogs that have saved human lives on this pass, time and again. They were very large, mostly tawny colored, extremely intelligent and kind.

The devoted lives of these monks, and these dogs, is something pathetically noble.

A pretty chapel or church is built on to the hospice, and in there one sees a fine marble statue of Marshal Saxe, the hero of Marengo, put there by the order of Napoleon.

*****

There are few large farms in Switzerland. Yet, we stayed last week at one that would do credit in size even to the United States--a couple of hundred acres, mostly given up to grass and stock; every foot as carefully looked after as if it were a gentleman's lawn in London. The owner is what they call a rich Bauer. He is a romantic-looking character, the red-cheeked, burly man, as he goes about among his hired people in the picturesque costume of other days. His wife and daughter also dress in unique costume. They all look very striking on the green meadows away up here on a mountain side, half as high as the Rigi. All this peasant's immediate ancestors were born in this old stone house, and, though he has grown rich here, his life is unchanged from theirs. There are many long, round-paned windows to the rooms, through which the sun pours in and warms the bright-colored flowers with which the window shelves are filled. An old eight-day clock of his grandfather's stands in the corner counting the seconds for these two hundred years. There is not a carpet or a table cloth in the house, but in their stead are old chests, wardrobes and chairs of rare carving, and queer pewter mugs of another age are on the walls.

Their lives are very simple. At dinner they gather around an uncovered pine table, and the family dip soup from the same big bowl. They have an abundance of sour wine, black bread, and such butter, cheese and milk as would make an epicure glad.

The high mountain air about them is bracing; they seem happy and healthful, and, more than most peasants, enjoy the grand scene of Alps and lakes around them.

They set a little side table for us in another room, where we had all the good things a farm affords for two francs a day. Over on the Rigi, just across the lake from us, the tourists and the fashionables are paying ten to twenty francs for food not so wholesome.

October 9, 1871.--"Chicago has burned to the ground and all your houses are burned with it," was the telegram that came to me for Brentano three nights ago. I went to his house at midnight, but he was gone to Freiburg. When he came back, he simply telegraphed, "Commence to rebuild at once." The Americanism of the order set all his Swiss friends to talking. "Had Chicago burned up in Europe," they said, "we would have spent a year mourning over it. Over there they simply rebuild the same day and say nothing."

I commenced a subscription list to help the unfortunate of Chicago, two weeks ago. I have raised 60,000 francs in sums as low as two cents each. I think no town of its population in Europe has given so liberally. To-morrow the cash goes on.

CHAPTER V
1872

LOUIS BLANC, THE STATESMAN--HIS NOVEL COURTSHIP--HIS APPEARANCE--INVITES US TO PARIS--JUST MISS VICTOR HUGO--HIS SPEECH AT MADAME BLANC'S GRAVE--LETTER FROM LOUIS BLANC--ALABAMA ARBITRATORS--SEE GAMBETTA AND JULES FAVRE.

May 9, 1872.--On this day Louis Blanc, the French statesman and historian, called. It was to thank me for a favor I had done on a time for his nephew, but the visit resulted in a friendship that lasted till his death, ten years later.

Louis Blanc had been to the old French Republic (1848) what Brentano had been to the revolution of South Germany. At one time he was the most powerful member of the French Assembly. His writings, more than all things else, brought about the revolution that for a time made him President. In this 1872, he is again in the Assembly of a new republic.

While he stayed at Zurich, we came to know his friend, the vivacious English writer and traveler, Hepworth Dixon. We met often. Once Louis Blanc gave us all a dinner in the Neptun, and Dixon kept the table in a roar, telling of his ridiculous experiences in American overland coaches, in Texas and elsewhere. Of Texas, he had views alarmingly like those of Sheridan. If he owned hell and Texas, he certainly would rent out Texas and live in hell. "And do you tell us *that* is manners down South in the United States?" queried Mr. Louis Blanc, in the naivest manner. "Indeed I do; surely, surely," said the traveler, glancing at Mrs. Blanc, "I saw it a hundred times. Pistols, bowie-knives and swearing. Nothing else in Texas." The kind Frenchman believed it all, for he believed all men honest as himself; only at the close of the dinner did Mr. Dixon let him know that part of his talk was good-natured champagne chaff.

Louis Blanc was the smallest big man I ever saw. He was only five feet high. His head was big enough for Alexander the Great. He was only fifty-nine years old now, but it seemed to me his life and actions went back to the Revolution. His hair was long and black and straight as an Indian's. He had no beard. His face was rosy as a girl's. His little hands were white as his white cravat; his feet were like a boy's; his eyes brown, large, and full of kindness; his voice sweet as a woman's. He dressed in full black broadcloth and wore a tall silk hat. He looked, when walking in the street, like a rosy-faced boy in man's clothes.

His little stature and apparent innocence of half that was going on about him, kept Madame Blanc in a constant worry for fear he would be run over by passing wagons when we were out walking together. "Now run over here quick," she would say to him at a crossing. "Do, my dear, be careful. See the horses coming." Out of doors, or on our little excursions to the mountains, he was perpetually and literally under her wing. She knew the treasure she had in him.

I constantly thought of the story of his past; for was not this little, low-voiced man, walking with us, he who had written "The Ten Years" that had helped destroy Louis Philippe; was not this the same voice that had enchained assemblies, and led France?

Once in a little log schoolhouse in the backwoods of the West, where, as a young fellow, I was teaching, I had read some of his books. Poor as I was, I would have given a month's salary then, to have taken Louis Blanc by the hand. How little I dreamed that some day I should not only take him by the hand, but have his warm friendship.

Louis Blanc's head was all there was to him--that and a great heart.

His marriage to Madame Blanc was a marvel. They met in London. She was German and could speak no French. He was French and could speak no German. He courted her in broken English; and he did well, for a better woman never lived.

Victor Hugo, standing at her grave years later, pronounced one of his noblest eulogies to womanhood. It was an outburst of remembered oratory.

Gambetta.

We were glad of the friendship of such a man as Louis Blanc. He wrote me many letters and invited us to Paris, where we spent some delightful days. His brother Charles was the director of Fine Arts and Theaters there. We had invitations to the best operas and plays. One night I had the pleasure of hearing Gounod lead the Grand Opera House orchestra in his own "Faust." Monsieur Blanc also took us out to see the National Assembly sitting at Versailles, where he was a senator. By good luck we saw and heard Gambetta and Jules Favre. There was no disorder that day, at least, and the speaking was moderate in tone. It was no noisier than our own senate. Louis Blanc also spoke a few words in a quiet way. He wished them to move the Assembly into Paris. "It is all nonsense," he said to me, "this pretense of fearing a Paris mob. 'Do right,' I might have said to them, 'and the mob will let you alone. Do wrong, and--well, it is not far from Paris to Versailles, and there was a time when a mob could escort a king even, from the one place to the other.'" He meant Louis XVI. and his queen, whom the mob led from this same palace to the Paris scaffold.

That evening we went late to dinner. The Blanc's lived on an upper floor of house No. 96, on the Rue du Rivoli. It was rather far. "But why didn't you come earlier?" said Mrs. Blanc, meeting us at the door. "You can't guess who was here." It was Victor Hugo. How sorry we were to have missed the opportunity of seeing the most famous man in France.

It happened later that I was in Paris the day after Victor Hugo's funeral. Everybody said it was like the funeral of a great king. I went up to the "Arc de Triomphe." The great monument built by Napoleon, in his own honor, was covered with wreaths in honor of Victor Hugo. Which man, I thought, does France, in her inmost heart, revere the most--the poet, or the conqueror?

I do not recall much that Louis Blanc said to me that first time in Paris, but something he said in reply to some words of Mr. Dixon's, at the banquet, I wrote down. Dixon was chaffing, in an exaggerated way, about the patriot's idea of liberty. "Ah!" replied Louis Blanc, quoting from another Frenchman, "there is but one thing only, which dreads not comparison with Glory; that is Liberty."

The nephew whom I had obliged, and through whom our friendship with the statesman came about, fell ill in Paris, and Louis Blanc wrote me this:

"PARIS, 96 Rue du Rivoli, Dec. 21, 1871.

"DEAR SIR: It grieves me to the very heart to have to say that my nephew is most dangerously ill. He has now been in bed for about a month, and his precarious state keeps both my poor wife and myself in a state of unspeakable anxiety. This domestic affliction, added to the necessity I am under to spend the whole of my time at Versailles, where the Assembly is now residing and threatens to *settle*, has as yet prevented me from seeing Mr. Washburne. But I have not lost sight of my promise, which I hope I shall be able to fulfill before long. Many thanks for the photographs. That of Mrs. Byers is very far, indeed, from doing her justice. We wish we had a better one. I will write to you soon. In the meantime, accept, my dear sir, our most cordial thanks for the kindness you and your dear wife have shown to our nephew and to ourselves. With my wife's best regards to Mrs. Byers and yourself, I remain, very truly yours,

LOUIS BLANC."

The youth got well, but he did not take much to the Zurich schools after all. He had gone home again, and the uncle decided on letting him go to sea.

"PARIS, 96 Rue du Rivoli, July 14, 1872.

"MY DEAR SIR: Many thanks for your very kind letter. Our nephew is quite recovered, and more than ever determined to be a sailor; so much so, that we have made up our minds to let him go as a midshipman. He will probably start in a month or two.

"My wife and myself speak often of you both and of the friendly reception we met at your hands. May we indulge the hope of returning it soon, on your visit to Paris?

"I would have been glad to make General Sherman's acquaintance, but, unfortunately, I found no opportunity to do so.

"Mrs. Louis Blanc and nephew unite with me in kindest regards to Mrs. Byers and yourself. Most sincerely yours,

"LOUIS BLANC."

September, 1872.--All this past summer the international arbitrators at Geneva have been trying to settle our difficulty with England over the Alabama pirate business. Our Mr. Evarts has won great honor in his management of our side of the matter. Still we have virtually lost the case. A few days ago, the 14th, the treaty was signed. True, it gives us fifteen millions, but we set out with claiming two hundred and fifty millions. What a bagatelle to have to accept after that. The testimony really tends to show that the Rebels never hurt the North with their cruisers a hundredth part as much as everybody supposed they had. It was only a little Captain Kidd sea robbery after all.

It is something, however, to make England come to time, if only a little, for only the other day a London paper declared England will never pay the Yankees a dollar, no matter what the arbitrators say. We shall see.

CHAPTER VI
1872

WILLIAM TELL--THE RIGI IN THE GOOD OLD TIMES--PILATUS--ROSE BUSHES FOR FUEL.

We spent this summer of 1872 at beautiful Bocken, an old castle-like chateau, sitting high above the lake, ten miles out from the city. It was once the home of the Zurich burgomasters, at the time when they exercised the authority of petty kings. The scene from Bocken is very grand. The chateau, with its big hall of knights, its old oak-paneled dining-room, its brick-paved corridors and leaded, round-paned windows, is very interesting. Paid 600 francs for the use of rooms all summer, and reserved the right to return other summers. The days were fair, and it seemed to me I had never seen so many clear, moonlight nights. The lake, shining in the clear moonlight, lay 1,000 feet below us, and, at times in the night, we could even faintly see the snow-covered mountains of Glarus. It was a delightful summer at Bocken, and our joy was doubled by the coming of our firstborn.

Bocken.

More than one of this summer's excursions was to the scene of the Tell legends on Lake Luzern. I knew the legends were already being doubted, even by some of the Swiss, but I hoped, by diligent searching among certain half-forgotten archives in the old arsenal at Altorf, to find something new. I was not wholly disappointed; I saw a musty document there that told of the building of the chapel to Tell on the "Axenstrasse." That was in 1388, only *thirty-one years after Tell's death*. The document gave the amount of wages paid to hands, the amount of wine furnished the workmen, and a statement that one hundred and fourteen persons who had known Tell were present at the dedication. On the supposed spot of Tell's birth, another stone chapel was erected in 1522. There is also in this museum a copy of a proclamation of four hundred and ninety-four years ago, by the Council of Uri, ordering all good Christians and patriots to make yearly pilgrimages to Burglen, because it was the birthplace of William Tell. This document was discovered in 1759, but was burned up in a fire at Altorf, about 1779. The copy, however, is regarded as genuine. The question arises, why did a poor little village community ever go to the expense of building these chapels, if they had no certain knowledge of the existence of their hero, and why were the citizens making these excursions to Tell's birthplace at that early time?

Buerglen, Tell's Birthplace.

In this old arsenal at Altorf are preserved the battle flags borne by the Swiss at Morgarten in 1315, only eight years after the death of Tell. The genuineness of these flags historians have not doubted. Neither is the old Swiss story of that battle in dispute. If the ancient Swiss could know of this battle, and save their flags, why should they not also know the facts as to Tell, at the time they were building chapels to him? If they do not, these chapels remain as monuments to the utter foolishness of a people.

The tradition as to his shooting an apple from his boy's head is of no earthly consequence; true or untrue, it has no more to do with the Swiss patriot's having served his country than the story of the cherry tree has to do with the patriotism of Washington. Tyrants, compelling enemies to tests of archery under great risks, were nothing uncommon in even other lands than Switzerland, and even this little incident in Tell's life may have been true. For myself, I am satisfied that a patriot named William Tell existed, and that his hot-headed love of freedom, and his recklessness, precipitated a revolution in the Alps. In these later days his killing even a tyrant would probably brand him as a common freak or an assassin. Time and history mollify many things.

The chapel at the Axenstrasse was about to fall into the lake, while I was in Switzerland. Its restoration was decided on. Knowing that I had interested myself in the Tell traditions, and at my request, the authorities allowed me to take away the stone step in front of the old altar, to place in the Washington monument. I secured official testimony as to the block, had a proper inscription put on it, and sent it to Washington as a souvenir of Switzerland's greatest tradition. It is now in the Smithsonian Institution, being regarded too valuable a relic to hide away in the monument.

Now that we could speak the language, we made delightful excursions to the mountains. I had determined to write a book on Switzerland,[1] and regarded it necessary to see, not only the Alps, but Alpine village life, and everything characteristic of the country. The result was that we went on foot to almost every valley and village, and climbed not a few of the famous mountains. I now became a member of the Alpine Club. The Rigi we climbed oftenest of all. There was no such thing as riding up, no easy railway carriages, then. People climbed mountains on foot, and the names burned on our Alpine stocks had a meaning. Many and many a Saturday noon we took the train at Luzern, climbed up the Rigi through the woods alone, on the Arth side, and stayed there till Monday morning. We usually got to the top in three hours. Daylight of Sunday saw us out on the high plateau, looking at that great sight, the rising of the sun in the Alps.

Living among the mountains was glorious then, and *cheap*. Many a time, in those days, we have had lodgings and meals at four francs a day, at the Rigi Staffell, where once the poet Wordsworth tarried. And at Michaels Kreutz, a height near by, two and one-half francs for pension was our usual expense. We traveled much in second-class cars. Everybody did this, and we were in the mode. Often when I was alone in the mountains, I went third-class even, and was as well off for sightseeing as I would have been in a Pullman palace car.

The Alpine views from the Rigi in good weather are almost beyond description. One must see them to realize their splendor. Chains of snow mountains are in the distance, and thirteen blue lakes shining at the Rigi's foot. It is only six thousand feet high, but unsurpassed as a point for seeing Swiss scenery.

Sometimes I went up Pilatus alone. It is higher than the Rigi, and near by. The climb was five hours, and I always slept in the little Senn hut, with the cowboys. The cattle, with their tinkling bells, occupied half the stone building. Cool autumn nights I have sat there till midnight, talking with the cowboys, before a big fire made of dried Alpine rose bushes. There were simply acres of roses on Pilatus then, and the Senns were glad to get rid of the shrubs by burning them. I never felt in such perfect health in my life, as in the bracing air on Pilatus Mountain, and the fact that tourists never knew the way up there made life among the goats and the roses immensely enjoyable. For years, ever since my imprisonment in the South, I had suffered horrors with headaches and migraine. These frequent stays in the air of the higher Alps were slowly curing them.

CHAPTER VII
1872

GENERAL SHERMAN VISITS US AT ZURICH--LETTERS FROM HIM--SWISS OFFICERS ENTERTAIN HIM--HIS LAKE EXCURSION--HE EXPLAINS HIS GREATEST CAMPAIGN TO THEM--HE IS ENTERTAINED AT THE SWISS CAPITAL--LETTER FROM GENERAL DUFOUR.

August, 1872.--General Sherman had written me late in the previous Autumn of his intention to visit Europe. Admiral Alden was appointed to the command of our squadron at Villa Franca, and invited the General to sail with him in his flagship, the "Wabash." They left on Nov. 11, 1871. In his note he had said, "I am certainly hoping to arrange my route so as to pay you a visit." This rejoiced us greatly. I heard nothing more till January 16th, when he sent me another little note from Marseilles:

"Marseilles, France, Jan. 14, 1872.

"Dear Byers: You will have seen in the public journals that I am adrift. Of course, during my travels I intend to come to Zurich to see you, but the time when is uncertain. Now the season is not favorable, and I find it to my interest to stay near the Mediterranean till spring. I left my ship at Gibraltar near a month ago. Have been through Spain and the south of France, and am now on my way to rejoin the ship at Nice. We expect to spend all of February in Italy, March in Egypt and the East, April in Prussia, and I expect to swing round by Dresden, Vienna and Munich to Zurich in May. I hope then to find you in good health. Should you have occasion to write me, a letter to the care of the United States Consul at Nice will be forwarded. With great respect, your friend,

W. T. Sherman."

In a month he wrote again, this time from Italy. On Feb. 8th I had written him of an intended military demonstration on the part of the authorities, in his honor, when he should come to Zurich. This he was adverse to, as his note indicates:

- 36 -

"NAPLES, Feb. 28, 1872.

"DEAR BYERS: I have received yours of Feb. 8th, and avail myself of about the last chance to write in reply. It will be some time before we can possibly approach Zurich from the direction of Vienna, and I suppose by that time I will be pretty well used up; yet, if I can do anything to please you, will do my best. Please say to the gentlemen of Zurich that when I reach Zurich, the less display of even a volunteer or militia force, the better; but I will leave it to your own good sense to do what is best for them, and for me. Maybe it would be better to postpone all preliminaries till you hear from me at Vienna. We embark to-morrow for Malta and Alexandria, Egypt, and it will be some time before we turn up again in the direction of Moscow and St. Petersburg. Our aim is to cross the Caucasus to the Caspian, to Astrachan by the Volga, to Nishni, and so on to Moscow; so, you see, I have a good, long journey yet before me. Meantime, I hope you will continue well. As ever, your friend,

W. T. SHERMAN."

Again there was a silence till spring. General Sherman did not carry a newspaper reporter around with him, to report his journeys and his doings. He was traveling as a private gentleman, seeing, and not being seen. At least, this was what he wished. He had gone to the far East, had come back to Constantinople and crossed the Caucasus Mountains. In May he wrote again from St. Petersburg:

"ST. PETERSBURG, May 30, 1872.

"DEAR BYERS: My party is now reduced to myself and Colonel Audenried, Fred Grant having gone to Copenhagen to see his aunt, Mrs. Cramer, who is now on the point of going to America. I don't now know whether Grant will rejoin me at Vienna or go direct to Paris, to see his sister Nellie, and await us there. At all events, Audenried and I start at noon to-day for Warsaw, then Berlin, Dresden, Vienna, etc., to Zurich, where we ought to arrive between the 15th and 20th of June. I prefer much not to be complicated with private engagements or displays of any kind, for it takes all my time to see the country, and it is awfully tiresome to be engaged day and night in receiving and returning calls. I hope you will appreciate this, and have no preparations made till we arrive, and then if I can do you any service by seeing your friends, I will do my best. Truly your friend,

W. T. Sherman."

Early in August he and Colonel Audenried were with us in Zurich. No public demonstration took place on his arrival. It was as he had wished. We took him out to Bocken, our home on the lake, and had a few delightful days with him there.

I recall that on the first day we had dinner spread underneath the trees, out on the terrace of Bocken. The blue lake lay a thousand feet below us, the white mountains shone in the distance, behind us were high hills covered with evergreen forests. About the chateau were bright meadows and rich vineyards. There is scarcely a scene more beautiful in this world. Yet, I was surprised how little it affected him. In the presence of such grandeur, he seemed at that moment unimpressionable. He was a man of moods. I called his attention to the glorious view. "Not more beautiful," he said at last, "than the lakes near Madison. I think of them when I see this. I like American scenery better than any of it. It is the real, native thing in our country. Man has done nothing there. Here, in Europe, so much is artificial." Yet there was nothing artificial around him here; unless it were the much-vaunted, little, red, wooden-looking Swiss strawberries on the table. He wondered how we could adopt the Swiss way of pouring wine on them, instead of cream and sugar. The big cake in the center of the table was decorated with preserved fruits. "How singular that is, isn't it?" he said; "real Dutch." But he liked it for all that. He liked, too, our simple table, though an American dish or two had been prepared in his honor; and he had a relish for good wine, but was moderate in its use. When we had the champagne, I proposed his health. "No," said he, gallantly, rising to his feet, "we drink the health of Mrs. Byers." "Both together then," I said.

He was happy when I gave him a cigar. The scene began to have some interest for him. It was finer than Madison after all. I think the dinner increased his appreciation. The practical side of what he saw was always in his mind. He measured the near hills with his eye and guessed their height. "North must be right over there," he said, pointing, though the sun was not shining. The snow mountains were twenty miles away--not thirty, as we had stated. He was sure he "never missed on distances." But he did this time. He climbed up to the winemill in the barn loft, examined the presses below, took hold of the queer scythes of the mowers, and undertook to describe an American mowing machine to a peasant, who did not understand a word of English. In an hour or so he was acquainted with everything practical about the place.

At supper he ridiculed the American ways of traveling abroad. "'Tourists' is the right word for them," he said. "They are not observing travelers at all. Their time and money is thrown away." He told of an American girl who rode one hundred miles in a railroad car with him, through the most interesting part of Spain, and read a yellow-backed novel all the way. "I never go to a new place, but I know all about it," he said; "its topography, geography, history. A thousand times my habit of observing has afterward been of use to me." He told how, when he was a young lieutenant in the army, stationed in Georgia, his comrades spent their leisure Sundays reading novels, card playing, or sleeping, while he himself went riding or walking everywhere, exploring every creek, valley, hill, mountain, in the neighborhood. *"Twenty years later the thing that most helped me to win battles in Georgia was my perfect knowledge of the country, picked up when I was there as a boy.* I knew more of Georgia than the rebels themselves did." He insisted on our acquiring a habit of observing everything, learning everything possible. "You don't know how soon you will have use for the seemingly useless thing that you can pick up by mere habit." He related how, when he captured a train and telegraph station down South once--[It happened that I had been present on the occasion]--he called for some one among the privates to try to take off messages. His own operator was not at hand. A young soldier, who had once picked up a little telegraphing as an amusement, stepped forward and took a rebel message from the wire that turned out to contain information of vast importance to the whole army.

August 4.--Yesterday, to make him more comfortable, Mrs. B. had had a bed placed for the General in our little front salon. "I won't have it there at all," he said. "There shall be no trouble for me. Back it goes into the bedroom. Give me a cot in the hall--that's what soldiers like." The bed went back.

At noon, a very swell company of cadets came up from Horgen to do the General a little honor. I happened to be away, and, as the captain could speak no English, and the General no German, a funny scene followed. They drew up in line and saluted, and the General saluted in return. Then he made a good-natured, funny, little speech in English. They all laughed, and seemed to think it good, gave him a cheer, fired their guns and went back to the lake. The captain afterward asked me what it was the General said. I told him that he praised their company as being one of the nicest he ever saw, and said if they would stack guns and come to the house, they should drink to his health in some good champagne. "Mein Gott! and did he say *that*," said the captain; "and we, big fools, just walked off and missed it all."

General Sherman's memory for names, places and incidents was certainly phenomenal. He had never been in Russia before, yet, in telling us of his delightful trip over the Caucasus Mountains, he recalled all the nearly unpronounceable names of villages and mountains along his route. He had seen and investigated everything along his way, and talked with half the people he met, whether they understood him or not. He was so kindly in his ways, so sincere, no one ever took his addressing him amiss. I could not help at times comparing him in my mind with what I had read of the Duke of Wellington.

Colonel Audenried amused us not a little, by telling, *confidentially*, at the supper table, of the great excursion the General and his party had tendered them by the Sultan on the Black Sea. The Sultan's magnificent private yacht, manned by sailors in gilt jackets, carried them everywhere. Wines and lunches and dinners were only to command. It was a beautiful, oriental time; but, when they got back, a bill of $600, I think, was presented to the General, on a silver platter. He gracefully paid it, and said nothing.

August 5.--To-day there was a flowing of champagne, in *fact*. The army officers, at Zurich and in neighboring towns, chartered a steamer and arranged for a banquet in the General's honor at the Castle of Rapperschwyl, at the upper end of the lake. The day was beautiful, and it was a fair sight, as the steamer, decorated with Swiss and American flags, filled with officers in gay uniforms, and with music playing, turned into Horgen, the landing nearest to Bocken. The villagers fired cannon, waved flags and cheered, as General Sherman, in full

American uniform, went down from Bocken to the landing. A naturalized Swiss-American kept a restaurant near to the landing. He had had an enormous American flag especially made, to hang out as the General went past his place to the steamer. The General took off his hat to it, called a pleasant word to the owner of the flag, and the man was happy. Years afterward he kept that flag as the one the great General had greeted. He hung it out only on great occasions. I doubt not it will be wrapped about him at his grave. How easy it is for the great to make men happy.

The excursion on the lake, and the banquet, were delightful. In the shadow of the old castle, the talk and the toasts were about two Republics. The name of William Tell was being spoken with the name of Washington. The Swiss Dufour and the American Sherman were linked together, as the Swiss officers touched glasses. It is an international episode like this that helps, more than all the tricky diplomacy of the world, to give peoples a kind understanding of each other.

Sherman was amazed to find out that these officers, all the preceding winter, had (at their officers' school) been studying his campaigns. Every move about Kenesaw Mountain, every day of his assaults on Atlanta, were as familiar to these men as to members of his own staff. I never in my life saw a more interesting scene than when, under an awning, on the deck of the steamer, these Swiss officers stood around him, while, with a big military map before him, he traced for them the route of the "March to the Sea." It was a picture for an artist. It was as if Napoleon had described to a listening group of American officers, the campaign of Italy. All were greatly impressed with the great simplicity of his talk, his kindness of manner, as with pencil he marked for them each interesting spot of the campaign. It was a great thing to have the most famous march of modern times explained to them in so friendly a way, by the commander himself.

"I will never forget this day," said more than one officer to me, as we left the steamer that evening.

They drew lots for the possession of the map with the General's pencil marks, and it fell to Colonel Schindler, the Consul for Austria. "It shall be an heirloom forever in my family," said the Colonel to me one evening at his tea table.

August 6, 1872.--In the evening, my wife and I gave a reception to General Sherman at the rooms of the Bellevue hotel in the city. It was attended by our personal friends, by Americans then in the city, by a number of officers and by many prominent people. The General was in full uniform. Numbers spoke English with him, and with others he spoke tolerable French, that he had learned, probably at West Point.

On the next day it rained, but he was off for the St. Gotthard pass. We protested against his starting in bad weather. "Weather never holds me back from a journey," he said. "If it is raining when I am starting, it is almost sure to clear up on the way, and when I most need it."

We were again out at Bocken. He had changed his mind about the scene. It was the finest view he ever saw. On leaving, he gave my wife an affectionate kiss, and said, "May God take care of you." It was to be years before she would see him again.

*****

August 20.--Horace Rublee, our minister at Bern, gave a public reception to General Sherman at the capital the other night. I was invited to attend. It was a rather elaborate affair, in the Bernerhof. Outside a band came and serenaded the General, playing some American airs very poorly. The General was in full uniform. Most of the prominent people of Bern and many public officials were present. The General, I noticed, talked quite a little French with some of the ladies. Nothing of note occurred at this reception, but there was a fine time, and the General enjoyed himself.

The next day was spent in seeing the sights of the city. At noon I saw a bit of Sherman's well-known gallantry for women. Numbers of us, mostly young men, were standing with him in the Bernerhof corridor. An elderly lady, alone, passed us and started up the grand stairway. She was half way up when Sherman's eye caught her. Instantly he sprang up the steps and offering his arm escorted her to her room. The rest of us looked on a little abashed that we had not thought to do this.

*****

While in Switzerland the General had met the famous old Dufour, the Wellington of the Swiss army, who had so promptly put down the Rebellion of 1847. With his 100,000 men and his 300 cannon he did more in a month than most generals do in a year. General Sherman sent him, through me, a map of his own campaigns. It gratified the old Swiss warrior greatly and elicited the following reply to me:

"G<small>ENEVE</small>, 23rd Janv., 1873.

"M<small>ONSIEUR LE</small> C<small>ONSUL</small>: J'ai reçu en parfait état le rouleau que vous m'avez fait l'honneur de m'annoncer par votre lettre du 21. Je vous en remercie.

"Cette carte est un précieux document pour éclairer l'histoire des glorieux événements de la dernière guerre d'Amerique.

"Je suis bien redevable a Mons. le Général Sherman d'avoir pensé à moi en cette circonstance et je vous prie de lui en exprimer toute ma reconnaissance quand vous aurez l'occasion de lui écrire.

"Agréez, monsieur le Consul, l'assurance de ma considération distinguée.

G. H. D<small>UFOUR</small>, Général."

CHAPTER VIII
1872

LETTER FROM GENERAL SHERMAN--VISIT AMERICA--SANDS OF BREMEN--STORMS AT SEA--ELIHU WASHBURNE--BANQUET TO HIM ON SHIP--I AM A GUEST AT THE SHERMAN HOME--MRS. SHERMAN--ARRANGE TO TAKE MISS SHERMAN TO EUROPE--MEET MR. BLAINE--MY SONG IS SUNG IN THE SHERMAN HOME--CONVERSATIONS WITH SHERMAN--MEET PRESIDENT GRANT--HOW I HAPPENED TO BE IN THE REBEL ARMY ONCE--LETTERS FROM GENERAL SHERMAN.

October, 1872.--As I had now been absent from home just three years, I secured a few weeks' leave to visit the United States. Dr. Terry was to go along. I arranged to sail on the "Deutschland," from Bremen, Oct. 10th. Early in September General Sherman wrote me from Ireland, asking me to bring his daughter Minnie (now Mrs. Fitch) back with me to Europe.

"DUBLIN, Sunday, Sept. 1, 1872.

"DEAR BYERS: As you can well understand, I have been kept busy and have not had a chance to write letters, save to my home. My trip is now drawing to a close, and by Thursday next we will be at Queenstown ready to take the steamer Baltic for home. I have letters from my family by which I learn that my daughter Minnie is very anxious to spend the winter in Europe. I remember that you proposed to come to Washington about this time, and if you have gone this letter will not find you at Zurich, and I shall hear of you on our side; but if this letter reaches you, please write me at Washington, as I would prefer she should make the trip across with you, and remain with you until she finds General and Mrs. Graham, who are somewhere in Italy. I know you would do this for me, and it only depends on your coming and the conclusion Minnie arrives at after I reach home. I am perfectly willing she should spend a winter in Europe, and only desire that she have the personal supervision of some friend of mine. She could easily join some party in New York, but she desires to stop long enough in some place to perfect herself in French, and to observe the customs and manners of strangers.

"I hope ere this Mrs. Byers has passed the first dread ordeal of mother, and that you have now a child to think of and dream about.

"Please give her my best congratulations and wishes for her continued health. Believe me, always your friend,

"W. T. SHERMAN."

When I went through the flat, sandy region of North Germany, to take the Bremen steamer, I thought I had never seen so desolate a country in my life. It was a rainy, windy day, and the train was slow, the scene sad; everybody looked poor. Women by hundreds, with red handkerchiefs on their heads, were out in the fields, digging potatoes in the rain and wind. The villages were sorry-looking places. Some day, when the Mojave desert in America has villages scattered all over it, and a poor American peasantry, the descendants of our children, dig potatoes from the drifting sand, the scene will be like that long stretch of ugliness in the rear of Bremen.

Our steamer stopped at Southampton for a day and a night. So Dr. Terry and I took a run over to the Isle of Wight. To this hour, I think, I never saw so lovely an island or a place where I should so like to live. Its clean roads and pretty hedges and beautiful trees, its quiet English villages, its rambles, interested us much. And then there was the blue sea beating all around it, and, passing it in the near distance, the ships of all nations. At the point was the lighthouse and the rocks, and nearer, the noble downs. Here were the rocks and the waves that Tennyson had looked at and walked beside for half his life-- the scenes that made his poetry. Not far away was Farringford, the poet's home. The whole island, that sunny day, seemed like a dream.

The next evening, at twilight, on our vessel's deck, far out at sea, I lingered and looked at the Isle of Wight, the lighthouse and the dim, gray crags, with the waves beating against them.

We were twelve days reaching New York, and had storms and hurricanes half the way over. The "Deutschland" survived them all, only to go to the bottom, on a later voyage, with three hundred people. That was in the Channel. One day, on this, our New York voyage, everything seemed to be going to pieces, and for an hour or so I knew how it felt to be very close to death. I was more alarmed than I had ever been in any battle. In war, one expects death almost. Here it was different. Not a human being could keep his feet a moment. There was more than one said good-by to comrades that day, as he supposed, forever. I had but one friend on board, Dr. C. T. Terry of New York, who lived in Zurich for many years, and with whom I had made hundreds of foot excursions in the mountains. He was a dentist, possibly in his calling not second to Dr. Evans in Paris. He had come to Switzerland a poor youth, and, by honor, skill and diligence, had amassed a fortune. He, like myself, had left a wife and child behind in Zurich. In the midst of the hurricane, we shook hands, and in a few words agreed what should be done, should either survive. Had that ship gone down, I would certainly not be writing here. No lifeboat there but was being torn to pieces; nothing of human hands could have withstood that sea's fury another hour. But it was a grand sight spite of the terror. It was ten in the morning, snowing, and the sun shining, every minute, turn about.

As the hurricane eased up, I hung on to a rope by the bridge, and miles away could see lofty white-caps, their shining crowns lighted by the sun, lift themselves and thunder together, or roll on toward us till they would strike the ship. The sea was rolling in deep, green valleys, and, as the ship would leap across these watery gorges, the view right and left was indescribably grand. I looked at the awful ocean, and thought of Switzerland. It was as if the valleys of the Alps had turned to green, rushing waters, and the mountains had commenced falling. I would almost take the risk again, to see so grand a sight.

October, 1872.--The morning after the storm, the sea was still running high, but passengers could keep their feet and, if well enough, talk together.

Pretty soon, a very large, grand-looking man, with a sea cloak about him, came on deck. "And who is he?" I said to the captain. "Why, that's your *greatest* American," he replied. "That's the man who cared for the Germans in the siege of Paris. That's Minister Washburne, the friend of Germany." Sure enough, on a day's notice, Mr. Washburne had come aboard when we touched at Southampton. He had been sick in his cabin till this moment. He guessed the storm had shaken the bile out of him, he said, when I introduced myself to him. He had been too sick to know the danger we had been in. Now he stayed on deck and was well. Mr. Washburne was General Grant's first and truest friend. Without his tireless support, from Galena to Appomattox, the name of General Grant had not gone farther than his father's tannery. Genius must have somebody to open the door for it. Washburne did it for Grant. John Sherman, in the House and Senate, did it for his illustrious brother. Barras did it for Napoleon. Even a cannon ball, rolling down hill, has to be started by somebody.

*****

It is the last day of the voyage. The captain gave a banquet last night to Mr. Washburne. All Germans are deep in their gratitude to him for his work in Paris.

Many speeches were made at the table, many toasts drunk. When Mr. Washburne rose to speak, he looked like the picture of Daniel Webster. The same large head, the same intellectual countenance. He looked like a statesman, not a politician. He was of the kindest manners, and loved to talk of the people he had known. I had the pleasure of walking for hours daily with him, up and down the deck, sometimes far into the night. He had been Lincoln's friend, as well as Grant's, and there was no end to the incidents he could tell of the great President. I regret now that I did not write them down. He also talked of the Commune in Paris, whose horrors he had witnessed. He believed socialism and mobism a disease. In Paris it was infectious. He told me much of his youth out West. He went to Galena a poor boy, and when he studied law in an office, making fires as pay for use of books, he had nothing but a buffalo robe to sleep on, spread on the office floor. Later, he was a Cabinet Minister. He was a true Republican, through and through. Hobnobbing with the nobility of France had made no snob of him. He asked me to make him acquainted with Terry. "I like and honor such men," he said; "they are the salt of the earth, these self-made Americans. They are what makes a republic possible."

A very rich American lady on the steamer with us was carrying in her trunks several dozen kid gloves, and asked him to help her get "easy" through the Custom House. He refused indignantly, adding, "And what right have you, a rich woman, madame, more than my wife, who never owned so many gloves in her whole life, to slip things through the custom-house? The law expects, compels, her to pay duty on her two or three pairs, and, trust me to see to it, you shall pay duty on your trunk full." She left him in high dudgeon, when he turned to me and said: "It is just such rich, ostentatious people evading law that is making the poorer classes mad and discontented with government."

"Lincoln," he said, "has been the people's friend more than any other man since Jesus Christ."

On reaching New York, Mr. Arthur and others of the custom-house came out with a tug to meet him, and take him ashore. I was asked to go along in the tug.

Mr. Washburne went to the Fifth Avenue Hotel. "Now don't you go because I do," he said to me. "It is a useless waste of money. I go because I have to. Come and see me there tomorrow." I went on the morrow and was introduced to Mr. Blaine, who had, I thought, the most magnetic personality of any man I ever saw. I thought, when he grasped my hand, he had mistaken me for some old-time friend, but shortly I saw the same hearty good-will toward all who entered the room. He knew how to make friends, and to keep them. What a golden secret! I never forgot that handshake.

November, 1872.--For a week or so now I was in Washington, a guest in General Sherman's home, then on I Street, corner of 3rd. He and Mrs. Sherman cordially insisted that whenever I came to Washington, I should make their house my home. This I often did, not at Washington only, but later at St. Louis and New York as well. Mrs. Sherman was always one of my sincerest and firmest friends.

General Sherman.

Mrs. General Sherman.

"Don't talk religion with her, though," said the General to me one morning in his study, after breakfast. "She is a very zealous Catholic, and you----" "I am a zealous nothing," I interrupted. "I like Catholics the same as other good Christians, and have gotten over the notion that all the salt of the earth is in the creed I accidentally was born in." "Then you are all right. As for myself, it's no difference," he went on. "Why, I guess, I don't believe in anything; so in this room talk as you please." Mrs. Sherman was a thousand times more than a good Catholic. She was in every sense a good woman. Here, as at her other later homes, she had a little room arranged as an office, where she worked and studied out plans for helping the poor. Probably no woman in the United States ever spent more time and money in doing good. Few had more true friends. Her religious zeal was well known, and never abated. She thoroughly believed the Catholic church the best church.

She was extremely bright and kind in her ways. The army officers all liked her, and her house stood open to every friend.

I recall one evening how she and the General gave a supper to the staff. All were in uniform. She had not invited them to come; she had just *told* them to come, and they came with their wives. Two or three civilians were present, Mr. Church, a famous war-song singer, and myself among them. After the supper there was some instrumental music in the drawing-room. "And now," said Mrs. Sherman, "Mr. Church is going to honor us with a song." My verses, "Sherman's March to the Sea," were still popular in the country, being sung everywhere. Mr. Church stepped to the front of the piano and sang the song in such a voice as I had never heard it sung in before. The splendid rendering of the music, his great, fine, patriotic tones, that sounded like the coming of an army with banners, moved everyone in that room deeply. For a moment, I entirely forgot that the words were my own. All applauded, so did I; why not? So did the General. Then a guest stepped forward and made a little speech. "I am happy," said he; "I speak for all. What a pleasure we have had--the first song of the war, sung by the first war-song singer in the land, in the presence of the one who wrote it, and in the home of the Commander who made the March."

General Sherman, too, made a little speech, praising the music, the words, the singer, and then he added: "Without this song, the campaign never would have had its picturesque name. Now," said he, "I want Mr. Church to sing that other favorite song of mine, 'Old Soldier, You've Played Out Your Time.'"

They were rugged verses Mr. Church now sang, and striking music, but, privately, I almost thought it a little cynical in the General to agree with the words that declared an unknown grave in a ditch a desirable ending for the true soldier. "But that's it, that's it," said the General. "Do your duty, have a good time and win glory, but don't kick when the end comes. That song is the true picture of a soldier's life."

It was a memorable evening, but, I fear, not half a dozen of that happy company are on earth now. Yet it seems so few years back. The voices of all of them still seem to sound in my ear. I write down the little record before the last memory fades. That night at General Sherman's house was an echo of the war days.

When the company left that night, the General asked me up to his little room. He was smoking constantly. The conversation turned on the origin of the "March to the Sea." "Yes, I know," he said, "some of Grant's friends are claiming that he suggested that, but no one ever heard Grant himself utter one word to claim it. True, he was chief commander over all the armies, when I cut loose for the South; but it would be just as senseless to attribute it to the President, who was over all of us, as to attribute it to Grant. Lincoln's letter to me, after the event, shows how completely he knew who originated the idea of my changing base and putting my army down by the ocean; and a letter from Lee, written after the war, shows what *he* thought of the importance of my getting this water base, and of its sequence, the march north in the Carolinas. 'The moment he reaches the Roanoke,' said Lee, 'Richmond is untenable, and I leave it.'"

One May morning (1864), away back by Chattanooga, a certain General Warner asked General Sherman, privately, what he was going to do when he got his army away down to Atlanta, without supplies, and with a lot of rebels behind. General Sherman suddenly stopped his pacing the floor, knocked the ashes from his cigar, and said, "*Salt water.*" "Do you mean Savannah or Charleston?" said the astonished staff officer. "*Yes*," replied Sherman, "I do." *That* was the origin of the "March to the Sea."

General Warner related the whole details of this conversation, in a letter to General Sherman's wife. Lincoln congratulated the great leader, and added, "*None of us, I believe, went further than to acquiesce.*" One of the interesting autograph letters of the war is that one to Sherman, saying: "I congratulate you on the splendid results of your campaign, the like of which is not heard of in past history. (Signed) U. S. Grant."

"Well," said the General at last, laughing, as he gave the fire a great stir with the poker: "I suppose they won't hardly doubt as to who really *made* the march."

*****

November, 1872.--Went out to my home in Iowa and visited my relatives. While there, received a couple of notes from General Sherman, saying Miss Sherman was getting ready to join me on my trip back to Europe, the 14th of December, by the "Celtic."

"WASHINGTON, D. C., Nov. 5, 1872.

"DEAR BYERS: I wrote to Mr. Sparks, agent, of the White Star Line, soon after you left us, but he had gone out on the plains. He is just back, and writes me promptly, offering the most liberal terms, more than I deem it prudent to accept. He offers the best rooms in any of his ships, and 'to accept your ticket on the Bremen Line in exchange.' I knew he would be glad to favor me, but I always prefer to pay the usual price, and to accept as a favor 'preferable accommodations.' Now, I have written to Sparks that I prefer to pay full passage for Minnie, and merely suggest for you that he charge you the usual fare to Paris, $95, and take your ticket at its cost, $63. This would leave you $32 to pay, and this will embrace railroad tickets from Liverpool to Paris. I also named the 'Celtic,' the finest ship afloat, which sails Dec. 14, and I guarantee she will put you in Liverpool in 8½ days, and in Paris Dec. 24, giving you barely time to take Christmas dinner with Mrs. Byers at Zurich. Write me as soon as you can that I may close the bargain. We will expect you to come to stay with us as long as you please before starting.

"I take it for granted you vote to-day, and will then have a full month to see your folks and come to us. Of course, I don't like to hurry you, but this programme seems so fair I trust it will suit your convenience.

"My best regards to your father.

Truly yours,
"W. T. SHERMAN."

*****

"WASHINGTON, D. C., Nov. 22, 1872.

"DEAR BYERS: I now have a letter from Mr. Sparks, agent of the White Star Line, saying he has all ready for your and Minnie's most comfortable passage in the 'Celtic.' Dec. 14, next. So I shall expect you here by the 10th of December, and will accompany you to New York and see you off.

"He also reports that the 'Celtic' has just made the run from New York to Queenstown in 8 days and 12 hours, with bad coal. So you may safely count on reaching Paris inside of ten days. Truly yours,

W. T. SHERMAN."

Shortly, I went back to the General's home at Washington. He took me to see President Grant. He seemed to have free access wherever he pleased to go, for, although others were waiting in the reception-room, he passed them with a bow, and conducted me into the cabinet-room. General Grant sat quite alone at the end of the historic table. The warmth of his reception showed very quickly how intimate the two great leaders were.

*****

The President asked me some questions about the service abroad, and my replies seemed to gratify him. Then there was a hint that Mr. Horace Rublee, the American Minister at Bern, was about to resign and come home. I had known that from Mr. Rublee direct, and I had quite an ambition to secure the place. Why not? I had performed the duties more than once in the Minister's absence, and the proposed promotion seemed perfectly natural. General Grant gave me every encouragement to believe that I should shortly have the post.

Shortly the President arose and asked General Sherman to let him know at once when the resignation of Rublee should be sent in. He saw no reason why I should not be promoted to the post.

"It looks like a very sure thing," said the General to me as we left the White House.

Alas, and alack! Mr. Rublee went home on a leave, found his affairs different from what he had anticipated, and did not resign at all. He simply got his leave extended and extended, and drew the pay, nearly to the end of Grant's term. My best good chance was gone.

December 9, 1872.--Went with the General and Mrs. Sherman to hear McDonald, the Scotch novelist, lecture on Burns. General Sherman introduced the speaker, and, in a little speech, showed his own familiarity with the Scotch bard. I knew this well enough, for I had seen him reading Burns by the hour. McDonald commenced with great feeling and enthusiasm. Once I had heard Charles Dickens read, but it seemed to me here, to-night, was a man more sincere with his subject. There was no effort at effect. I recall Dickens in his dress suit, his enormous white shirt front, his big, red rose on his lapel, his dainty, foppish movements on the stage, his undisguised pauses and signals for applause, as much as to say: "That is good; now clap your hands." With McDonald, all was different, all sincere. Burns seemed to be there in person that night.

After the lecture we sat up till midnight, telling reminiscences of the war. The year before, in our home at Zurich, we had spoken of an escape I had once made from the prison pen at Macon, and of how near I had come to changing the whole siege of Atlanta. He asked me for some more of the details. I had been captured from his army in the assault on Missionary Ridge, and had endured many months of imprisonment at Libby. When they put us in the stockade at Macon, I resolved on getting away. The first time I tried it, the guards fired and killed another officer, who happened to be near me, in the dark. Then, by hook and crook, I got hold of a gray rebel uniform, and in this disguise, one bright July morning, walked over the dead line, past the guards, and, eventually, got off into the rebel army at Atlanta, a hundred miles away. For ten days I walked up and down among the troops, the forts, observing the position of the besieged army. I dared not stop, or rest, or sleep. If spoken to, or stopped, I was forever just going to the Ninth Alabama, where I claimed to belong. Naturally, I never went near that regiment. My intent was to collect all information possible concerning the rebel troops and forts, and then, in the excitement of the first battle, escape through the lines. I well knew the value my knowledge now could be to

Sherman. I had dozens of incidents every day that for a moment put my life in peril. Once I saw the lines of the enemy so thinned, Sherman's army could have entered almost without a shot. Then came the terrible battle of the 22d of July. I followed the Rebel troops in the attack on Sherman's rear, but failed to make my escape. The next morning I changed my course, and, passing their left flank, and down close by the Chattahoochie river, there in the woods, within sight of the Union banners, was captured as a spy. Every stitch of my clothing was searched. I was brutally treated and sent to Hood's headquarters for trial. Unfortunately for me, some of the very officers who captured me had seen me in one of the forts the preceding Sunday. Army headquarters were fixed on the green lawn of a city mansion. The officers' desks were out on the grass, and the papers describing me as a dangerous spy were put into one of the pigeonholes. These had been shown to me on my way to headquarters by a foolish guard. All was excitement, for fighting was still going on. As for me, I was put into a little tent, with two deserters, who were to be shot the next morning. During the night, one of these condemned boys got out of the tent on some pretext, and, when morning came, and I was brought out for a hearing, all the incriminating papers were gone. There was not a particle of proof as to who I was. I instantly acknowledged myself to be a Union soldier, and claimed the rights of a prisoner of war. The astonished officials reminded me that they had a right to shoot me, I being discovered inside their lines in their uniform; that only a few months previous our General Rosecrans had shot two Southern officers for doing what I was now doing. I was in great peril, when a Colonel Hill, Chief Provost Marshal of their army, said, for the present, anyway, I should be put back among the prisoners at Macon. Almost the same night, I was selected, with some two hundred others, to be taken to Charleston, to be put under the fire of the Yankee fleet, then bombarding the city. The barbarism of the act, the excitement and confusion soon following, led to a complete forgetfulness of me. I never heard again of the charges against me.

General Sherman had listened to the story in perfect silence. Then rising and giving the coals in the fire a violent stir with the poker, he exclaimed: "By God! that was an experience. Had you gotten through the lines that day, it might have changed everything. It might have saved ten thousand lives."[2]

Christmas Eve.--The voyage on the "Celtic" is over, and to-night finds Miss Sherman and myself in Merry England.

I soon left Miss Sherman with friends in Paris, and hurried home to Switzerland. Later, after some rambling in Italy, she came and spent a month with us in our home by the lake. Two or three letters from her father at this time, though purely personal, are not without interest:

"WASHINGTON, D. C., Jan. 3, 1873.

"DEAR BYERS: We have all written to Minnie several times, but, I fear, we have overlooked the fact that you must have separated in Paris soon after Christmas, but I hope she was thoughtful enough to write you our several general messages of respect and fond wishes. I was in New York last Monday, Dec. 23d; called at the office of the White Line, and got the agent, Mr. Sparks, to promise to give me the first possible news of the 'Celtic.' That night I was at the New England dinner at Delmonico's, and received a note from Sparks saying the 'Celtic' was reported off Queenstown that night at 10:30, and that is all I know of her, and of the details of your passage, up to the present moment. The next morning I telegraphed to Mrs. Sherman here, and to your father at Oskaloosa. All the ships that came over at the same time report heavy westerly weather, so I suspect you had a rough passage after passing the banks of Newfoundland, though the westerly wind rather favored your speed. My supposition is that you did not enter Queenstown, but put the mails on some tug that went outside, and that you put into Liverpool the 24th, too late for London or Paris for Christmas Day, and I hope you found out General Fairchild and spent the day with him and Mrs. Fairchild. We will begin to look for letters from Minnie about Monday next--this is Thursday. The weather in all North America has been severe since you left us, except for two or three days after you sailed. The ground is covered with heavy snow. Yesterday (New Year's) was, however, strictly observed, and we had a full house of visitors all day.

"All my folks are well, and send to you and Mrs. Byers and the baby all sorts of messages of love and respect. Yours truly,

W. T. SHERMAN."

*****

"WASHINGTON, D. C., Jan. 21, 1873.

"DEAR BYERS: I was very glad to receive your letter of Dec. 29, from Zurich, and I see why you were unusually anxious to reach Zurich, with a clerk deranged, and short in his accounts. I am glad, of course, his deficiency has been so promptly covered by his father, as I suppose you are personally liable for his act.

"We have several letters from Minnie, telling us of her voyage and safe arrival in Paris.

"The weather all December was so bad here that we feared you had a hard time, but, on the whole, ten days was a good trip at that season, and you were especially fortunate in having so smooth a passage of the straits at Dover. Minnie is beginning to figure on her trip to Italy, and is already in communication with General and Mrs. Graham at Florence. I suppose she will go there in February, and I hope a month or so there will satisfy her, and then she will turn toward Switzerland. I think she has secured the services of a most excellent French maid, who will enable her to travel with great ease and comfort. At this distance I cannot well advise her, and think it best to let her shape her own course.

"All things in Washington remain as you left them. A little more visiting and more dinners, and this will continue till after the inauguration of the 4th of March, when we will settle down to our chronic state again.

"I propose to remain quietly at home till the North Pacific Road has progressed far enough to justify me in crossing the continent by that line.

"Give my best love to your wife, and believe me always, your friend,

W. T. SHERMAN."

*****

"WASHINGTON, D. C., March 7, 1873.

"Dear Byers: I have your letter of Feb. 11, and can see you and your little family settled down in your quaint home by Zurich's fair waters.

"We have letters from Minnie at Florence, and she is now with our old friends, General and Mrs. Graham, and we feel absolute confidence. She says they go to Rome about the 1st of March, and she proposes to spend March and April there and at Naples, and their project is to go to Vienna via Venice and Trieste. It certainly will be a happy incident if you can go along and take her to Zurich. I am afraid she will find less time to settle down to her French studies and music at Zurich than she first proposed. But let time settle that. She is now on the right track, and will have her whole summer to put in in the Swiss cantons. There is no good reason why she should come home till October.

"We have just got through the ceremonies of inauguration, and, as all the papers are filled with it, I feel certain you will get some by telegraph, and the whole details by the New York papers. Thus far no changes have been made in the Consular or Foreign appointments. The senate is in extra session, and if General Grant proposes to make any material changes he must do so within a few days, but of this you will also learn by telegraph. He surely keeps his council well, as his most intimate friends do not know his purpose.

"I think the Washington bonds are good, as the debt is limited to ten per cent of the aggregate value of taxable property.

"Master Cumpy still flourishes, and asks innumerable questions of Europe, Asia and America. At present rate he will know geography before he reads.

"Present my kindest regards to your good wife, and believe me always anxious to hear from you and to serve you. Sincerely,

W. T. Sherman."

CHAPTER IX
1873

LETTER FROM GENERAL SHERMAN--LOSS OF THE "ATLANTIC"--THE BOYHOOD HOME OF NAPOLEON III. AND OF HIS MOTHER, QUEEN HORTENSE--A COMPANION TELLS OF THE PRINCE'S PRANKS AND STUDIES--JOSEPHINE'S HARP--ARENABERG FULL OF NAPOLEON RELICS--WE HAVE A LONG INTERVIEW WITH THE EX-EMPRESS EUGENIE--LETTER FROM GENERAL SHERMAN--SPEAKS OF THIERS.

May Day, 1873.--The terrible wreck of the White Star Liner "Atlantic," took place two weeks since. Five hundred souls lost. I had secured passage for our young friend, Hirzel. He writes how he clung to the rigging that cold morning, and witnessed poor human beings gradually freezing, letting loose their hold, and dropping from the rigging down into the sea. He was almost the last one taken off on to the rocks.

General Sherman speaks of this disaster, as well as of the Modoc war:

"WASHINGTON, D. C., April 24, 1873.

"DEAR BYERS: Your last letter came promptly, and I have sent it out to Mrs. Sherman, who is on a visit to Ohio, and, of course, demands prompt notice of everything concerning Minnie. We get from her letters regularly and promptly, the last being dated at Castellamare, near Naples. She seemed unusually well, and said she would soon return to Rome, and then begin her northward progress. The Grahams will probably move slower than she wants to, and she will probably catch a favorable opportunity to reach you in Switzerland. I advise her to take this course; get near you, and then maneuver from that as her base for the summer. She does not seem very anxious to go to Vienna, though I advise it for no other reason than to see the Fair and the city, and also to see the family of our Minister, Mr. Jay. I want her to come home in September or October, and to arrange for her passage as early as possible, for there will be a rush in the autumn westward. Notwithstanding the loss of the 'Atlantic,' I have not lost faith in the White Star Line. It was not the fault of the ship that she was foundered on the rock at a twelve-mile speed. No ship could stand that; still, if she is afraid, then the Cunard Line will be preferable.

"Our spring has been very backward, indeed, but the trees are trying now to blossom and to leaf. The grass is very green, and I hope that winter is past. The President is away at the West and the Secretary of War in Texas, so times here are dull, although we find the Indians are trying their annual spring business; not very peaceful. You will have heard of the killing of General Canby, and the treacherous conduct of the Modocs. I hope the last one of them will be hunted out of their rocks and killed. I have not heard of the actual coming of Mr. Rublee, but notice that Consul Upton of Geneva has been named as chargé during his (Rublee's) absence. If I hear of his resignation, I will endeavor to remind the President of your claims, but must warn you that against political combinations I find my influence very weak.

"Present me kindly to Mrs. Byers, and, believe me, truly your friend,

W. T. SHERMAN."

The home of Queen Hortense, Napoleon's stepdaughter, is on the Rhine, only a couple of hours' ride from Zurich. One of our delightful excursions was to go and see the falls at Schaffhausen, and then take a little steamer up the river to "Arenaberg," the beautiful chateau where the Queen lived for twenty years, and where she died. Here, too, her son, Napoleon III., lived, as a youth. In the stable building, close to the chateau, were his sleeping-rooms and study. Louis Napoleon once said he would rather be a fine country gentleman than Emperor of France. He got his tastes for the beautiful in nature in this boyhood home. The chateau sits above the Rhine, with beautiful hills behind it, and the historic lake of Constance close by. It is on Swiss territory, and is a spot of perfect loveliness. It is the one spot where Napoleon's days were all happy days, and the one spot where Queen Hortense led a happy life. The scene is so perfectly enchanting, any one, not burdened with a crown, should find delight in just existing there. The Queen's room, in the upper corner of the villa and overlooking the river and the lake, and with ravishing vistas beyond, is just as she left it at her death. There are her harp and her paint-brushes and her table. In this room she wrote the famous song of "Partant Pour la Syrie," that moved all France. Walter Scott translated it into exquisite English.

Napoleon III.

Empress Eugenie.

I went often to Constance, and among my acquaintances was one who had been a boyhood friend of the Emperor. It was Dr. J. Marmor, a retired linen merchant in the town. He still corresponded with France's ex-ruler, for Sedan's day was over, as was the terrible scene in that little farmhouse by Donghery. Dr. Marmor showed me his letters from Napoleon, and gave me the wax impress of his private seal from one, together with some writing of the Emperor's.

No one in Constance will forget the day when Napoleon, at the height of his power, came from Paris, to visit the home of his childhood. What grand preparations there were, what decorations, banners, bands, cannon; what a gilded equipage, for the Emperor to head the procession in! Suddenly the train whistle shrieks. "The Emperor! The Emperor!" cries the crowd, as he descends to the carpeted platform. The big, gilded carriage and the flunkies wait. "Where is my friend, Dr. Marmor?" asks the Emperor. He is sitting out there, in his old, one-horse buggy, looking at the scene, hoping for just a glance at Napoleon, as he will pass among the self-appointed bigwigs and flunkies. Suddenly the Emperor sees him, grasps him by the hand, and, springing into the old buggy, cries: "Drive on. To-day I ride with Marmor." Then Marmor's one-horse chaise, with nobody in it but the Emperor and himself, heads the procession through the city. At first, everybody stared, and then everybody cheered. Marmor, in five minutes, had become the first man in Constance. That incident has been his pride ever since.

When I called on him, and told him I wanted to write for a magazine something about Napoleon's boyhood, he gave himself wholly to my service, went with me everywhere, and told of a hundred frolics he and the young prince had had in the neighborhood. Prince Napoleon would have been a poor secretary for the Y. M. C. A. He was an awfully fast boy, according to one who "had been there" and knew all about it. Some other old folks whom I met in Constance, knew things also peppery to relate, were they more than big pranks, or worth the writing down.

Hortense's chateau is two miles or so outside the town. "Many a time," said Marmor, "after half a night's frolic with a few of us here in town, have I galloped with him out home, yelling half the way. It must have been the beer. When we got there, I slept till morning with him in the barn, the place where he had his study. He studied, too, spite of his fastness," said the doctor. "How he read books! just as people nowadays read newspapers. He read everything, and he remembered it all. He was a generous soul, too; everybody said that. He was a famous youth for his kindness to the poor, just like his mother; only she was better. What a swimmer he was, what a wrestler, what a horseman, what a rake! As to horses," the doctor went on, "why it was a common habit of his to mount, not by the stirrup, but by a single bound over the crupper and into the saddle." It is curious now to know that Louis Napoleon once was a captain of militia here, and also a member of the school board. "Bismarck never hatched out more schemes in Berlin, than the young prince did out there in the barn, over the horses. In his mind's eye, he was Emperor of France a dozen times out there. I guess all men do that, who have ambition," continued the doctor, "and he was the most ambitious boy I ever knew. But nobody thought he had any chance for anything."

The attendants showed us all the rooms in the Queen's villa. Here, in the upper east corner, is the one she died in, in 1837. The sun comes into it, and it has enchanting views. At the end of the room stands, not only her harp, but, near by it, the harp of Josephine. The villa is full of souvenirs of the great Napoleon, too; the clock that stood still the night he died at St. Helena; swords, banners, presents from kings, etc. In the garden, in a chapel, is a white marble figure of Hortense, kneeling before the altar. It is one of the beautiful things of Europe.

The Empress Eugenie comes here summers. No wonder; all is so enchanting. All except the memories. Right over there, almost in sight, on an island in the lake, is a castle, the summer home of the old German Emperor, who crushed out her husband's life. Greatness must all be paid for.

*****

What we had seen, made us now the more anxious to see the ex-Empress herself. Sometimes she was here at the chateau; oftener, at the little watering place of Baden, half an hour from Zurich.

Our chance came. Miss Sherman, the daughter of General Sherman, was visiting for a month at our home by the lake (July and August, 1873). She was a good Catholic, and her mother was the only American woman on whom the Pope had conferred the order of the "Golden Rose." Eugenie, also, was a zealous Catholic. Would she receive the daughter of General Sherman, and the Consul and his wife? The Duke Bassano arranged it all. "Her majesty will receive you on Tuesday morning, at ten o'clock," said a little perfumed note in French. We were not so sure of our Gallic verbs and pronouns; still, we could speak some French, and would risk the visit. Tuesday morning found us in our best toilettes, waiting in a little anteroom, at the annex of the Hotel in Baden. It was a simple enough old stone house, half of it built by the Romans, in the times when they, too, came to these springs for their aches and pains. In a few minutes, the friendly old Duke Bassano came in to announce that all was ready. Major Cunningham and his wife were with us. "And how shall we address her," we innocently inquired of the Duke, remembering that the Emperor was dead, and France a republic. "Oh, as her majesty, of course, only as her majesty." He opened the door to a small, simply furnished sitting-room, and we entered. Almost at the same moment, Eugenie entered from an adjoining apartment. She walked to the center of the room, took each of us by the hand, and bade us a cordial welcome. She was dressed in full black, partly décolleté and trimmed with some white lace. She motioned us to some chairs arranged in a semi-circle, in front of a little divan. On this sofa she seated herself, and possibly never looked more beautiful on the throne of France.

"And now what language shall we speak in?" she smilingly asked in the most perfect English. "Your majesty's perfect accomplishment in our own tongue, settles that," one of our party answered. "Good. Oh, yes, I learned English in school, you know, after I left Madrid as a girl; and my master was Scotch; and then I lived a time in London, too. I like the English, and I like the English people; but I like the American people just as well, only I never knew why your country kept slaves, and had no respect for black people. I am sure color makes no difference, if it is only a good man. Would you not invite a black man to your table? I am sure I would, and did; and once, when a diplomat who was dining with me also, objected a little to my courtesy to a 'negro,' as he called him, I gave him quickly to understand that possibly the negro was better than he was."

Then she talked to Miss Sherman (now Mrs. Fitch) about her mother, of whose Catholic zeal and perpetual charity to the poor she had heard so much.

To each one in turn she addressed some pertinent word, and then, laughing, turned to me as a representative of my country, and exclaimed numerous things not very complimentary to our system of high tariff.

"Why, we make the most beautiful things in the world in Paris; you Americans all say so, and yet you won't let your people buy them without paying twice what they are worth, by your fearful custom-house rules.

"Americans are so clever; they ought to know they hurt their own people, and they hurt us in Paris, too. Our poor work for such small wages, and would always be happy, if you would only let them sell to you; and, after all, your rich importers just add your tariff fees on to the price of our goods, and who has the benefit?"

I answered: "Ours is a prosperous country, with our protective tariff system." "Yes, I know, in *spite* of your tariff. I have heard that, a hundred times. Some day, you will be just like us, and get where you can get the cheapest. You don't think making things dear helps anybody, do you?" Politeness prevented much discussion. It was all one way. Besides, was it not to hear her talk, not ourselves, that we were there?

She went back to the black man, or the black woman rather. "I had a good laugh on my dear husband, the Emperor, once. He lived in your country awhile, you know, and he was always fancying your pretty women. One day at New Orleans he saw a beautiful female form ahead of him in the street. It was all grace of movement, and elegance of apparel. He was struck by the figure. I think he was half in love. 'I must see her face,' he exclaimed to his companion. 'I must see her. She is my divinity, running away.' He hurried his pace, passed her, and the moment politeness would permit, glanced back. It was a 'mulatto.' I don't think he always regarded black people quite in the light I did."

Shortly we proposed to go, though she made no sign that the interview was at an end. "No," she said. "Wait; I have leisure, nothing but leisure and rheumatism." But she had no rheumatic look; a more charming-looking woman of fifty, I never saw. Her bright eyes were as blue as the sky, her complexion exceeding fair, her hair still golden, her vivacity of manner and cleverness of speech surprising beyond measure; and then her kindness made us feel that we were talking with a friend. All of us were led on to say much, and the visit lasted for two hours. Much of the talk was about Switzerland and health resorts, and so much at random as not to be remembered or noted down.

When at last we arose to go, she again came to the middle of the room and took us each by the hand. And then I asked her a word about her future plans. "There are none," she said. "All is over. I have only my son, and he and I will spend our lives in quiet and peace." Alas! only a few years went by and that son was lying dead in an African cornfield, his body pierced by Zulu lances.

*****

In June General Sherman has written again about Miss S.'s travels, and also something about the French Republic, and the Modoc War:

"WASHINGTON, D. C., June 9, 1873.

"DEAR BYERS: I am just in receipt of your letter of May 20. Mr. Rublee was here not long since en route for Rome, and from what he said I think he has made no business arrangements, and that he will stay there his full term.

"We have letters from Minnie up to May 20, at Rome, at which time she had joined the Healys, and will accompany them to Venice, Milan, Nice and Pau, France, a route that takes her well away from Zurich, but she begs to be allowed to remain abroad longer, say till next spring, so as to enable her to have more time to stay with you and to visit England and Ireland. I suppose she ought to reach Switzerland in July or August and stay with you a month or more. I have given her my consent, and hope before she reaches you you will have all our letters on the subject. If she stays beyond October, she had better not attempt a winter passage, but wait till April or May. This will make a long visit, but I suppose it will be the only chance she will ever have, and she might as well profit by it.

"Mrs. Sherman did intend to take the family to Carlisle for the summer, but the season is so pleasant here that she has almost concluded to remain at home and make short excursions. So that we will be here in Washington all summer.

"I rather like the change in France, and I think General McMahon will make a better president than Thiers, for he can keep out of the corps legislatif, which Thiers could not do. If France can stand a republic she must endure such presidents as time offers. It is easier to get a good president than a good dynasty.

"Our Modoc war is over, and soon the principal chiefs will be hung by due course of law (military), and the balance of the tribe will be dispersed among other tribes easily watched. We always have something of this sort every spring. Give my best love to Mrs. Byers, and believe me always your friend,

W. T. SHERMAN."

CHAPTER X
1873

THE SOURCE OF THE RHINE--STRANGE VILLAGES THERE--A REPUBLIC FOUR HUNDRED YEARS OLD--THE "GRAY LEAGUE"--"THE LEAGUE OF THE HOUSE OF GOD"--LOUIS PHILIPPE'S HIDING PLACE --A TOUR IN THE VALLEY OF THE INN--LETTER FROM GENERAL SHERMAN--REGRETS HIS CAREER SEEMS OVER.

This summer we determined to see the source of the River Rhine. For all that tourists seemed to know, it was only a mist among the clouds. It was far away in the upper and unfrequented Alps. We went on foot, and found all the upper Rhine scenery ten times as grand as anything below Schaffhausen and the Falls. Except the classic scenery from Bingen to Coblenz no scene there is to be at all compared with a hundred places on the Rhine, among the Swiss Alps. What is called the German Rhine, is far less striking. It is the Swiss Rhine, far above where it flows through Lake Constance, that is truly picturesque. At Chur, we turned to the right, into the mountains, and followed up the branch known as the "Vorder Rhine."

Every morning at the sunrise, we were trudging along the way with our knapsacks and staffs, with the wildest mountain scenery all about us. We passed many ruins of castles, and numerous picturesque little villages--Reichenau, Ilianz, Trois, Disentis.

We always rested a few hours in the middle of the day, slept awhile, and had simple dinners of trout and bread, with honey and wine.

Rich Peasant's House.

Right and left the scenery is gorgeous, certainly, but this grand nature is also man's enemy in these higher Alps. Flood and avalanche are forever threatening; the fields produce little, the villages are poor and wretched, and we ask ourselves, why do people seek such places to live in?

The answer is, they can't get away; they are too poor. Besides, here is where their ancestors lived always; why should they not live here, too, they answer. Years later, a girl from one of these places came and lived in our home as a domestic; but she was forever lamenting her mountains and her wretched village, spite of the fact that it had been three times overwhelmed by avalanches. That was the town of Selva.

Near to this Selva, is the hamlet of Gesten, and there eighty-four souls were lost by an avalanche in a single night. The big grave containing them all was shown to us, outside of the village.

Tourists who travel by coach and railway in Switzerland, have little conception of what real, Swiss, Alpine scenery or Alpine life is like. It is just judging the moon by looking through a telescope. Life in these almost unknown valleys, differs from all the rest of Switzerland. Here the commune is the government. Of national laws, or presidents and parliaments, the people know nothing. The village mayor is the king. Not many years ago, these mayors and their village advisers in the Vorder Rhine countries, could hang men and women of their own accord.

The people are a species of Italian and speak an Italian dialect. Five hundred years ago, they had petty republics up here. Here were the "Gray League," the "Ten Jurisdictions" and the "House of God."

In 1396, the liberty-loving people of the high Rhine valleys fought for liberty, and founded a little nation called Rhaetia, that lasted four hundred years, when it became united to Switzerland. Ilanz, their old capital, stands here still, a novel picture of past ages. The snow-capped mountains, the fine forests, the picturesque river Rhine, are there as they were then, and the sons and daughters of these old liberty athletes have changed almost as little as the scene of their fathers.

We walked on to Selva and spent the night. I could have thought myself living among Roman peasants in the time of Julius Cæsar. Everything was antique, simple, different from the nineteenth century. Corn grows up there, but the people live mostly from their flocks. I noticed the men wore earrings, and men and women, with their ruddy, brown faces and black hair, look like a better class of Southern gipsies. They have almost no books, few schools, and only a single newspaper in the whole valley. No human being, outside of the Upper Rhine, would think of calling that journal a newspaper. The houses are built of hewn logs, turned brown as a Cincinnati ham, and the clapboard roofs are held on by big stones.

Spite of their surroundings, these peasants and villagers are happy, and sing and dance as did their ancestors on the plains of Tuscany.

They fear the avalanches every night. They call them "The White Death," and look on them as sent by spirits.

They know little, and care less, about what is going on in the world, and would give more to wake up any morning, and find a new kid or lamb born, than to hear of the discovery of a new continent. Their only ambition is to get their cribs full for the winter, and at last to mix their bones with the dust of their fathers, beyond the village church.

Near to one of these villages, and farther down the valley, is the tiny lake of "Tama," and there the river Rhine begins. The natives here call it *"Running Water."* The stream is dark and green, and the lake is surrounded by dreary rocks and ice-clad mountains. It is 7,690 feet above the sea. Tourists on the palace steamers of the Rhine, down by the sands of Holland, should see the historic river at its cradle, if they would have memories to last forever.

We followed another branch of the Rhine that joins this one at Reichenau. It, too, is born among the grand mountain scenes, and sweeps through deep gorges, among them the famous Via Mala. Here at Reichenau, too, is the first bridge over the united Rhine. It is of wood, eighty feet high and 238 feet long, in a single arch.

Near it, we were shown a little, old castle that has become historic. There was a school kept there upon a time. One October evening of 1793, a wandering pilgrim, with a pack on his back, knocked at the door and begged the old schoolmaster to give him work. He could cipher and talk French, and write a decent hand. For many months, the humble stranger helped to teach the boys, and earned his daily bread. No one troubled himself to find out who he was. He signed his name Chabourd Latour. One evening, the boys saw the undermaster in tears. He was reading a newspaper, wherein was the account of his father's being beheaded on a Paris scaffold. The secret of the poor teacher was soon out. It was not Latour, but Louis Philippe, a coming king of France. He had wandered everywhere in disguise, for after his escape from banishment, no nation had dared give him a resting place.

This little Rhine valley had no more romantic story.

*****

One evening after we were back at Zurich a kindly faced gentleman called at the consulate. The fatal card hung on the door, "Office closed till 9 to-morrow." I was in the court below, with just ten minutes between me and train time. I was to hurry out home to a party by the lake. I saw the look of disappointment on the man's face, and something told me I ought to stop. The gentleman was a traveling American. Some papers of importance had to be signed by him immediately before a consul. Of course I missed the party, but I made a friend. It was Mr. A. D. Jessup, a Philadelphia millionaire. He lingered about Zurich a few days, and we met and talked together often. Sometimes we had our lunch and beer together at the famous little café Orsini. Then Mr. Jessup said good-by and left on his travels. A month from then a telegram came from him at Paris. It was an invitation to be his guest on a ten days' drive in the Austrian Tyrol, with a wind-up at the World's Fair in Vienna. He was a friend of President Grant's, the message continued, and he could arrange for my leave of absence.

A few mornings later a four-horse carriage halted by the consulate and we started for the Engadine, that lofty Alpine valley that is coursed for a hundred miles by the river Inn. This is not a valley of desolation. It is broad and productive, and once had many people and a little government of its own. To-day there are pretty villages at long distances and Insbruck is a picturesque and historic town. But the Inn valley is sky high compared with other rich valleys of Europe. We had bright sunshine and a delicious mountain air all the way. The Inn is rapid and beautiful, and right and left, for twenty miles at a stretch, rise high green hills, or else abrupt and lofty mountains, with sometimes bold and almost perpendicular crags. If we saw a rock that looked extraordinarily picturesque, away up toward the blue sky, there were sure to be also there the romantic ruins of some old castle. It seemed that we passed a hundred of these lofty ruins, with broken towers and fallen walls, through whose tall arches we sometimes saw patches of blue sky. Eagles soared around many of these lofty and deserted ruins. As we two drove for miles and miles along the white winding road by the river we constantly looked up at the romantic heights, and in our minds re-peopled the gray old castles and thought of the time, a thousand years ago, when all the peasantry of the rich valley were the serfs of masters who reveled in these castles built with the toil of the poor. A time came when the enslaved rose and all these castles were overthrown or burned and left as they are to-day. There are ruins high up above this Inn valley that, doubtless, have not been visited by a human footstep in a hundred years. Most of them are inaccessible. The former roads cut up the rocky mountain sides to them, are gone and forgotten, and the heights with their awful ridges against the sky look as desolate as the desert.

We closed our delightful journey with a visit to the World's Fair at Vienna. Barring the Swiss National Exhibition, I have never seen anything so fine.

On my return I found this letter from General Sherman waiting me. In it, he expresses regret that his active career seems over:

"WASHINGTON, D. C., July 14, 1873.

"DEAR BYERS: I received your letter some days ago and sent it from my office to the house, for the perusal of Mrs. Sherman, therefore it is not before me now. I take it for granted that Minnie is, or must be, at Zurich or near there. Since she has been traveling from Italy her letters have been less frequent, and I fear some of our letters to her have miscarried, or been delayed. It is now pretty well determined that she will remain over the winter, so that she will have plenty of time to see all things that can be of interest. I hope that she will give Switzerland a good long visit, and that from there she will make the excursions that are so convenient. We all write to her often, so she must feel perfectly easy on our behalf. Instead of going to Carlisle, as Mrs. S. first intended, the family have remained here in Washington, and I see no cause to regret it, for we have had but little oppressive weather, and our house is so large and airy that I doubt if any change would be for the better. Of course, all the fashionable people, including most of the officers, have gone to the seashore or mountains, so that Washington is comparatively dull, but the many changes here in the streets, and abundance of flowing water have added much to the comfort of those who remain and can't get away.

"Elly and Rachel, the two smaller girls, who were at school when you were here, are now at home, and are busy all day with their companions, playing croquet in our yard. Tom is putting in his vacation by riding horseback with two of his companions up through Pennsylvania. At last date he was near Altoona, and will be gone all of July and part of August. I suppose the return of Minister Rublee to his post has disappointed you, but you must have patience and do well that which is appointed for you, leaving for time that advancement which all ambitious men should aim for. I sometimes regret that I am at the end of my rope, for it is an old saying that there is more real pleasure in the pursuit than in reaching the goal. Although you may hear of cholera in this country, I assure you that it is not serious. I suppose the same is true of Europe, though it is reported the Shah of Persia declined to visit Vienna on account of cholera. I think Minnie ought to visit Vienna, if only for a week, to see that really beautiful city, and to visit Mr. Jay's family. My best love to Mrs. Byers. Truly your friend,

W. T. SHERMAN."

CHAPTER XI
1874

SHERMAN ON CUBA--VISIT ITALY--GARIBALDI'S WONDERFUL RECEPTION AT ROME--THE ARTIST FREEMAN--FIRST AMERICAN PAINTER TO LIVE IN ROME--ROME IN 1840--SEE VICTOR EMMANUEL--JOAQUIN MILLER--HIS CONVERSATION AND APPEARANCE--NEW SWISS CONSTITUTION--MORE LETTERS FROM GENERAL SHERMAN--TOO MANY COMMANDERS IN WASHINGTON FOR HIM--WILL GO TO ST. LOUIS--HIS VIEWS OF WAR HISTORIES.

A hint once that if I preferred to be in the Army instead of the Consular service the matter could be arranged, led me to think of one of the Paymasterships then being created by Congress. The General wrote me as to these plans. His letter has value only because of the prophecy as to Cuba.

"WASHINGTON, D. C., Nov. 28, 1873.

"DEAR BYERS:--I was very glad to get your letter of November 12th this morning, as it reminds me of a duty neglected to write you, renewing my thanks to you for your extreme kindness to Minnie. She arrived home about the 1st of November perfectly well, and she has been quietly at home ever since. The winter season is about to begin, and she must do her share in society. We begin to-night by a large reception at Mr. Fish's, and I suppose must keep it up through the winter. I suppose that Mr. Rublee will remain where he is, and the Department regarding you as fixed, will not voluntarily promote you to a larger Consulate.

"As to the Army, things are somewhat confused. There is a law forbidding any appointments or promotions in the staff corps and Departments, including the Paymasters. Of these there are for duty about forty-seven, and I understand the Paymaster-General, Alvord, says he must have fifty-three to do the necessary work. And in his annual report to be submitted to Congress next Monday he will ask for that number, and I believe the Secretary of War and the President both approve, but for these six places there are more than a hundred conspicuous applicants. Yet I will submit your letter, or so much of it as refers to that subject, to General Belknap, who knows you and whose recommendation will be conclusive. Of course I, too, will endorse. But don't build any castles on this, for I know what a rush there will be on the first symptom of Congress opening the subject. Everybody here is on the qui vive for Cuba, but I don't get excited, for I believe the diplomatists will settle it, but sooner or later Cuba will cause trouble in that quarter. I will give your message to Mrs. Sherman, to Lizzie, Minnie, etc., and will always be glad to hear such good news of the baby and Mrs. Byers. Give them my best love, and believe me,

"Truly, etc.,
W. T. SHERMAN."

March, 1874.--Went to Italy for a month, via the Mont Ceni. I was surprised at the beauty of the river boulevard in Pisa, for travelers rarely mention it. To my mind, it is finer than the Lung Arno of Florence. Besides, it is something to see a big bridge made wholly of marble.

The one man of all men in Italy I hoped to see, was Garibaldi, the Ulysses of the modern world.

He was not to be seen; but I tried to console myself by looking over to his little island of Caprera, near the Sardinian coast. Dumas' Life of Garibaldi set my mind on fire with the story of this man. My inn-keeper at Naples, too, had been with the patriot in all his campaigns. Listening to him talk was as entertaining as reading Homer.

Garibaldi.

King Victor Emmanuel.

The scene, when Garibaldi came to Rome from the solitude of his little island, to enter parliament the next year, was worthy the brush of a great artist. The Italy that he had made, and presented to Victor Emmanuel, had seemed to have forgotten the old man of Caprera. He was feeble and poor and rheumatic. Suddenly all Italy, *his* Italy, remembered him. The King sent a gilded chariot drawn by six white horses, to take him through the streets of Rome. As the old cripple, wearing his Garibaldi mantle, limped into the Parliament house, every member rose to do him honor. I would rather have been Garibaldi in Rome that day, than to have been Cæsar, riding along the same streets, with slaves and subjugated peoples in his train.

March 5.--Looked at numbers of the historic Roman palaces. The one that affected me most was the dingy and neglected old building in the Ghetto, where the Cenci lived. This immense and half-empty pile, in an obscure part of Rome, would attract nobody, save for the story of a beautiful girl, immortalized by the pencil of Guido Reni. All the time I was within the building, my mind was on a scene in a prison, where this same girl hung in torments before her cruel tormentors, crying to be let down, and she "would tell it all"--the killing of her own father.

And then came that morning before daylight, the morning of her execution. Herself and an artist are in a cell. A little candle burns, the executioners wait outside the door, and Guido Reni, to make her picture striking, drapes a sheet about her head and shoulders, while all the time she is waiting there for death. Saddest tale of Rome!

Next morning I called at the American Legation. Mr. W----, the secretary, affected the utmost ignorance and indifference as to who I was, or whether my card would finally reach Mr. Marsh, our Minister. I asked him to hand the card back to me, and walked over to the Rospigliosi palace, where Mr. Marsh promptly received me, and in the kindest manner. I was in the presence of a statesman and a scholar--not a snob.

Mr. Marsh had followed the Italian court all about Italy--to Turin, Florence, Rome. He stood high in the estimation of the Italian court and foreign diplomats. His genius and scholarship were now casting luster on the American name.

"Don't tell anybody at home what a palace I live in," he said to me, jocosely. "They will think me an aristocrat over there, whereas I am the plainest of republicans. Here in Rome a palace is just as cheap as anything. Everybody lives in a palace here."

In another part of the palace, I saw Guido's great picture of Aurora. I noticed the mark of the French cannon ball that went through it when Garibaldi was defending Rome.

Bought a copy of Guido's Cenci, and then went and looked at the Angelo bridge, where they cut off the head of Beatrice.

I went often to Mr. Freeman's studio. He was the first American painter to live in Rome. He was, too, the first U.S. Consul to Italy, and he it was who protected Margaret Fuller, on a time, from the danger of a mob. It was at the time the French forced their way into Rome. He planted the Stars and Stripes on her balcony, and the mob fell back. That was in 1849.

Freeman painted a picture for me that has inspired a poem by J. Buchanan Read. It was "The Princess." The model was a blonde, with hair like gold. Freeman corrected my notion that there were no blondes in Italy. There are many, just as there were in the time of the earlier masters. Yellow was Titian's favorite color.

Freeman told me much of Rome, as it was when he first went there, in 1840. He lived there under three popes, Gregory, Pius IX and Leo XIII.

Rome was entirely different from to-day. The houses had open entrances, or, where there were doors, they swung outward to the street, like American barn doors. There were almost no sidewalks, and the few seen were only wide enough for one person. The streets were dimly lighted by occasional oil lamps, great distances apart. Of course, assassination in such streets was of common occurrence. The water spouts of the houses were so projected as to empty themselves in cataracts on the heads of passers-by.

The pavements were made of cobble stones, that had to be covered with straw or earth when the Pope went abroad in his grandeur.

The city was full of foreign artists, along in the fifties, as now. Among them were Crawford and Greenough, Story and *West*, whom Byron called *"Europe's worst painter and poor England's best."*

The fact is, West was a Pennsylvania Quaker, though he became King George's court artist, and at last got buried in St. Paul's Cathedral.

I went often to the Vatican, not to see the palace itself, for that impressed me not at all, or only as a great and miscellaneous pile, but to see a certain picture there. The artist who made it was but thirty-seven years old when he died. Yet, it has been said that in the "Transfiguration" one sees "the last perfection of art." This picture seems to be one of those things that no one ever thinks to try to emulate. Like the Iliad and Paradise Lost, nothing of their kind came before them, and nothing is looked for to follow them.

One morning I was drinking my coffee in a little den in the Via Condotti. A very singular-looking man came in and sat down at the little table next to mine. Hearing me speak English with a friend, he addressed me. "You are the Consul at Zurich, are you not? You were pointed out to me the other day in the street. I am Joaquin Miller of California. Let us get acquainted." I moved my chair and coffee over to his table. I was greatly gratified at meeting a poet who seemed to me to have some of the genius of Byron. His "Songs of the Sierras" have the ring of the master. Last summer I read them in Switzerland. Their freshness, their flavor of the prairie and the mountain, their passionate utterance, took me by storm. What the English said of him, in their extravagant joy at "discovering" a live genius in the wilds of the United States, did not affect me, it was the stirring passion of the verse itself. The buffalo, the Indian scout, the burning prairie, the people of the desert, the women with bronzed arms and palpitating hearts, the men in sombreros, with brave lives, and love worth the dying for--that was what he was writing about, and they were all alive before me.

Sitting here at the little white marble table of an Italian café, he seemed all out of place. There was nothing in the surroundings of which this half-wild looking poet-scout of the prairies was a part. His yellow locks, flashing blue eyes, stormy face, athletic form, careless dress, and broad-brimmed hat on the floor by his feet, all told of another kind of life.

Much of his talk was cynical in the extreme. He was ridiculing everything, everybody, even himself, and he looked about him as if constantly thinking to grab his hat, bound for the door, and rush over the Tiber with a yell. He hated restraint of any kind whatever--dress, custom, language.

Miller was now writing in some little attic in Rome, but none of his friends knew where. He would not tell them; he wanted to be alone.

A boy brought us the morning journal, and we talked of newspapers. I asked him what English and American papers he read. He smiled, and answered ironically: "When I want *seriousness*, I read the London *Punch*, and for *truth*, I take the New York *Herald*."

There was no talk that morning with him about poetry, but he was jocose and cynical.

He asked me what I was doing. I told him I was getting ready to try my hand at a drama. "Don't do it--all damned nonsense!" he cried. "Dramas worth anything are not wanted, and if you write in blank verse, as you say you propose, not one actor in five hundred knows how to recite the lines. It must be *mighty plain prose* for these wind sawyers."

Just then a tall, fine looking young man came and sat down by our table. Mr. Miller nudged me, and whispered, "Bingen on the Rhine." "That is young Norton, son of the woman who wrote 'Bingen on the Rhine.'" I looked at him with interest; but he was English, and I was a stranger, so conversation at that particular table suddenly stopped.

It was on this visit to Rome that I often saw Victor Emmanuel, Italy's first King. Every Sunday afternoon he drove on the Pincian Hill. The extreme Catholics of Rome, the Pope's party, paid him little or no attention, and scarcely greeted him when he passed; but all the rest of Rome and all Italy nearly worshiped the "Re Galantuomo." He was a stout, dark looking man, with black eyes and a mustache like a horse's mane. He was fifty-six years old then, and had been twelve years King of Sardinia, and sixteen years King of Italy.

At this time our Minister, Mr. Marsh, arranged to have a friend and myself presented to Pope Pius IX, but a sudden attack of Roman fever deprived me of the pleasure.

Two men have existed in my life-time whom I should have given much to know,--Mr. Gladstone and Abraham Lincoln. Once I was a bearer of dispatches to Mr. Lincoln, but illness led me to hurry away, after giving the trust to General Grant. It has been the regret of my life that I missed grasping the hand of, possibly, the greatest man that ever lived.

BACK IN SWITZERLAND. Great excitement on this May Day, 1874, for on the 19th of last month, by a popular vote, the people changed the Swiss Constitution. Instead of twenty-two little cantons, doing just as they pleased, they will now have a centralized republic, more like the United States.

Some interesting features of the new Swiss system are these: The President is chosen for but a year, and can not succeed himself in office. No military surrender is allowed. The post and telegraph and telephone belong to the government, which also controls all railroads and owns some. Schools are free and compulsory. Salt and gunpowder are government monopolies, and factories are under national control or regulation. Abuse of the freedom of the press may be punished by the general council. Supreme Court Judges are elected, but from the legislative body. National laws must be submitted to popular vote if demanded by 30,000 people. The President must be chosen by the Assembly from among its own members. Members of the Cabinet have seats and votes in the Assembly.

August 18, 1874.--Had a long letter some time since from General Sherman. He says: "Don't rely too much on my influence here in Washington. Privately, we feel here that President Grant has somewhat gone back on his old friends, in trying to make alliances with new ones. Besides, I am compelled to endorse a good many on their war record, and would not like to be found to choose among them." He also says that this fall he will probably move to St. Louis. "There are too many commanding officers here in Washington."

On the 7th he writes interestingly about the histories of the war.

"WASHINGTON, D. C., August 7, 1874.

"DEAR BYERS:--I was glad to receive your letter of the 19th of July, and, with you, think the Centennial of Philadelphia will prove a lamentable failure. Congress will not probably adopt it as a national affair, and it will degenerate into a mere state or city affair.

"Economy is now the cry here, and it may be that it is forced on us by the vast cost of the Civil War, which was bridged over by paper money, that now calls for interest and principal. As in former years, the first blow falls on the Army and Navy, that are treated as mere pensioners, and every cent is begrudged.

"No one who was an actor in the Grand Drama of the Civil War, seems willing to risk its history. I have endeavored to interest Members of Congress in the preliminary steps of preparing and printing in convenient form the official dispatches, but find great opposition, lest the task should fall on some prejudiced person who would in the preparation and compilation favor McClellan or Grant or some one party.

"All histories thus far, of which Draper's is the best, are based for facts on the newspaper reports, which were necessarily hasty and imperfect. Till the official reports are accessible, it would be unsafe for any one to attempt a narration of events beyond his personal vision, and no single person saw a tenth part of the whole. I have some notes of my own part in manuscript, and copies of all my reports and letters, but am unwilling to have them printed lest it should involve me in personal controversies.

"Minnie will be married Oct. 1st, and we will all remove to St. Louis soon thereafter.

"All send you and Mrs. Byers the assurance of their affection. Believe me always your friend,

"W. T. SHERMAN."

CHAPTER XII
1875

LETTERS FROM MRS. SHERMAN AND THE GENERAL--HE TELLS ME HE IS WRITING HIS LIFE--THE NEGRO QUESTION--A CHATEAU BY LAKE ZURICH--I WRITE A BOOK ON SWITZERLAND--ALSO WRITE A PLAY--A CITY OF DEAD KINGS--GO TO LONDON--MEET COLONEL FORNEY--DINNER AT GEO. W. SMALLEY'S--KATE FIELD--VISIT BOUCICAULT--CONVERSATIONS WITH THE NEWER SHAKESPEARE--THE BEAUTIFUL MINNIE WALTON--BREAKFAST AT HER HOME--PROF. FICK--HIS HOUSE BUILT IN THE OLD ROMAN WALL--LECTURES--HOLIDAYS AT THE CONSULATE--MRS. CONGRESSMAN KELLEY--A STUDENT COMMERS--BEER DRINKING--DUKES OF THE REPUBLIC--DUELS--LETTER FROM GENERAL SHERMAN--PRUSSIAN ARMY MANEUVERS.

March 24, 1875.--Received a welcome and gossipy letter from Mrs. General Sherman. It reads:

"ST. LOUIS, MO., March 12, 1875.

"MY DEAR MAJOR:--Your welcome letter would have been answered immediately, but I have not been well. My general health is very good, but the weather this Winter has been exceptionally cold.

"Minnie and her good husband, with whom she is very happy, live a few squares from us, and we see them every day; Minnie having learned to be a great walker, during her sojourn in Europe. We find our circle of friends and acquaintances very large, and we find that almost as much time has to be devoted to visiting here as in Washington. We are delightfully situated in the home we occupied for several years, before we removed to Washington, and which belongs to us. We have plenty of spare room for friends, and shall certainly claim a good, long visit from you and Mrs. Byers and the children, when you return to your own country. Should the next Administration be Democratic, that may not be very long hence. Pray remember that I shall expect you.

"I have seen, and admire very much, your poem on 'The Sea' in the 'Navy Journal.'

"I am very glad you were gratified to receive the pretty copy of your grand song, 'When Sherman Marched Down to the Sea.' I shall have something else to send you soon. The General's Memoirs are in the hands of the publishers, Appleton & Co., of N. Y., and will be out in May. It will be in two volumes, excellent print, and I am sure you will find it entertaining. I will see that you get an early copy. Please write to me when you receive it, without waiting to read it, because I shall be anxious to know if it has gone safely. Should you not receive it by the last of May, let me know. Do not buy a copy, for I wish to send you one. The book begins in 1846 and extends to the close of the war. The chapters that I have read are *highly interesting*.

"The General seems to be growing older in appearance, but his health is good, and his spirits are the same; his vivacity has not sensibly diminished. To-night he is off to the theater, to see Charlotte Cushman, who makes her last appearance in St. Louis to-morrow. We have had a great many attractive actors and actresses here this Winter, and we have yet in store a greater treat than all. Ristori is playing in New York and will be here some time during the Spring. The General and Lizzie both admired Albani exceedingly, and think her a superior actress to Nielson and as good a singer. I did not see her, as the weather was bad and my cold was severe during her stay here.

"St. Louis is a city of great commercial enterprise and has a wonderful future before her. Perhaps you will select this as a place of residence on your return home. We would be very glad to have you here.

"I hope Mrs. Byers and the children are well and that your own health grows stronger. Lizzie joins me in best love to all. She and I are alone to-night. Elly and Rachel are away at school, Minnie in a home of her own, and Cumpsy in bed.

"Believe me very truly and warmly your friend,

"ELLEN EWING SHERMAN."

I find this in my diary. On returning from Italy, we went over to "Wangensbach" by Kussnacht, on Lake Zurich, to live for a Summer or two. Wangensbach is an old chateau, or half castle-place, built by the Knights of St. John in the long, long ago. The walls are three feet thick, in places more, and there are all sorts of vaulted wine cellars and mysterious, walled-in places, under the building. The view from the windows and terrace, of blue lake and snowy mountains, is superb in the extreme. The chateau is now owned by Conrad Meyer, the Swiss poet and novelist. It is six miles to my office in the city, and I walk in and out daily, though I could go on the pretty steamers for a sixpence. Here, on a May day, "Baby Hélène" came into the world, to gladden eight sweet years for us.

Wangensbach.

Spite of Joaquin Miller's prognostications at Rome about plays, I was foolish enough to go ahead, and write a melodrama in blank verse. Schultz-Beuthen, a friend of Liszt and follower of Wagner, wrote delightful music for its songs. I went up to Mannheim, and attended the plays in the old theater where Schiller was once a director, and where some of his best plays were brought out.

Miller wrote me about this little play of mine as follows:

"N. Y. HOTEL, N. Y., U. S. A., Feb. 11, 1879.

"MY DEAR MR. BYERS:--I remember you with pleasure, remember the compliment you paid me in preferring a visit to me before the good Pope.

"I have read your pretty play with pleasure, and have the opinion of able managers. And I am bound to say, my dear boy, that it is for the leisure, not for the stage. Like all your work, it is well done, verses *especially*, but how on earth do you expect to present five scenes in one act in this swift modern day? All modern plays have, as a rule, but one scene to the act. Then you have almost altogether omitted *humor*. Try again. By the by, I last night brought forth a play. See enclosed bill. It was most emphatically *damned*. Write me if I can do ought for you, and believe me

Truly yours,
J. W. MILLER."

My libretto and the music had pleased Minnie Hauk, the singer, and she herself thought of using it, but the objection to the Wagner kind of music came up. Her husband, Count Wartegg, wrote me from Paris: "The libretto is very interesting, so original, and so well written that its success is assured."

Minnie Hauk.

Minnie Hauk was just now at the height of her fame. In Scotland and England she was very popular. At Edinburg the college students one night, at the close of the opera, unhitched the horses from her carriage and pulled her to the hotel themselves. I knew her quite well in Switzerland. In fact, her secret marriage with Count Wartegg had taken place in my office, and I had been a part of the little adventure. She was a wife for years before the public found it out. Her husband had an historic old castle over in the mountains of the Tyrol.

In the meantime I had prepared another little play, and Miss Kate Field had given them both to Genevieve Ward, who sent me this about them:

"232 RUE DE RIVOLI, PARIS, 26 Dec., 1875.

"DEAR SIR:--I received the plays you confided to Miss Field, and read them with much pleasure. Pocahontas should be very popular in America, and I trust you will be fortunate in having it well produced. The sympathies of the public should also be warmly enlisted for the 'Princess Tula,' a charming character, which requires delicate handling. Miss Clara Morris would personate it most charmingly. I regret that they are both lighter than my line of business, which is the heaviest. I feel none the less honored that you should have sent them to me, and again thanking you, and wishing you every success, I remain

Yours truly,
"GENEVIEVE WARD."

The second drama was not offered to the managers at all, and the two plays were laid away forever.

While on the Rhine I also visited Speyer, "The City of Dead Kings." In one crypt seven German monarchs lie side by side. Next to Westminster Abbey in London, and the Capuchin Church in Vienna, no one spot can show so much royal dust, and nowhere on earth can one feel so much the fleeting littleness of man as in these three places.

*****

I had spent much time in preparing my book, called "Switzerland and the Swiss." Now when I asked permission of our State Department to print it they promptly telegraphed me a refusal.

A Consul, not long before, had published a book on Turkey that was not liked by some of the satraps of the Sultan. So a veto was put on all books by Consuls.

My book was then printed anonymously, but received most favorable comment. "Whoever the author is," said the "Zurcher Zeitung," the principal Swiss journal, "he has shown more thorough knowledge of the Swiss people than any foreigner who has written about us." The large edition was sold, spite of its being published anonymously.3

The London papers have much to say now about the mixed condition of party affairs in America. Yesterday I had a letter from General Sherman bearing on the same subject. It also tells me he is writing a history of his life. It also gives his views of negroes voting.

"ST. LOUIS, MO., Jan. 26, 1875.

"DEAR BYERS:--Your letter of Nov. 21st, sending a copy of the London Saturday Review, has been in my pigeon hole 'For answer' so long that I am ashamed. I have always intended to avail myself of the opportunity to write you a long, gossipy letter, but have as usual put it off from day to day, so that now I hardly know what to tell you. We are now most comfortably established in St. Louis, a large, growing and most dirty city, but which in my opinion is a far better place for the children than the clean and aristocratic Washington. Minnie, also, is domiciled near us in a comfortable home, whilst her husband seems busy on his new work in connection with a manufactory of wire.

"I have no doubt that General Grant and the Cabinet think me less enthusiastic in the political management than I ought to be. And they may be right. In some respects they have been selfish and arrogant, and are fast losing that hold on public respect they used to enjoy, and there is now but little doubt but that they have thrown the political power into an opposition that the old Democratic party will utilize for itself. The mistake began in 1865 when they gave votes to the negroes, and then legislated so as to make the negro dominant at the South where the old Rebel whites represent eight millions to the four of the blacks, and the first have united solidly into a dangerous opposition. In our form of Government, when the majority rules in local Government, it is hard for the National

Government to coerce this majority to be docile and submissive to a party outside, however respectable.

"I had seen that article in the Review, as also many others of mine which, on the whole, are flattering. I have, after considerable hesitation, agreed to publish the whole, of which that one was the conclusion. The book, still in manuscript, is estimated to make two octavo volumes of about four hundred pages each, and I have given the manuscript of the first volume to the Appletons of New York, and will send the balance this week. The whole should be out in about three months, when I trust it will afford you a couple of days of pleasant reading. Thus far the public has no knowledge of this thing, but I suppose I can not conceal it much longer.

"We are all well. Give our best love to Mrs. Byers, and believe me truly your friend,

"W. T. SHERMAN."

After a while the book appeared, and again the General wrote about it.

"ST. LOUIS, MO., Aug. 31, 1875.

"MY DEAR FRIEND:--I have received your welcome favor of July 31st. Mrs. Sherman has since got one of later date, in which you acknowledge the receipt of the Memoirs. I am glad, of course, that they pleased you in form and substance. Such is the general judgment of those who embraced the whole book, whilst others, picking out a paragraph here and there, find great fault. When I had made up my mind to publish, I prepared myself for the inevitable consequences of offending some. I tried to make a truthful picture of the case, as it was left in my mind, without fear, favor or affection, and though it may cause bad feelings now, will in the end be vindicated. I want no friend to eulogize or apologize, but leave the volumes to fight out their own battle.

"We are all now at home except Minnie, who has her own home not far from us. Her baby is growing and beginning to assume the form of humanity, recognizing objects and manifesting a will and purpose of his own.

"Early in September all the children will resume their schools--Tom at Yale, Elly at Manhattanville, N. Y., the rest here in St. Louis. With the exception of some minor excursions I will remain close at home. Our annual meeting of the Army of the Tennessee will be at Des Moines this year--Sept. 29–30. We don't expect much, only to keep it alive. We look for a stormy political Winter, and next year another of the hurricanes that test our strength every four years.

"My best love to Mrs. B. and the children.

"Yours,
W. T. SHERMAN."

January, 1875.--I went to London to see about my play. Stopped at 10 Duchess Street. General Schenck was our Minister then, and he and Colonel John W. Forney gave me letters to theatrical people. Mr. Geo. W. Smalley was also polite to me.

It was a nice American dinner-party I participated in at Mr. Smalley's home, and while there was a little air of stiffness in the white-gloved, side-whiskered waiters, it was a hospitable, jolly occasion. Among the guests were Kate Field, Col. Forney, Secretary McCullough, and some English literary people. Kate Field was wide awake, and she, and Col. Forney, one of the best talkers and best informed men I ever knew, kept things lively till midnight. Col. Forney was one of the handsomest men I ever met, and was loyally faithful to friends.

One of my letters was to Dion Boucicault, the actor, probably the biggest dramatic plagiarist since Shakespeare. His name was to about two hundred plays, of which he certainly never wrote a dozen complete. He was of immense talent in the way of absorbing, or transposing, or cribbing outright other people's work, without their even knowing it. In a sense, he did make things his own. If what he afterward said to me about there not being an absolutely new idea in the world is true, then he was not a stage plagiarist, as much as a first class boiler-over.

In this Winter of 1874–5 he was the most popular actor in London, and Joe Jefferson was playing there too, as was Henry Irving. At Drury Lane theater, there was nothing but standing room, day or night, when Boucicault was on the boards. His wife was playing with him. Several times I stood up among a crowd of Londoners whose hands were too pressed in to clap, but they made it up in crying or laughing. It was melodrama in perfection. All the immense crowd felt themselves actual participants in the play. What a bag full of money the English-American must have lugged home this winter.

One evening a note came for me to call on him at his house, at 9 o'clock next morning. It was foggy and almost dark on the streets when I rang the door bell. I was shown into a drawing room dimly lighted, where, sitting in the half dark, by a low open fire, was a man I could have taken for William Shakespeare. The lofty brow, the intellectual face, the partly bald head, looked like no other. He did not see me as I entered, nor did he turn around, but went on looking into the fireplace. I looked at him a moment sitting there, and then said good morning. "Ah," he said, looking up as calmly as if his whole attitude had been affected. "Good morning, take a seat. I read your play, it is melodrama, it is no account; that is, as it stands, you know. You had best hire a good stage man to go over it for you. You haven't studied the stage, that's clear, and that is what is the matter of our countrymen, Mr. ---- and Mr. ----. They can write, but they know no more about the stage plays than new-born babes." I sat there and listened to him in astonishment.

He talked much of himself, and related some of his methods of making plays *play*. But the real secret, he could not translate for me further than to say, "The way to write a play, is to *write a play*."

I could not help thinking, as I sat there listening to the voice by the firelight, of the time when Boucicault had to sell a play for from $200 to $300, and of that later time when a play with his name to it brought him almost $50,000.

I took his advice as to my melodrama and had a playwright go through it with pencil and shears.

When I got home to Zurich a telegram asked that I forward the music at once. A London theater had accepted my play. Shortly the theatrical hard times set in; my theater closed doors, and that was the last of "Pocahontas," a melodrama.

Thomas' orchestra took some of the music later, and played it with success at the Philadelphia Centennial.

Minnie Walton.

One morning when in London, I was invited to breakfast with Minnie Walton, the actress. She was at the "Hay-market," playing with Byron, I think. She was noted then as the most beautiful actress in London. At the appointed hour I was at her house, but she was still in bed. I entertained myself in the drawing room for half an hour with her two pretty children. Then she herself came in, and I certainly saw a brilliantly beautiful woman. Her features were smooth and perfect, her complexion very fair, and her manners most captivating. She wore a white morning dress with network bodice that outlined a form as beautiful as her face. She had no wonderful reputation as an actress, but her beauty attracted many Londoners to the theater. Everywhere in the shop windows, one saw pictures of "The pretty Minnie Walton." She had a power in London, all her own. It was "the fatal gift of beauty," but a gift more attractive to women than birthrights and coronets.

November, 1875.--Upon my return from London, we went back into town for the winter. House rent has doubled here in four years. We now pay 2,500 francs for a centrally located apartment of seven rooms. Everything has grown dearer. The pension where we used to live for four francs a day now charges seven and eight and nine francs.

Zurich too is becoming a fine, modern, commercial city. The railway station is almost the finest in the world, and big, granite business blocks are building, that would do credit to New York or London. Where the city moat and a graveyard used to be, is now one of the finest short streets in Europe.

Almost the only house on this street, left of the olden time, is the "Ringmauer," the home of our friend, Prof. Fick. Its front is an absolute wall of ivy, from the pavement to the gables. The whole front wall of the house is a part of the ancient city wall itself, built possibly by the Romans. The rooms are low, and the windows used to be ironed like a prison. Near by, still stands one of the old wall towers. Inside this ivy-covered old domicile, we have spent many happy hours. Many a time, over the walnuts and the wine, with the genial Professor and his family, we have sat far into the night and conjured up the people who were wining and dining here in this same room, may be a thousand years ago. Fick, a brother-in-law of Frankland, the English scientist, was a distinguished law professor in the University. He originated the Swiss railroad law, and knew more of American affairs than any German I met abroad.

In late years, he suffered horribly with rheumatism, and he had a queer habit, when severe attacks came on, of sitting down and comparing the severity of each attack with one in some previous month. He kept his watch lying open before him, and carefully recorded each twang and pain in a diary.

Spite of my sympathy for his suffering, I could at times hardly refrain from smiling, on hearing him exclaim: "Ah! that was a whacker, that catch was--must write that down. Let me see--lasted two minutes, pulse 80; this day, last year, minute and a half, pulse 100." So for an hour he would sit, his feet wrapped in flannel, and his mind occupied in measuring and timing his pains.

"What do you do that for, Professor?" I asked him once. "My God!" he replied, "it helps busy my mind. I would die without this watch and diary."

In the afternoon the attack would cease, and in the evening the students would see the loved Professor delivering his lecture as smilingly as if he had never had a pain in his life.

December, 1875.--Through Fick, Kinkel, Scherr and others of our friends among the University professors, we had free entrée to lectures when we pleased; could come or go. Scherr's on France, and Kinkel's on art, we heard throughout, as also Henne's on Swiss history. There were numbers of American students too in the Polytechnic and University, so that our relations with teachers and taught were very friendly. The American students were always at our home on all American holidays, when the Consulate and our apartment were opened up together and decorated with our national colors. Speeches were made, toasts drunk, and a general good American time had. We ourselves greatly enjoyed these reunions on a foreign soil, and the students and American residents gave many proofs that they enjoyed them too.

I recall how just before one Christmas, Mrs. Kelley, wife of Congressman Kelley, of Philadelphia, who was then living in Zurich, asked me to go with her to help select a picture for an American friend. I felt honored that she should consult my taste. A very fine and expensive engraving of Dante at Florence was selected.

What was my surprise, on Christmas evening, to see her head the American party to our house, with this picture and a speech to the Consul.

The treasured gift hangs in my Iowa home, but the kind words of that Christmas evening are stored away in the depths of our hearts. It was the sign, not the gift itself, that gratified us most.

Most of us mortals are so constituted that to have the esteem of our fellow beings gives us a most comfortable feeling *here*, anyway, whatever it may do for us *hereafter*.

December 7.--Last night Prof. Kinkel invited me to attend a Students' Commers or festival. There must have been a thousand students present in the big skating rink. They sat at long tables; the corps students in high boots, and wearing their corps caps, badges and ribbons. In front of every one stood a mighty schooner of beer. All smoked, and the narcotic cloud was so dense I could scarcely see to the stage. There were decorations everywhere, and a band of music in the gallery. There were sentinels outside at the door, and whenever a particularly popular professor was about to enter, signals were waved along the tables and to the band. Then, as he walked blushing through the aisles to the stage, pandemonium itself was let loose in the way of clanging glasses, band playing, pounding tables, hurrahing and singing, until the conquering hero was seated on the platform. It was a great time for the professors. Lunge, the chemist; Kinkel, the poet; Hermann, the physiologist; Scherr, the historian; Meyer, the chemist; Klebs, the bacteriologist, and other men with names that sound all over Europe, were literally carried to the stage on the wings of noise, smoke, music and lager beer.

These great Zurich professors are the men whom Hepworth Dixon calls the "Dukes of the Republic." They are the only people in Switzerland appointed to their places for life.

Students near me got away with a dozen and more schooners of Munich's best. I don't know where it went to, but they have been known to drink twenty glasses at a sitting. For myself, to keep up appearances I did away with three glasses and a half, and absorbed smoke enough, without touching a cigar, to give me the headache for a week.

Here, as at the German Universities, the corps students fought duels. The most self-important young man in the city is the one with the little red corps cap, the big top boots, the ribbon across his breast, and the fresh patch of muslin on his nose, showing a recent engagement.

If the duelist has attended still other universities, he will probably have a half a dozen welts and scars across his face. He may not know much about text-books, but these unseemly welts on the face are signs of great honor; and as the man of danger struts down the street with a big-mouthed bull-dog in tow, he is a spectacle to behold. His greatest happiness in life is to have some passer-by turn and gaze on him.

And this was what Bismarck was doing at twenty; this, and shooting off pistols in his bedroom!

These University warriors are not so dangerous as their slit-up noses indicate. I have known of fifty duels in the past few years and not a soul, save one, was badly hurt. He *did* get really killed.

The offenses for which the students bleed and die are all petty, fanciful, and even provoked. Sometimes corps members are simply compelled by their different societies to go out and seek a fight and try their mettle. Ill feeling or enmity, I have noticed, has not of necessity anything to do with student dueling.

*****

November 20.--Had this from General Sherman:

"WASHINGTON, D. C., Nov. 9, 1875.

"DEAR BYERS:--I am indebted to you two letters, the last one enclosing the comments on the Prussian Army as developed in the Autumn maneuvers in Silesia. There is no doubt Prussia, otherwise the German Empire, is determined to keep up the physique, organization and instruction to meet any possible conflict, thus necessitating much loss of labor, and constant trouble in furnishing arms and food. We cannot attempt to follow her example, though of course we can learn much from their experience. General Meigs was present on the occasion of these maneuvers and will on his return make an official report which will be in book form, easy of preservation.

"Republican successes here this fall make the officials feel better, but the fact that the House of Representatives is Democratic will cause much confusion and heartburning this Winter, and until the nominations are made next Summer.

"My best love to Mrs. Byers.

"Yours truly,
W. T. SHERMAN."

CHAPTER XIII
1876

STORM IN THE ALPS--MR. BENJAMIN--KATE SHERWOOD BONNER--ICEBERGS--A SCOTCH POET--HORATIO KING'S LITERARY EVENINGS--COL. FORNEY--MR. ROBERT--A NEW YORK MILLIONAIRE'S HOME--A CHRISTMAS NIGHT HURRICANE AT SEA--THE TILDEN-HAYES FIGHT--CIVIL WAR FEARED IN WASHINGTON--DENNISON, THE INVENTOR--A STRANGE MURDER--THE WRECK OF THE SCHILLER AND LOSS OF MISS DIMMICK.

September 1.--Spent a day or so of each week this summer up at the Alpine hamlet, Obstalden, where we could look down a thousand feet into a blue lake, or up five thousand to the tops of snow peaks. Tried to read Milton up there on the green grass above the lake; stopped when half way through. I got it into my head that it was only a poetical paraphrase of the Bible. That is what Goethe thought once of doing, turning parts of the Holy Book into verse; but as the Bible is already done well, why not let it alone? Where is there anything in Goethe, or Milton either, to compare with the magnificent language of the Scriptures, and no human being would *dare* to change the *thought*. Curious, Byron, too, thought of putting Job into verse. Is not the book of Job already the grandest poem of the world? When among the Alps, I never cared to read anybody's description of them; language is too weak, unless the language were Lord Byron's.

One night near Obstalden, a terrible storm of thunder and lightning was leaping back and forth across the lake, and at moments every peak was illuminated. In the darkness the lake was at an immeasurable depth below us; a clap of thunder, a flash, and it seemed for an instant a bright mirror shining in the air. We had been coming down the path from Amden and had lost our way in the darkness, and when the lightning flashed, it was so vivid, we were afraid to go ahead. We took shelter under a projecting rock there on the mountain side, and watched the spectacle. All the artificial things that man ever dreamed of would be nothing in the presence of these elements, battling with each other over the mountain tops.

From peak to peak, the rattling crags among
Leaps the live thunder. Not from one lone cloud,
But every mountain now hath found a tongue,
And Jura answers, through her misty shroud,
Back to the joyous Alps, who call to her aloud.

It was nearly morning before we could find the way down the rocky path to our little inn; but anyway we had seen a storm in the higher Alps.

A pretty little incident occurred here one day with our children. My wife, Helen and Lawrence were at dinner out under the castanien trees on the terrace above the lake. Two strangers got out of a rickety old chaise that had brought them up the mountain. "May we eat dinner here with you under the trees?" said the eldest of the strangers, a kindly faced, white-haired gentleman, to the children. Extra plates were brought by the landlady of the inn, and the children and the strangers had a good time together.

"And your name is Helen," said her new friend at parting. "Yes, and what is your name?" answered the little girl. "Just Albert, please," said the man, smiling. "Good-bye, little folks," he called as he climbed into his one-horse wagon. "Good-bye, Mr. Albert," called out the little girl, waving her hands, "Aufwiedersehen."

The Frau Minster, Zurich.

In a few moments a rider hurrying up from the lake told the landlady in bated breath that it was Albert, King of Saxony, she had been entertaining. He was traveling in the Alps incognito. "Good gracious," cried the landlady, "had I known that, what a different charge I might have made."

September 25, 1876.--We are in the middle of the Atlantic. On the 16th, we left London on the Anglia. Mr. Benjamin, the marine artist (afterward Minister to Persia), is among the passengers. He made sea sketches, all the way. Kate Sherwood Bonner, a Southern literary woman, who put staid old Boston in an uproar last year by stirring up some of the effete clubs of culture that did not cultivate, is also on board. She is bright and beautiful, with her golden hair, and has the fairest white hands imaginable. A strange incident made us acquainted. She mentioned her home in Holly Springs, Mississippi, and in a moment I knew that once in the war times I was a sick soldier in that very house. I saw death scenes in its elegant chambers, in her own boudoir, of friend and foe, too horrible to relate.

The weather is perfect. We sail to Canada. There is not a sick soul on board. Everybody knows everybody, and there are concerts and recitations and fun in the cabin every night. All the day we play games on the deck. Nobody wants this journey to come to an end.

We saw an iceberg, and we saw a whale (yesterday). We offered the Captain $20 to stop the ship, put us down in life boats and let us row close to the iceberg. He refused. "Company at London would raise a row," he said. We were so close, however, we could see beautiful little inlets and bays worn in among the high walls of the crystal island, against which the sea was dashing. The ice was several hundred feet high, clear blue-green, and the sight, with the evening sun striking it, was altogether novel and beautiful. We stood on the deck and watched it for twenty miles. When we were near to it, the Captain said there was a terrible drop in the temperature of the sea water. We were sixteen days reaching New York.

October 4.--Visiting the Centennial. By mere accident, found telegrams telling us of the sudden death of my wife's father, while we have been having so long a voyage at sea. He was buried the day we reached New York. Owing to the length of the voyage they had given up finding us. William Gilmour was an educated Scotchman and a noble man, from near Burns' home, where his brother John had been one of Scotia's young bards.

In October, we visited home friends in the West, and returning East, staid a time in Washington, visiting at the home of General Sherman and elsewhere.

Horatio King, then having weekly "Literary Evenings" at his home, invited us often. These evenings did more to enliven a taste in Washington society for books and high culture than any other one thing in that whirl of politics and pretentiousness. King had been President Buchanan's Postmaster-General. He knew almost everybody in art and literature in the country, and the people one met at his home were always interesting. I regarded it a great pleasure to go to his "Evenings." He was growing older, but his intellect was bright as in youth, and his young wife attracted people of taste into their charming circle.

Colonel John W. Forney we also met again in Philadelphia, though I had known him in London. He was a man of great intellectual vigor, of magnificent presence. I once heard a Londoner say, "Your Colonel Forney is the finest looking American I ever saw." He, too, like Horatio King, knew everybody. He had been Secretary of the Senate and was a famous newspaper man, who in his day ranked with Greeley and Raymond and Bennett. His self-possession was wonderful, his talk enthralled, and he had a heart kind as a woman's. Our Government sent John W. Forney abroad as a Commissioner, just to "talk Europe into showing her wares at Philadelphia," some one said. A better talker could not have been found between the two oceans. He was emphatically, too, a "woman's man," and he knew how to influence the public men through their better natures--their wives.

In December, at New York, we visited at the home of Mr. Christopher Robert, who, as already mentioned, built "Robert College" at Constantinople. He was a retired millionaire, and his home life must have been a contrast to the lives of most New York money men. It was the life of one of the patriarchs, not on a desert among his flocks, but in a luxurious home, in a fashionable quarter of New York City. He was a splendid looking "old-time gentleman" of seventy-five years. I never saw white hair so becoming and honorable to a man as his was, not seventy-five years carried so upright and with so much dignity. His large, smooth-shaven face was as rosy as a child's, his eye clear as a boy's of twenty.

He had earned money in his life, and he used it in doing good. His house was a sort of religious Mecca, where a poor man could go and be sure of help. His daily life was that of a Christian gentleman. Mornings, after breakfast, a bell rang, when every member of the family, guests and servants, were expected to assemble in a room for devotion. In a fine, clear voice, Mr. Robert read the Scriptures, and though surrounded by wealth, dilated on the littleness of riches and the greatness of a true heart. Then he prayed. It was like a morning mass. And I thought what a city New York would be, were it filled with rich men like to Mr. Robert. His zeal for sowing good seed was boundless. No man hung an overcoat in that luxurious house entrance, but on going away would discover the pockets filled with sensible pamphlets appealing for a higher life.

Evenings, there were always a number of pleasant people at dinner, and some delightful music. I recall an evening there with the Reverend Doctors Taylor and Ormiston.

Knowing Mr. Robert to be a man of deep sincerity and thought, I once asked him "if he thought the dead ever returned to be near us?" This was when out walking in the fields of Switzerland. "Most assuredly I do," was his answer. "My lost ones are near me now--there in those roses, in the sweet grass, in all beautiful things. They come near to us when we are in a mood to want them to come. They don't speak--but they hear our inward breathings--and when we worship beautiful nature, we are talking with them."

I could not help thinking of that beautiful custom in certain parts of India, where at funerals a vacant place is left in the procession for the dead one who is supposed to be invisibly walking along with them.

On December 16, we had left New York on the "Elysia" and had tempests all the way across the ocean. On Christmas night, a hurricane set in, such as is not seen outside of the Indian seas. Everything on the outside of the ship was torn to pieces--not a life boat, nor bridge, nor boom pole, nor sail left. Everything gone. We were blown back thirty miles towards New York. The sea was churned into mountains of milk, and the thunder and lightning at midnight was something perfectly terrific. The ship's hatches were all battened down with tarpaulins, and we were fastened in below. Spite of the precautions, water rushed down the ship's stairways by hogsheads full. Two or three passengers lost their minds. Many said farewell to each other, including the ship's officers, and we all thought ourselves lost.

On New Year's Day we reached England, just ahead of another storm such as Britain had not seen in a hundred years. Hundreds and hundreds of coast vessels went to the bottom, carrying unnumbered British sailors and passengers with them.

As we passed the great pier of Dover, we saw how the mighty rocks composing it had been hurled in vast piles by the storm, as if they were boxes made of straw. The work of the engineers had been as nothing.

Man marks the earth with ruin; his control
Stops with the shore.

*****

While I had been in Washington, the contest was going on over the election of Governor Hayes and Samuel Tilden to the Presidency.

In official circles at Washington, the fear of disorder, rebellion, revolution, was extremely grave. Troops were being silently, secretly slipped to Washington. Many looked for an immediate storm. General Sherman told me privately he was preparing for it the best he could. "If a civil war breaks out," said he, "it will be a thousand times *worse* than the other war. It will be the fighting of neighbor against neighbor, friend against friend." He grew almost pessimistic in his views for the future of our country. "It is only a question of time," said he, "till the politicians will ruin all of us. *Partisanship is a curse.* These men are not howling for their country's good, but their own political advantage, and the people are too big fools to see it. We are liable to smash into a thousand pieces every time we have an election." He was greatly moved, and almost wept at the thought of what would happen, were the violence then threatened really to break out.

January 4, 1877.--Again in Zurich. When we reached our home, we found the servants had returned, the house was warmed for us, and everything was in place as if we had not been gone a day; yet we had traveled 13,000 miles. Above the hall door, in evergreen and holly, were the words--"Welcome Home!"

How many of our American servants think of such a pretty, feeling act as that, for their employers!

*****

Some of our first Winter evenings here we spent in playing whist at the Dennison home. They are worth mentioning, for the people who played with us, and the story of some of them. Mr. Dennison had once been manager of the Waltham Watch Works, and it was he who *invented* watch making by machinery. He is called the "father of American watch making." He is a tall, fine looking gentleman of seventy, with kind eyes, pleasant speech, modest manners, and universal genius. He seemed to know everything that concerns the working of a machine.

Our best whist-player at the table was Mr. Sadler, a kind old English gentleman who brought Christmas cake to my wife, regularly as the holiday came. He kept the story of his life secret. He was a mystery, and no one dared to pry into his past. We knew him to be rich, though he lived like a poor man in an obscure pension.

One day, just as I was in Liverpool on my way home from New York, he was murdered in a quiet park; no soul suspects by whom. Then we found out that he had been a member of the English Parliament, who for some mysterious misdemeanor, in association with his brother, also in Parliament, had to fly England. He got away by feigning sickness and death, having himself carried out of the hospital in a coffin. His wife, of whom we had never heard before, appeared suddenly at his death, like a specter. She claimed his money, which can not be found, though I personally knew he had thousands, and as suddenly and specter-like departed. It is all mystery, even to-day. His banker, shortly after the murder, received a mysterious and unsigned telegram from New York City, saying: "Give yourself no trouble as to who killed Sadler. He will not be found." The murderer had not had time to reach New York. Who sent the telegram?

Another of that card quartette was the lovely Miss Dimmick, of Boston, a medical student at the University here. She was the first young lady graduate at Zurich, and she finished with great honors. Then she went home on a visit. On her return, we arranged to meet her in Paris, but one morning came the shocking news that she and five hundred others had drowned at the wreck of the "Schiller."

Early one morning, in a terrible fog, the steamer Schiller struck a rock off the Scilly isles. Almost everybody was lost. The last seen of Miss Dimmick she was on the deck, kneeling in her night robe, her hands clasped, her face turned to heaven in prayer. When the peasants of the island found her body, there was a beauty and a peace in her countenance that touched them, and moved them to treat her tenderly. They placed her by herself, and when the officers came later to take some of the bodies away, they prayed permission to bear her coffin on their shoulders to the ship.

Boston City Hospital voted some money and named one of the free ward beds in honor of Miss Dimmick.

Now I recall those little card evenings at the Dennison's with strange feelings.

CHAPTER XIV
1877

GENERAL GRANT VISITS LAKE LUZERN--CONVERSATIONS WITH HIM--HOW I BROUGHT THE GOOD NEWS OF SHERMAN'S SUCCESSES IN THE CAROLINAS TO GENERAL GRANT AT RICHMOND--GRANT'S SIMPLICITY IN HIS TRAVELS--A STRANGE EXPERIENCE ON THE RIGI--LONDON PAPERS AMAZED AT THE POPULATION OF THE UNITED STATES--FIRST TELEPHONE.

July 1, 1877.--Last week there was some talk among the prominent people here, including the few Americans, of having a public reception for General Grant. Knowing that he was stopping at Luzern, I went to see him for the committee. In a little lake-excursion near to the Rigi, it happened that I was on the same boat with him. The seats on the deck of the steamer were filled with tourists, gazing in wonder at the inspiring scenery we were passing in the bay of Uri. The water is two thousand feet deep, the lake a wonderful blue, and the dark, majestic mountains near by, a contrast to the slopes of snow and the ice fields a little further off.

It was summer, but the day was dark and cool. "Where is the General?" I said to General Badeau, who was traveling with him.

Lake Luzern--Tell's Chapel.

"Do you see that man sitting down there at the right, alone, with his coat collar turned up?" I went nearer, and recognized the familiar features. But to me, he looked none at all like the General Grant of war times, the one I had seen on critical battlefields. He wore a black cylinder hat, his overcoat collar, turned up, hid half his face, he sat earnest and speechless with arms folded, apparently barely glancing at the mighty scenes the vessel was hurrying past--scenes that were exciting exclamations of wonder from half the people on the deck.

General Badeau pronounced my name, but General Grant did not, at first, remember me. When I recalled the time I brought the dispatches from Sherman to City Point, and the long talk we had together in the little back room of his cabin, about Sherman's army, he brightened up, interested himself, and seemed glad to talk of old war days.

I think not one reference was made to the scenery we were passing. I must think, too, he was getting tired of all the attentions heaped upon him by European cities, for he preferred, when I spoke of it, that the Zurich people should do nothing in the way of receiving him.

"Look at that great, foolish lot of people hurrying to be first at the gangway," he remarked to me, as the steamer turned landwards at Luzern. "They might as well sit still; nine times out of ten, hurry helps nobody--the boat stays at the landing, everybody will get off, and to-morrow it will be all the same who is off first."

I have often thought of that remark. His taking time for things may have been one of the keys to his success.

We were the very last to go ashore. That evening at the Schweizerhof, I had some pleasant conversation with him again.

He regretted that he was not at the White House, just a few hours, to put the deserved quietus on the strikers in Pennsylvania who were shamelessly destroying other people's property. One hundred and twenty-five locomotives and ten million dollars worth of railroad stock were destroyed at Pittsburg in one night. "That is what an army will be wanted for yet, in our country," he added, "an army to make ourselves behave."

He spoke of silver and free coinage. I admitted my ignorance of the whole subject. "I don't understand subjects on which the experts themselves differ," I said. "It is simple enough," he replied. "I can explain some things that will make it clear to you;" and he asked me to come and be seated on a garden bench, on the terrace overlooking that wonderful lake.

It was 9 o'clock at night. Behind us, in zigzag lines, were the picturesque city walls and towers, built in the Middle Ages. The lights from the quays and bridges reflected themselves on the lake; not far away stood the eternal mountains. The scene, the time, seemed all out of keeping with talks on politics. But General Grant lighted a cigar and gave me more clear-headed notions about what makes money than I had learned from listening to, or reading, the buncombe of half the politicians in the country. It was because he was simple, and honest, and sincere, and because he knew what he was talking about. I had, in some way, long before concluded that Grant was only a military man. That night's conversation led me to think him also a statesman. Any way, he was sincere.

After smoking quite a little time in silence, he said, abruptly: "I was just thinking of the letters you brought me that time from Sherman. How did you get to me at City Point? Sherman must have been entirely cut off from the North." I told him, in a few words, how I had long been a prisoner of war, how I had escaped my captors at Macon, and my experiences in the Rebel Army at the battle of Atlanta; my recapture, my escape again at Columbia, South Carolina, and my being appointed to a place on General Sherman's staff at the time; how one morning General Sherman ordered me to get ready to run down the Cape Fear River in the night, to carry dispatches to General Grant and the President; how half a dozen of us got aboard a tug, covered its lights and its engine with cotton bales, and passed down the river in the darkness, without a shot being fired at us; how I reached City Point in a quick ocean steamer, and his reception of me in the little back room; the excitement of General Ord at the news I brought. It was the first news that the North had of Sherman, after he entered the swamps of the Carolinas.

All at once, the whole incident came back to General Grant's mind, for there in his cabin that time, many years before, he had questioned me about the details of my final escape from prison, and my means of reaching him in the North.4

"Yes," he said, "I remember it all now. You had a letter, too, from Sherman to Mr. Lincoln, who came down from Washington that very night. We were all tremendously moved and gratified by the news you brought of Sherman's constant successes.

"Many of my generals feared always that Lee might slip away from me, and jump on to Sherman down about Raleigh. I had, myself, more fears of that, than I had about my ability to take Richmond, if Lee would only stay there and fight me."

Pretty soon, a steamer landed with a lot of passengers, and I walked with the General back into the hotel. We found General Badeau deep in newspapers, and Jesse, the General's son, playing billiards and smoking.

The next morning, after an early breakfast, I visited Mrs. Grant and the General in their rooms. Mrs. Grant was as kindly mannered as the General himself. One would not have thought them fresh from the attentions of princes and potentates. They told me in an enjoyable way, much about their travels. The General dropped some remarks, too, showing me that the grand scenery he had passed the day before had been noticed very closely by him, silent though he had been.

The contrast between these simple, great people, upstairs in the hotel, and some of the great people downstairs, was very impressive to me. There was not one particle of stiffness or formality in General and Mrs. Grant's reception of me. It was as if his rank were no greater in the world than my own; simply as if he and his wife had met an unpretentious man to whom they liked to talk, and who would go away feeling that they were friends.

All over Europe, I understand, General Grant and his wife have impressed people in the same way. In every sense, they were preserving their unostentatious, homely American ways.

"Certain comforts and things, I want in traveling, just as at home," said the General. "I want my little sitting room. I want my ham and eggs for breakfast--and nothing is so hard to get cooked right in Europe, as just these ham and eggs."

*****

I had a strange trip down the Rigi last Monday morning. I had been staying at the Staffel over Sunday. At ten of Monday, I was to be in Luzern, as an official, to help marry a couple, one of whom was an American. Long before daylight, I was starting down the steep path. It was starlight overhead, and a warm summer morning. Down below, however, the whole valley and all the lakes and hills seemed hidden by a mantle of fog. Every few moments we heard a clap of thunder away down there, or saw a flash of lightning dart along the gray surface. My wife urged me not to descend into clouds that looked so dangerous; but my presence in Luzern was a necessity, and I went ahead. For half an hour my path down the mountain side was dry and beautiful. It was just breaking dawn, when suddenly, and within a few feet distance, I stepped down into a cloud full of water. Instantly I was in a perfect Noah's flood, and yet I knew a hundred feet above me the stars were shining. The peals of thunder soon seemed to shake the mountains, and the lightning became terrific. A few moments' walk had brought me out of a dry atmosphere and a quiet morning, into this storm of the Alps. I tried to get back and up the mountain, but I was fairly washed from my feet and the path. In five minutes I was completely lost, and, fearing to tumble off some precipice, I stood stock still. I had reached what seemed a level plateau of tall grass. There I stood till daylight came, and the storm went partly by, when, to my horror, I saw that had I walked another dozen steps I would have gone over a cliff and fallen a thousand feet.

I caught a steamer, however, and reached the city, where the groom divided some of his drier garments with me, and the wedding went merrily on.

*****

Some of the London newspapers are in great wonder over the United States census. A country only a hundred years old, and yet mustering thirty-eight and a half millions of people!! Few European states so large, and none of them so rich and great.

*****

Our friend, Mr. Witt, had a telephone put up in his house yesterday. It is probably the first one in the country. Great curiosity and interest is manifested here in this invention of a talking apparatus, by which the human voice may be carried a hundred miles.

CHAPTER XV
1877

GENERAL GRANT AND THE SWISS PRESIDENT--BANQUET TO GRANT AT BERN--GOOD ROADS--CHARGE D'AFFAIRES FOR SWITZERLAND--WRITING FOR THE MAGAZINES.

July 27, 1877.--General Grant arranged to visit the Swiss capital on the 24th. Our minister being absent, I, as senior consul, went up to Bern to offer him the courtesies of the legation. Quite a crowd of people surrounded him as he came in at the station, and we drove to the Bernerhof hotel. General Adam Badeau was with him, as was also his son Jesse.

At 10 o'clock of the morning of the 25th, I had the pleasure of presenting General Grant to the Swiss President, at the palace. President Heer spoke but little English, and General Grant no German at all, so it devolved on me to act as interpreter during the half hour's conversation. The Swiss Parliament house, called the palace, is a very noble structure, standing on a commanding height, with the Bernese snow mountains spread out in perfect view from windows and terrace.

The reception of General Grant was simple in the extreme. A common business interview between two or three private gentlemen could hardly be more devoid of official airs.

President Heer himself is a simple, kindly man, a statesman loved by his people, and very well acquainted with the affairs of other countries. He had evidently "read up" on General Grant, for he had kept track of his travels, and referred to some incidents of his life in the war. As ex-President of the United States, General Grant was just as simple and kindly as was his Swiss entertainer. Each expressed gratitude at meeting here on Republican soil. "We are not so great as you Americans," said the President, "but we are a much older Republic." They referred to the fact that the system of a second house in Parliament was adopted from the American plan. They talked about the advantages of two houses a little, and then the General was asked to go and look at the view from the window. There is not another view like that from any other executive mansion on earth.

The Swiss President does not live here. It is the official business building of the government. An American would be surprised to see President Heer's own little private home in the suburbs of the city.

"I will return this call, General Grant, in just an hour," said the President. So we went back to the Bernerhof and waited.

The return call was as simple as the first. It lasted but a few minutes, and ended in General Grant's accepting an invitation to a banquet that the President would give in his honor that evening. I had the honor to be included in the invitation. General Badeau and Mr. Jesse Grant were also to take part.

The afternoon of that day was dark and rainy; still I went walking far outside the suburbs of the town.

Near to an old bridge, I came across a man standing absolutely alone, in the rain, carefully examining the queer structure. It was General Grant.

He did not observe me, and I, believing that he wished to be alone, went my way down a different path.

It was fully an hour before he returned to the hotel, wet and muddy. That evening at the dinner, I heard him telling a cabinet officer of a delightful walk he had in the outskirts of the city.

There was no little surprise to know that the world's guest, instead of being escorted around by committees and brass bands, had spent half the afternoon out on a country road alone in the rain.

General Grant had no reputation as an after-dinner speaker, but he made two little speeches on this occasion, one in reply to the toast of the President to the distinguished visitor, and a longer one, when he himself proposed "Switzerland."

The dinner was in a private room of the Bernerhof hotel. Besides those already mentioned, the Vice President and the Cabinet were at the table, and all made short speeches. Short speeches were also made by General Badeau, by Jesse Grant and by myself. Nearly all spoke, or at least understood, English, so the toasts were in our own tongue. Only the President spoke in German, thanking General Grant for the honor he had done the sister republic, by leaving his resting place in the mountains and coming to the capital. There was general good feeling and plenty of hilarity about the board. The Swiss understand the art of having a good time at the table. Save a few words concerning the Darien Canal and the Pennsylvania strike, no politics and no high affairs were touched on that night.

When some specially fine cigars were passed along the table, General Grant helped himself, and smiled in a way that said, "Now I am indeed happy."

At midnight, the guest rose and made a move as if about to speak again. The President rapped on his wine glass for attention. "Hear, hear," said one or two guests, and every eye turned to where General Grant was standing. To our surprise, he simply bowed to the President, said goodnight, and quietly walked out of the room.

Chateau, Neuchatel.

August, 1877.--Bankruptcy seems to be threatening everywhere in Switzerland this summer; not here only, but everywhere else. The worst times, the people say, in a hundred years. To make it ten times worse, the horrible war between Russia and Turkey is developing into Turkish massacres of innocent people. There is nothing in Swiss newspapers now save war news, and on the streets men talk of little else, fearing all Europe may yet explode. It is the sentiment here that this war, with all its atrocities, can be laid at England's door, that it is from her that Turkish assassins get their encouragement and help.

December, 1877.--The reports of losses in the war continue fearful. Seven thousand men were destroyed at Plevna, in thirty-five minutes. Our American armies knew little of such sudden destruction. Fifty thousand and more on both sides were shot at Gettysburg, but the fight lasted two or three days. At Iuka, my own regiment (the Fifth Iowa) lost *217* out of only *482* engaged, pretty nearly every other man killed or wounded, in an hour. Plevna was not much worse than that. One cannot help, too, thinking of the English at Jellabad, where only one man out of sixteen thousand got away alive. No wonder the better sense of a people opposes war.

Christmas, 1877.--Like everybody else in Switzerland, we had a "*tree*" last night. Twenty children besides our own little ones, and some Swiss friends, were present. Naturally all was done in the Swiss way. The tree, immense in size, had its one hundred and one candles, its drooping chains of silver and gold tinsel, its little gorgeous colored ornaments of metal and glass, and its white cotton snowflakes. The tree stood in the consulate. The folding doors to our apartment opened up for the purpose. Nothing is on the tree but ornaments and lights. The gifts are on a side table. The bell rings; Kris Kringle, robed, and jingling with bells, bounds in. The children are absolutely in a paradise of joy, and the joy of the grown folks, on hearing the exclamations of delight, is scarcely less. The servants get a great proportion of the presents, for these gifts are a part of the wages. Pretty soon all join hands, grown folks and children and servants, and circle about the tree singing

"Christ is born,
Christ is born."

What a happy time it is! It is Christmas night all the time for a week, in Switzerland. There is nothing but good times and joy. Families come together, and far-wandering sons come home for the glad reunion. I have known young men to cross the Atlantic from New York, just to be in the dear, old home for a week in the Christmas time.

The Christmas lights shine in every house, the villa of the rich, the cottage of the poor. A Christmas tree is in every home. No rich man would go to bed and sleep, knowing some poor child had no Christmas tree. The public squares and side streets are filled with green trees for sale. A happy smile is on every face, and a "Gott grüss euch," on every lip.

That one week of comradeship and kindly feeling does as much to bring peace on earth and goodwill to men, in Switzerland, as does the church itself. It is religion mixed with joy.

*****

We are back on the lake again at Küssnacht, and such moonlight nights! Occasionally American friends come out by boat, to see us at Wangensbach, and walk home, the six miles, in the moonlight. The little, white, clean roads along the lake shore are perfect, and a delight to walk on. Will America ever know what a road is? We excel in almost everything else, why cannot we do this one thing? Nothing to-day would make the American people so happy, so prosperous, as good roads. People of Switzerland save millions and millions yearly by their fine turnpikes.

The other day I got orders from Washington to go to Bern and take charge of the legation as acting Chargé d'Affaires, during the absence of Mr. Nicholas Fish, going home on a furlough. Mr. Fish is a son of Grant's Secretary of State, Hamilton Fish, and is as accomplished and zealous in affairs of diplomacy as his father is in statesmanship.

I have an American friend who calls at the office at 2 P.M. every day now, to tell me in detail all the war news that I have just finished reading in the papers. It requires an hour, but he does it up thoroughly, and this, of all things, has made me wish the war would hurry to a close. But are not *Consuls* paid to *listen* to their countrymen sometimes?

While at home last winter, I arranged to continue writing articles for some of the magazines, and the labor makes pleasant employment for leisure hours. Many reports for the Government, too, on all conceivable subjects, continue to be asked for and are printed as fast as sent in. They are the result of a good deal of careful looking about.

CHAPTER XVI
1877

FRANZ LISZT AT ZURICH--SWISS, GREAT LOVERS OF MUSIC--WAGNER ONCE LIVED HERE--HIS SINGULAR WAYS--DR. WILLI--MADAME LUCCA'S VILLA--LISZT'S KISSING BEES--JEFFERSON DAVIS' DAUGHTER--A LAUGHABLE MISTAKE.

September, 1877.--The Swiss have almost as much love for music as the Italians, though they have no composers of great reputation. Every city, town, and hamlet has its Music Guilds and clubs. The whole male population seems to sing. There are many fine instrumental performers among the women, but few good singers. The male bird is the vocalist here. Zurich is a center for great concerts, oratorios, etc., where Europe's greatest artists appear. The "Tonhalle" orchestra is one of the best in Europe. These are the men who first rehearsed and played Wagner's earlier operas. Seven years of Wagner's life were spent in Zurich, in exile. The people here still talk of his singular ways as a citizen. Zurich was then, as now, a Wagner-music loving place, even at a time when London and Paris would not listen to a Wagner opera.

My friend here, Schulz-Beuthen, himself a composer, is the happy possessor of Wagner's old piano, at which he composed some of his immortal works.

Wagner was poor when in Zurich, and lived by writing musical criticisms. For his own music, there was no sale. He had one or two rich friends here, however, notably the Wiesendoncks and the Willis, who encouraged not only his music, but a most singular method he had of getting rid of debts. It was a pretty way he had of calling on these opulent friends and, by the merest accident, leaving his grocer's, tailor's or hostler's bills lying on the drawing-room table. His kind friends naturally discovered the missives, and quietly *paid* them. It was a little joke whispered about that the number of Wagner's calls at rich men's houses was entirely numbered by the bills he was owing. All the same, he had rather good times by the beautiful lake.

Dr. Willi had Wagner one whole season at his lakeside home. Just across the lake was the villa of the Wiesendoncks, and

Wagner kept a little boat very busy, carrying his operatic "Motives" back and forth between his kind musical patrons.

Every now and then the "Tonhalle" has a red letter day. It is when artists like Sarasate play the violin, or when Franz Liszt or Rubinstein is at the piano.

Last week Franz Liszt was here. It was a great occasion, though not his first visit. At the close of the afternoon concert, I noticed many of the ladies gathered about him to have him kiss them, as he stood down in an aisle among the seats, holding an impromptu reception. Pretty soon they had him seated. They could get at him better that way. The men had little chance that afternoon, though in the evening I was one of those who had the honor of being presented to him. He received me very kindly, and spoke of certain clever Americans who had been pupils of his.

I had had a glimpse of him the morning before. Being an early riser, I was, as usual, down walking by the lake, near to the celebrated Baur-au-lac hotel. I happened to glance toward a window of the hotel that I heard open. I saw an astounding looking figure in a white night dress, leaning far out of the window, looking at the mountains. It was a great, smooth, ash-colored face that might have represented Charity in marble, set in a frame of long, white, silken hair. I knew from pictures that it was Franz Liszt, and so stopped and gazed.

I never saw so striking a picture of a human being before. His figure in its loose gown nearly filled the window. His great eyes seemed to be shining a "good morning" to the lake and the mountains. It was the face of genius, illuminated and happy by the beauty of the morning and the glory of the scene.

I should like to have heard Franz Liszt sit down and improvise a fantasia at the piano, the moment he left that window. I am sure there would have been tones born of the morning, for his whole face reflected the powerful emotion within him. I wondered to myself that evening, when he was holding the vast audience in the charm of his music, if he were not thinking of that fair scene from his window in the morning.

When the concert was over the other night, a few friends gathered with Franz Liszt in a little back room of the "Tonhalle." There was a little dinner and much champagne. And there was much bowing and kissing and getting down before this king of the piano. Men and women absolutely got down on their knees and kissed his hand, as if he were an object of adoration.

It was not exactly getting down before a "totem pole," though almost as extravagant, for there were nobler ways of worshiping the genius of music than by being ridiculous. The great master, though, was used to that sort of thing--in fact, rather liked it--and so went on with his wine and his kisses till midnight, adding to the delight of his worshipers by at last seating himself at the piano and playing one of his own compositions.5

Another artist with world-wide reputation, who summers about Lake Zurich even now, is Madame Lucca, the prima donna. She owns beautiful Villa Goldenberg at the upper end of the lake. I often see her about town, on foot, shopping.

One day as I was passing "Goldenberg" on the steamer, I pointed to it, remarking to a fine-looking German with whom I was conversing, that it was "one of the prettiest spots of all." "Yes," he answered, "I have never regretted owning it." "Owning it," I exclaimed; "why Madame Lucca lives there, and I supposed *she* owned it." "So she does," he answered smilingly, as he gave me a little nudge; "so she does, but I own *her*. I am her husband."

I meet many well-known characters in my frequent trips up and down the lake.

One evening lately, as I sat on the steamer deck, nearing my home at Küssnacht, a rather prepossessing young lady inquired of me in English if that were the home of William Tell. After a little conversation she walked to the bow of the boat, and the middle-aged lady who seemed to be her companion, said to me: "Do you know who that is you were talking with? That is the daughter of Jefferson Davis."

Pretty soon the girl came back, and I had the pleasure of communicating a bit of news to her that must have been of interest. I had read in the telegrams, that very day, of some famous admirer in America presenting to her father the magnificent estate of Bellevoir, on the Mississippi.

Amusing incidents occur, too, almost daily, from American travelers, going up and down the lake, supposing me to be a native, not acquainted with the American tongue. They are sometimes very free in their remarks about people they see on the boat.

The other evening, while sitting on the deck on my way home, I noticed a little party of three ladies and a gentleman, excitedly wringing their hands, talking English, and wondering what on earth they would do. They had lost the name of the place they were going to, and could not tell even how to get home again. Not a soul on the boat spoke a word of English; they were sure of that.

"Notice that man sitting there with a newspaper," said the gentleman of the party, indicating myself. "Kate, you talk a little German," he went on; "try your Dutch on him." "Not for the world," answered the lady appealed to. "That might be a prince, or a baron, or somebody." "Well, his clothes don't look like it, anyway," chirped in a second of the young ladies. "Did you ever see such an unfashionable necktie in your life?" "An odd looking genius that, anyway. I would not be afraid of him." "Go right up to him and blurt it out; he's good natured, I'll bet a dollar," chimed in the gentleman. "Never mind his necktie; it's information we're after." "Yes, but my German--I don't know," said the lady; "I don't know three words, and you *know* I don't." "Oh! go on--nonsense--walk right up to him, and see how pretty he'd smile on you," said all three.

She cleared her throat, and approached me, and in a few unintelligible words of bad German, spoke. I did smile, and answered her in plain American English, remarking that I had noticed that her party were Americans.

There was a sudden collapse of spirits, a queer winking and nudging of each other, and an inclination to walk away to the other end of the boat.

As I was leaving the steamer, the gentleman returned to me. "Excuse me, sir," said he, "but you astonished our little party. May I not ask where on earth you, a Swiss, learned such perfect English? It is almost American." "Oh! in knocking about the country here," I answered, "and I see lots of Americans on the steamer and, when they talk, especially if it is about me, I always listen to them. Goodnight."

I suppose that little quartette still think about the Swiss they met, with the queer necktie, who spoke the American English.

Lake Geneva.

CHAPTER XVII
1878

SOME RECOLLECTIONS OF MINE ABOUT GENERAL GRANT IN THE WAR--GRANT AT CHAMPION HILLS --SHERMAN'S LETTER ON CONFISCATION BY TAXATION IN AMERICA--SILVER NO "CURE ALL"-- GRANT AT RAGATZ--I GIVE A BANQUET IN HIS HONOR AT ZURICH.

January, 1878.--To-day made New Year's calls on some American friends; but it is not customary among the Swiss.

Received copies of my "Recollections of Grant and Sherman," printed in the Philadelphia *Times*. It so happened that I had seen General Grant often in the Vicksburg campaign, and he personally directed a charge made by our brigade at the battle of Champion Hills. The battle had been going on for some time, when he rode up close behind the line of my regiment. He dismounted from his bay horse and stood within a few yards of where I was in the line, leaning on my gun. He was under a heavy fire of musketry, and we boys all feared for his life. There was some suspense, before the order to "charge" was given. My company stood there in line on the green grass, just as it did on the village green in Newton, the morning we started for the war. Grant leaned against his horse and smoked, and looked simply as a man would, who had a little piece of tough business before him to consider. Aides rode up to him and rode away. He spoke to them in a low voice, that even I, who was so close to him, could not hear. The awful musketry rattle of terrific combat was a little to the left and right of us, and there was no great noise immediately in our front; but well we all knew that ten thousand rebels were over there in the timber, waiting our advance. There was no cannonading of our line, as we stood there unresistingly, feeling the shots from their rifles, and firing not a shot in return. Grant was not quite ready. I saw him glance, I thought half pityingly, at a few of our wounded who were carried back past him, and he looked very close at one man near me who was shot in the leg and who limped past him to the rear. I think he recognized his face, but he did not speak to him. He spoke to none of us; there was no posing, no sword waving, or hat swinging. I have almost forgotten if he even had a sword on. None but those near by knew that he was within a mile of us. It was just a little plain business he was then looking after, but I know some of us wished he would go out of range of the bullets.

Shortly I saw our colonel walk back to him. There were a few nods and low words, and as the colonel passed me returning, he said to me: "I want you to act as Sergeant Major." (I was with Company B). "Run to the left of the regiment and yell, 'Fix bayonets.'" I ran as ordered, crying all the time "Fix bayonets." Glancing back, I saw Grant mounting his horse. That instant I heard all the officers yelling, "*Double quick!*"--"*Charge!*"

We went into the woods and over the rough ground on the run, the bullets of the enemy all the time coming into us like hail. Suddenly, there was in front of us and all around us, a terrific roar of cannon. For nearly two mortal hours, we stood in battle line in that wood, and emptied our rifles into the rebel line of gray as fast as we could load them. They did not seem 200 yards away, though the battle smoke soon partly hid them. We carried muzzle-loading Whitney rifles and forty cartridges. In my regiment, every man's cartridge box was emptied, and some of us took cartridges from the bodies of the dead. A third of my command were shot.

When it was all over and nearly dark, we were out on the Black river road, resting. General Grant came riding up to where our flags hung on the guns, and stopped. We all jumped up out of the dust to cheer; some one caught up the flag and held it in front of his horse. He simply smiled, and said to the colonel, "Good for the Fifth Iowa," and then rode off into the darkness.

February, 1878.--Hard times is still the cry everywhere in Europe. A letter from General Sherman shows that now at last our people are finding out what the Civil War cost us, in the way of dollars and cents.

"WASHINGTON, D. C., Jan. 17, 1878.

"DEAR BYERS:--I have just received your letter of January 3d, with your clipping from the London *News*, for which I am much obliged. I had previously received the letter of December 28th, which I had taken down to my rooms for the perusal of

Mrs. Sherman, who is a more reliable correspondent than I am. She and Elly are here from St. Louis for a visit, and will probably remain all of February, to enjoy the social advantages of the capital, now at their height. Though everybody is crying at the hard times, yet extravagance in dress and living has not received a quietus. I wish it was otherwise, but no single man, or set of men, can change the habits of a people in a day or a season.

"Those who clamor for a silver coinage think it will cure all evils, but I am sure no measure that can be concocted by our legislators can change the state of facts, which is the necessary result of the war. Wages and prices of all things necessary, rose to a standard far above the real value. Now all must come down, and each class struggles to go right along as before, demanding that others must make the necessary sacrifices. Meantime also states, counties and municipalities have 'improved' by spending borrowed money, which must now be paid, principal or interest. The cost of Government, like all other things, has increased. Local taxation, to meet this cost and interest, is a burden heavier than property can bear, so that real property now everywhere, instead of being a source of income, is the very reverse, and I do not know but that all real property in this great land is 'confiscate.' I know that all my property that used to pay me some revenue is now unable to pay its own taxes. I do not see how silver coinage is going to mend this, but such is now the cry, and in some form or other the experiment will be tried. Our papers keep us well advised as to the progress of the war in Turkey, and I have a good map at hand, which enables me to follow the movements of the several columns pretty well.

"I am glad to learn that Mrs. Byers is in better health, and that you content yourself with what you have, for want of better. I hope ere your return to us, things will mend and prosperity once more return to Iowa and the West.

"As ever your friend,
W. T. SHERMAN."

September 21, 1878.--Yesterday, while up on the Rigi, I received this telegram from General Grant:

"I accept your invitation for Monday.

It was in reply to an invitation of mine to a dinner party that I wished to give in his honor at Zurich. He had been stopping at Ragatz for some weeks, that beautiful resort on the upper Rhine.

A Swiss paper had this little item the other day: "Among the crowd of fashionables at the resort of Ragatz, one does not notice a certain smallish, plain looking, sturdy man, who takes long walks alone, and who lives the simplest, least conspicuous life of any one there. No wonder few know who the quiet gentleman is. His name, possibly, is not even on the hotel register, but he is the first man in the great sister Republic beyond the sea. It is U. S. Grant."

September 25, 1878.--Had another telegram from General Grant on the 22d, saying he would reach Zurich at 12:36 next morning. I took train and met him at Horgen. Mr. Corning, the Vice Consul, went with me. Mrs. Grant was with her husband. No one on the train seemed to know of their presence. We found them sitting alone in a little, first class coupé. I had flowers for Mrs. Grant, and they both received us very kindly. We rode together to Zurich and talked only about Ragatz and the pretty scenes they had just passed. Mrs. Grant was especially enthusiastic over the picturesque journey.

A great crowd assembled about the station where we entered. General Grant took my arm and walked to the carriage. Mr. Corning escorted Mrs. Grant. Just as the General was stepping into the carriage, a rough-looking fellow suddenly ran up, caught the General's arm and cried out, "You are going to speak to me, hain't you?" There was a momentary fright, and thought of assassination, among all of us. A policeman jumped forward, swinging a club, to arrest him. "Don't you never mind," the man cried out in English to the policeman. "I'm one of Grant's old soldiers." The policeman halted, seeing the General smile and reach his hand to the apparent ruffian. "Yes, General, I was with you and Johnny Logan at Vicksburg," the excited man exclaimed, "and look *here.*" He commenced rolling up his sleeve and showed a wrist shot half in two. The sight of that soldier's wound sent a quick thrill through every one of us. "The past of the nation was speaking there."

The ceremony of the occasion was all forgotten. Had there been room, Mrs. Grant would have taken him into the carriage. For myself, I could have gladly walked, to let this wounded hero ride with his General. "Come and see me at my hotel," said General Grant, "and we will talk it all over." Again, he shook the stranger soldier's hand, and the horses started.

"Three cheers for General Grant," cried the soldier, swinging his hat to the crowd, that answered in a loud Swiss huzza.

In the afternoon, Mr. Nicholas Fish, the American Minister, who had come down from the capital to be at my dinner, went with me to the hotel, and we took the General driving about the town. Mrs. Grant preferred to rest. We went up on the terrace in front of the University, where is spread out to view one of the fairest sights in the world. The city lay below us, in front the chain of the Albis hills, to the left the blue lake, and beyond it the snow mountains.

The General was impressed with the view, but he was getting used to grand scenes in Switzerland; they are everywhere. He looked in silence. Shortly, he commenced talking about the spires and towers of the city below us; asked the name of almost every one of them, and spent a long time studying out the meaning of certain big, red letters on the roof of an orphan asylum under the terrace. He would not give that up. He asked the different German names for such things, how they were spelled, and finally guessed the riddle that neither I nor Mr. Fish (both knowing German) had been able to explain. This noticing everything and trying to solve it, is even to a greater extent a trait of General Sherman's. May it not be genius' method of intuitively making things its own?

He examined carefully the architecture of the University building, and talked with Mr. Fish about his father, the ex-Secretary of State. There was also a little reference to his own youth at West Point, not far away from the Fish's country home.

We went down the terrace steps. Now I noticed that Grant was growing old. His elasticity of movement was all gone. He was getting stoop shouldered, too.

He told me of a stone quarry he had, I think in Jersey. "On the continued profits of that," he said, "depends whether I shall stay very long abroad, or go back home."

To the dinner that night, I had invited some representative members of the Swiss army, press, learned professions, etc. Colonel Voegli was there; Dr. Willi, the friend of Wagner; Gottfried Kinkel, the professor and poet; Orelli, the banker; Feer, of the Swiss Senate; Vogt, the journalist; Mr. Fish, the American Minister; Mayor Roemer and others.

It was a gentlemen's dinner. Mrs. Grant remained in her room, after a brief glance at the table and the flowers downstairs.

It was an ideal place for a happy party. Inside the room the Swiss and American colors were blended, and some of the French dishes were rebaptized with American names for the occasion.

Outside, the almost tropical garden reached out into the lake. There was no music in the rooms, but almost every one present made a little speech. General Grant not only answered to the toast in his honor, but in a second speech proposed Switzerland, and especially Zurich, which he had heard spoken of as a "Swiss Athens." At no time did I ever see him in such good spirits. The table was not so large but all could plainly hear. Numbers of the guests addressed remarks and inquiries about our country to General Grant. He answered kindly, and proposed many questions of his own, until conversation became extremely lively. In short, his reputation for being no talker was smashed all to pieces that evening. He talked much, and he talked well, and was very happy; so were all of us. The two Republics were one around that table, and we were all democrats. General Grant drank wine with the rest of us, but with moderation. President Hayes, he related to me, had a great reputation for drinking absolutely nothing but water. "It is a mistake," said the General, and he told me how at a dinner at the White House, the night before the inauguration, President Hayes emptied his wine glass very much in the way that all other people did, who had no reputations for total abstinence. He was amused at some of the French-American names on the menu at his plate. I interpreted some of them for him, and, after the dinner, put his menu with its pretty picture of the lake into my breast pocket, as a little souvenir of the occasion.

We separated at midnight, and the next morning some of the same guests and myself escorted him and Mrs. Grant to their train for Paris.

CHAPTER XVIII
1878

THE ST. GOTHARD TUNNEL--I DESCRIBE IT FOR HARPER'S MAGAZINE--ITS COST--A GREAT SCARE IN THE TUNNEL.

October, 1878.--The great tunnel through the St. Gothard Alps is reaching completion. Nothing like it was ever accomplished before in the world. It happens that Mr. Hellwag, the chief engineer of the stupendous undertaking, is a personal friend, and he gave me every facility for visiting it. His courtesy and hints have helped me in preparing my article for Harper's (October) Magazine. Hellwag is already famous as the builder of the tunnels for the Brenner pass. He is also the inventor of the Auger, or Spiral tunnel system, by which railway trains reach high elevations up tunnel slopes, winding around and up the inside of mountains. He gave me letters and permits to go everywhere, and, so far as I know, I am the first American to have been inside the tunnel.

The undertaking of this tunnel is something vast. It takes the surplus cash of three governments to build it, Italy, Germany and Switzerland.

The line reaches from Lake Luzern in Switzerland to Lake Maggiore in Italy, one hundred and eight miles. One hundred and twenty thousand feet of this is tunneled through mountains of granite. The longest tunnel in the series is 48,936 feet. Few of the smaller tunnels are less than 7,000 feet long.

It was thought one hundred and eighty-seven million francs would pay for it, but two hundred and eighty-nine millions are now required. It is the usual blundering in figures that comes with most public enterprises. This particular blundering has bankrupted thousands of innocent people who have bought shares. The extra money is now raised, however, and the awful barrier of granite peaks and fields of snow and ice, between Italy and Switzerland, is to be overcome by skill of man.

There was no road over the Gothard for five hundred years, and not until a century ago was a vehicle of any kind ever seen up there. Even now, the wagon road is one of great peril, as I have myself experienced, a whole sledge load of us once barely missing being overwhelmed by an avalanche that fell a hundred feet ahead of us. There were granite boulders in that slide of snow, big as our horses, and the thing fell without a warning, and with a crash that was stupendous. Many lives have been lost in this pass; half the year, even now, it is abandoned entirely to the winds that howl among its mountains of desolation.

The tunnel was not quite finished when I was there. The boring machines inside are worked by compressed air, furnished by enormous air compressors outside. These also force air in for ventilation. They compress air also for the peculiar locomotives that are moved by air, not steam.

My guide and I got on the front platform of one of these air engines, and were shot into the tunnel for miles through a black cloud of smoke and gas that I thought would kill me, or cause me to fall off the engine. It was Cimmerian darkness. The engineer said: "You shall now see a glimpse of the bowels of hell." I saw nothing for miles, and then suddenly we came to the weird lights, the big air machines boring into the granite walls, and the half-naked workmen. It was a gruesome picture in there, with the yellow lights, the racket of the machines, and the occasional explosion of dynamite. The water in places burst from the rocks in streams as big as my arm, and with force enough to knock the workmen from their feet. At one spot, the torrent broke through fine crevices, at the rate of four thousand gallons a minute. A special canal was made under the railroad tracks, to carry this river of water out of the tunnel.

I was greatly impressed, not only by the scene inside, but to think that at that moment avalanches were falling five thousand feet above our heads, storms were raging among the cold peaks up there, and a rapid mountain river was rushing right along over us. It seemed a perilous place. Indeed, it was often feared that some mighty torrent might be struck suddenly, some day, and destroy every life in the tunnel.

Far in, where the compressed air left the pipes, the ventilation seemed better, but it would kill most men to stay in there at all for any length of time. It is well known that the health of these unfortunate workmen is being ruined. An early death stares every one of them in the face.

Something is always threatening to happen, and my conductor relates an incident that shows how easily alarm sets in. He was one day walking along in the half darkness, inspecting something near the mouth of the tunnel, when he heard far behind him what sounded like the tramping of a herd of buffalo, or the bursting of a torrent. Suddenly, he saw quick moving lights and heard human voices. Whatever it could be, exploding gas, demons, or torrent, it was rushing towards him like an avalanche. He jumped into a niche at the side of the tunnel, to save his life. Then he heard the cry, "The *mine*, the *mine!* run for your life!" He, too, then ran till he broke down and saw the terrible army of half-naked, begrimed men, with the coal lamps on their heads, rush by him in terror. A jutting rock had saved his life, but the herd of men, still screaming "gas," "the mine," "run, run!" tumbled over each other and tramped each other down, till the mouth of the tunnel was reached.

When my informant picked himself up, and went down to the company's offices, he found the whole crowd gesticulating and talking loudly. There had been no "explosion"--no "mine"--no "gas." It was simply a *strike*. The leaders had adopted this plan to scare everybody out of the tunnel.

The next day, and the next, the strikers refused to either work or disperse. They were trying "the dog in the manger" system of the United States strikers, neither working nor letting work. A regiment of militia was sent there, and, unlike American militia, did their duty. A very few musket volleys, and the poor, deluded strikers went away, though a good many staid there in their blood.

CHAPTER XIX
1879

AMERICAN ARTISTS AT MUNICH--I MEET MARK TWAIN--TAKE HIM TO AN ARTISTS' CLUB--CONVERSATIONS WITH HIM--BEER DRINKING--HE READS THE ORIGINAL OF "WHAT I KNOW ABOUT THE GERMAN LANGUAGE"--WE ENTERTAIN THE AMERICANS AT ZURICH--A LETTER FROM GENERAL SHERMAN--CONFEDERATES MORE POPULAR THAN UNION MEN--SHERMAN READY TO SURRENDER.

February 1, 1879.--Spent part of January in Munich, and very much of the time among the studios of the American artists. There are not less than fifty of our countrymen here, either practicing art or learning it.

Frank Duveneck (later widely known) had a large class of devoted students, who were also his followers in a style of painting peculiar to himself. There was a strong belief that he was a man of genius, but he spent much time teaching, when he ought to have been painting. Duveneck's students followed him later to Florence, where I saw them again.

Chase was also at Munich at this time. I can imagine no city more desirable for a student of art. The social atmosphere breathes of art; the galleries, of course, are unsurpassed. There are plenty of teachers--and models are plenty, and all very cheap.

I was introduced to Carl Piloty, head of the Academy of Arts. It was on the street a friend and I met him. The day was cold, the wind blowing. There could be little conversation. He wore a big paletot wrapped about him, and his face and head were so covered that I could not tell what he looked like. Saw him the same evening on the platform in the academy, posing models for the students. There was great enthusiasm for him.

Like most strangers, we visited the famous breweries, and at the "Hof Brauerei" waded around over the wet, stone floors and helped ourselves to beer, as was the custom. The place was full of loud-talking people, with many soldiers among them, some sitting at tables with schooners of beer before them, others carrying their beer glasses about with them as they gesticulated together in groups. A band played all the time. It was to me a wet, noisy, half-lighted, disagreeable place; but it was "the thing" to go there and help yourself to the world-renowned beer.

This brewery, too, is a great place, where one can see German types of many curious kinds, and know what German beer-drinking really is. As we came out into the court, we were near being drowned by some careless employee's turning loose several barrels of dirty water, from a spout over the doorway. Some soldiers in the vicinity laughed at the speed with which we escaped the flood of beer and water.

Out in the street we noticed a not uncommon Munich sight. It was a little parade of University students in open carriages. They wore their corps uniforms of high boots, jaunty caps, and ribbon across the breast. Some of them held aloft a schooner of beer. The front seat, or the place of honor, in each carriage was occupied by a stately bull-dog, arrayed in ribbons and brass collar.

The great bronze foundry was a place that entertained us greatly. The method of casting statues and monuments was explained to us, and the copies of noted American figures they had cast at different times, now in the exhibition room, made us feel very proud.

It was a group of great men who long ago won for our country the respect of the world. There is not a spot in America, or elsewhere, where one can see more of American genius represented in one room than is seen here in the museum of this foundry.

The sights of the city were not so different from the sights of other cities. King Otto drove by us a time or two on his way to that wonderful palace of his, with its gardens and lake and swans, and all that, up in the top of the building.

One of his Cabinet had spent a summer with us at Obstalden, in Switzerland. His family invited us to a little lunch, where we could talk much about the King; but it had to be in a complimentary way, for these good people saw nothing of what everybody else saw--that is, that he was a very unique personage, and probably going crazy. All the world, though, has been glad that he was sane enough to give it Wagner, for without Otto's long and splendid patronage, Wagner's music would still have been "a music of the *future.*"

One of King Otto's freaks is his wonderful fairy castle, built high up in the Bavarian Alps. When the snow is deep on the mountains, and the wind blows, he goes sleigh-riding late at night, and quite alone, in his wonderful sleigh. This sleigh is a gorgeous little coupé on runners. Inside, it is all cushions, luxury and shining lights. Outside, it is illuminated too, and when the mountaineers hear the jingling of bells late at midnight, and see the apparition passing, they cross themselves, and say: "God keep King Otto in his right mind."

We heard Wagner's operas given by his own trained orchestra, almost nightly. They were so long as to be absolutely fatiguing, and made me wonder if this craze for his music is not in part affectation. Enough is enough of anything. We went to bed nights, tired to death; but "it was the thing" to hear Wagner to the end, so we heard.

I think few things interested me so much in Munich as to stand and look at the river Iser. It was full, and dark, and rapid, and great cakes of broken ice floated past. I thought of that night at Hohenlinden

When dark as Winter was the flow
Of Iser rolling rapidly.

Later, as a souvenir of the visit, we bought a little painting by Wex, representing a pretty scene on the upper Iser River.

One of the pleasant incidents of the Munich visit was the meeting with Mark Twain. I copy a few lines from my diary:

Saw Mark Twain several times, and one night had the pleasure of taking him to the American Artists' Club. The young men had insisted on my asking him to come and make a speech. I went to his apartments, near my own, and together we walked clear across the city. It must have been miles, but I was glad of it. He talked all the way, not with the humor that has made him famous, but in an earnest, thoughtful, sincere mood. He told me how he did his literary work, when in Munich. "I hire a room," said he, "away off in some obscure quarter of the town, far away from where we live; where no one, not even Mrs. Clemens, could find me. The people who let the room do not know who I am. I go there mornings, stay all day, and work till evening. When at my book-writing, I never sleep a wink, no matter how many days or weeks the undertaking. It is now two weeks since I have slept one single hour." I wondered such a life was not killing him.

As we trudged along under the lamp lights of the streets, we had much small talk of the West, of the time when he was young and when he was "roughing it." I amused him by relating how I kept a copy of his "Roughing It" at the consulate, to lend to travelers who came along with the "hypo" and like afflictions.

Castle Chillon.

Something was said of certain American writers, recently sprung to fame. I mentioned a letter Charles Dickens, just before his death, wrote to Bret Harte. The letter, in fact, only reached Harte after Dickens' death, and was followed by Harte's beautiful verses, "Dickens in Camp."

"Dickens could well afford to write nice letters to Bret Harte," said he, "for he has no more faithful admirer and student, and he has adopted the Englishman's style. Why not? He could not find a better model, and even as great a genius as Balzac boasted of his dependence on the style of Victor Hugo. Solomon, when he said there was nothing new, meant also there were no new literary styles under the sun, either."

My own belief is that Bret Harte's short California sketches are better than anything Dickens ever wrote.

When we reached the new art room that night, the artists and students were already assembled, and were sitting at a couple of long tables, drinking beer and smoking. An enormous schooner full of beer stood at every plate, and the smoke in the room was almost thick enough to slice up and carry out.

The students all rose as we entered, and gave Mark Twain a little cheer. As he hung his overcoat up in the corner, he took from the pocket an enormous roll of manuscript. The young men saw it, and possibly began to tremble a little. "Don't be alarmed," he cried out, holding the mighty roll up to their view. "I don't intend to read all this." The place of honor at the center of one of the tables was waiting him, and the largest beer schooner of all stood in front of it. I was amazed to see him empty it almost before he sat down. "Let's have some beer, gentlemen," he said laughing, and schooner after schooner came and disappeared.

The paper was "What I Know About the German Language." It was the first time this now famous bit of humor saw the light. It did not seem to me so very funny in itself, but his way of reading it made it exceedingly droll.

When he had finished, every one had something equally ridiculous to tell of the bulls and blunders of ignorant Teutons writing English. Some had received wonderful letters that bordered on uttermost farce. Mark Twain begged possession of all these fool epistles, and possibly made his paper funnier than before from their contents.

The smoke, and the beer, and the jokes went on till midnight. In fact, these beer drinking Americans could beat a Heidelberg students' "Kneipe" all to pieces, and Mark Twain did not propose to be left wholly in the rear.

At last, we all shook hands and started homewards. It was a good hour's walk he and I had before us, but the cool night air was refreshing. For my own part, I was glad to get out of the dense smoke, and have a chance to talk alone with the humorist.

I liked Mark Twain. He is a small, slight man, with big, blue eyes and a great shock of reddish hair. He has a habit of saying

"Thank you kindly." He has youth yet, lots of money and a very pretty wife.

February 23.--On coming back from Munich, wrote a paper about the Iser. Also wrote for the Atlantic Monthly the account of my experiences inside Atlanta.

Last evening we had all the Americans who are in town at our home, celebrating Washington's birthday. A few Swiss and German friends were also with us--among the Germans the family of Director Witt. These were among our first and truest friends abroad. We have spent whole summers together at Bocken, Wangensbach and elsewhere, and we are god parents to one of the little girls. Numbers of guests made speeches last night. Sure it is, the flag never seems so dear to Americans as when they can touch it with their hands in a foreign land. Kinkel, the poet, and his wife and son also, were present.

April, 1879.--There are a million Northern soldiers still living in the United States who were true to the Union, and yet the United States Senate elects a clerk whose principal recommendation is disloyalty to his country. It seems to me a nation is in danger of collapse that can not tell its friends from its enemies.

General Sherman writes thus of the situation:

"WASHINGTON, D. C., March 22, 1879.

"DEAR BYERS:--I was glad to receive your letter this morning, and have sent it down to Mrs. Sherman, who is always glad to see your letters. And now without waiting, will answer your inquiries. We are still here in Washington at the Ebbitt House, Mrs. Sherman, Elly, Rachel and I. Cumpsey is at Baltimore at school, and Mrs. Sherman goes over quite often to look after him. Minnie lives in St. Louis, and at this minute of time Lizzie is there also on a visit. I took Elly and Lizzie with me South, but on our return, as I was somewhat in a hurry and could not well take St. Louis in my route, Lizzie switched off in West Tennessee and went straight to St. Louis. We hear from her daily. All are well there. I suppose you, in common with others, may have seen reports of the illness and death of General and Mrs. T. W. Sherman, but I suppose you recognized the difference of initials. It was another General Sherman, who was on the Army Retired List, who died last week at Newport,

R. I. Politics are now awfully mixed. We have an extra session of Congress in which the Democrats have majorities in both branches, and the Southern members, mostly all Confederate officers, are in the majority of the Democrats, and thus rule all. So at this minute the rebels have conquered us, and we are at their mercy. Who would have thought this in 1865? Our paper announced yesterday the election of a clerk of the Senate, with the recommendation that 'he had served *faithfully* on Lee's staff.' Little by little it has come about, and we find that it is popular to have belonged to the Confederate Army, and correspondingly suspicious to have served in the Union Army. Popular revolutions are hard to comprehend. For this reason I hold myself ready to surrender when called on, which may be at any day.

"My trip South was pleasant and I am glad I made it. Of course I confined myself to purely social matters. Love to Mrs. Byers and the children.

"Yours truly,
W. T. SHERMAN."

CHAPTER XX
1879

A TRIP THROUGH THE BLACK FOREST--STEIN ON THE RHINE--A FAMOUS CASTLE--"ALL BLOWN UP" --GOOD ROADS--FOX HUNTING.

June 4, 1879.--Two weeks since, friends invited us to accompany them on an extended drive through the Black Forest. Such a drive, through charming scenery, and with perfect June weather, was a pleasure nobody thought of declining.

We entered the Black Forest at Stein on the Rhine, and staid all night there. The scenery of the fair Rhine, the ancient castles, the picturesque hills, and the little town with its architecture of an age long past, gave us great enjoyment. The still perfect castle of Hohenklingen, far up on the rocks above us, is a thousand years old. This would be a spot for romance and poetry.

Long years ago I was here in Stein, but passing years make no change in the perfectly romantic appearance of the place.

Very shortly we were in the midst of what in earlier times was only a vast forest, dangerous for travelers to enter. Even now, away from the old towns and villages, the clean, white highway winds among forests of pine trees whose resinous odor is delightful to the senses. The woods are full of game, and at rare intervals we see a fox.

Parts of these vast woods are owned by rich landlords who hold them as "game preserves," and who lease them out to lovers of the hunt in the cities of Switzerland and Germany.

Many a delightful and exciting time have I had with my friends, the Witts or the Schwarzenbachs, hunting foxes and deer in those same Black Forest woods.

Usually we came with our guns on the train, to the hamlet of Singen. The gamekeeper would meet us at the station, and the next morning he had a dozen peasants beating the bush for us, while we stood like sentinels, at obscure hidden pathways in the woods, waiting to fire on the fleeing game. Those who could shoot at all, had good luck always. At noon, servants would bring baskets of lunch, including good wine, from the village to us. A rousing fire was made of brushwood, the slaughtered hares, deer, pheasants and foxes were put in piles to look at, and then a picnic was enjoyed such as only hunters with appetites dream of. There was more chasing again in the afternoon. Often a friend who owned an old-time castle on the hills near by took us home with him, when a night was made of it--such a night as must have made some of his ancestors (whose bones lay under the floor at our feet, in the big hall) wish themselves alive again.

Our friends took us from Stein to Hohentwyl, one of the greatest castle ruins in the world. It must have been an imposing sight in the Middle Ages. It sits like a high and isolated island on the level land in the Duchy of Baden. Yet it belongs to another kingdom (Würtemberg). Once, at the close of a war, the conqueror left it to the conquered, just for sweet honor's sake, and for the brave fighting of its defenders.

One wonders now how the princes and peasants of these valleys were rich enough to build such stupendous affairs. The peasants are poor here, now. What were they in the Middle Ages, with a baron and his castle sitting on every hill?

This particular castle, however, dating from the ninth century, was built and owned by rich German lords. Once it was the home of the beautiful Duchess Hadwig, the heroine of "Ekkehard," that most beautiful of German novels.

I must relate a joke. Mrs. C---- and my wife had been conducted over the vast ruins one forenoon. In the afternoon, I climbed on to the rocky height where the castle sits. When I rang at the castle door, the guide who came seemed to have spent his last pourboire for whisky. He showed me to the main tower, remarking in bad and muddled Dutch that it was once great, but the "French Army had blown it all up--all up." He walked ahead of me, constantly smoking and muttering to himself--"Yes--Ja, by Gott! blown up--all blown up." Each wall or tower or room he conducted me to, was "great," but he quickly added "blown up." I wondered where the ladies were, and inquired of my maudlin guide if he had seen two women that afternoon, with dark dresses and white parasols. "Ja," he answered, "saw them"--paused a moment, took his cob out of his mouth and continued--"*all blown up.*"

The French invasion of some old century had been too much for him. He had talked of it and the exploded castle until he could think of nothing else, and as he closed the door behind, looking at the little coin I had dropped into his hand, I heard him mutter, "Ja--*all blown up.*"

June 8.--As we drive through out of the way places, and to unfrequented hamlets in the Black Forest, far away from railroads, we find a simplicity of life that possibly has changed little in centuries.

Living is very cheap. We never pay more than twenty cents for breakfast. The brooks are all full of delicious trout, and at wayside inns they take them right out of the brook for us, and charge but a trifle for all we can eat.

The scene is everywhere entirely different from Switzerland; yet the green hills, the great woods, the white roads, the flash of hundreds of bright waterfalls, the village church towers, with a stork's nest on the top of every one, are almost as interesting to us as the Alps themselves.

Often when our showy equipage passed some farm, the peasants stopped work and stood stock still, leaning on their hoes and looking at us. Many men doff their caps and the women courtesy, guessing no doubt, from the showy four-horse drag, it was the Kaiser himself passing.

The seclusion of the old, old hamlets in the woods, the quiet everywhere, almost makes us lonesome.

Yesterday we were invited to visit a big farmhouse a little distance from the road. The owner was a rich bauer--"very rich," his neighbors said. Yet, his big, good-looking daughter in wooden shoes and *very* short petticoats, was engaged in cleaning out the stables. She came to us with the big stable fork in her hand, and in the most agreeable way showed us about the place. She was all smiles and jokes and good humor. She was "smart" too. I thought of "M'liss" in one of Bret Harte's stories.

We saw an enormous fire-place in the kitchen, without any chimney. The smoke simply ascended, or tried to ascend, through a pyramid of boards. The room was too much for us. "Don't the smoke hurt your eyes terribly?" said my wife to the girl's mother, as she wiped the tears away and tried to get her breath. "Oh! yes," answered the good woman, "it's terrible on the eyes, but just splendid for smoking hams."

At many places along the country roads, we passed children with baskets, gathering the manure up from the highways. This they carry into their father's fields. But every twig, stick or stone that can deface a white smooth road, is gathered up and taken away. Each farmer, for certain fixed distances along the highway, is a "care taker" of the road, and his little income from his farm is increased by a small allowance from the public treasury.

In the vicinity of Friberg, with its wonderful waterfalls and green mountains, we see as beautiful scenery as the heart could wish.

Little of the Black Forest life or scenery is even guessed at by a traveler on the train. The characteristic things of continental life in general are no longer on the routes of public travel.

CHAPTER XXI
1879

BRET HARTE--LETTERS FROM HIM--VISITS US--STAY AT BOCKEN--CONVERSATIONS--MRS. SENATOR SHERMAN--EVENINGS AT BOCKEN--WE ALL GO TO THE RIGI--HOW WE GOT THE "PRINCE'S" ROOMS--HARTE GOES WITH US TO OBSTALDEN IN THE ALPS--VERY SIMPLE LIFE--A STRANGE FUNERAL--HARTE FINDS HIS STORIES IN A VILLAGE INN--MORE LETTERS--WE VISIT THE MOSELLE RIVER--FINER THAN THE RHINE--A WONDERFUL CASTLE OF THE MIDDLE AGES--ALL FURNISHED AND FRESH AS WHEN NEW--THE FRENCH DID NOT FIND IT WHEN THEY WERE DEMOLISHING GERMAN CASTLES--AN EXQUISITE GOTHIC CHURCH FIVE HUNDRED YEARS OLD--WONDERFUL ROMAN RUINS AT TREVES--MORE LETTERS FROM BRET HARTE--A HAPPY MAN.

May 30.--One day I was wandering quite alone in the Jura Mountains. I had little with me save my umbrella, my overcoat, and a pocket copy of Bret Harte's poems. When I rested, here and there, under a tree at the roadside, I read the poems--all of them; but "John Burns of Gettysburg," "Dickens in Camp," "The Reveille" and "Her Letter," I read often, and felt them to be the rarest verses any American had ever written.

His "Heathen Chinee" had given him fame, while these other great things were but little known.

I believe I had never asked a man for an autograph in my life, but I did want Bret Harte's own name at the foot of "Burns of Gettysburg;" for I had read it with a thrill, and with tears. I sent him the very same little book I had carried around with me.

He returned the copy with these words written on the margin:

"Phrases such as camps may teach,
Sabre cuts of Saxon speech."

He also wrote me. He was now U. S. Consul at Crefeld, near the lower Rhine.

"United States Consulate, Crefeld, May 28, 1879.

"My Dear Mr. Byers:--I have written my name in your book, and return it to you by to-day's post. I beg you to believe that I have never performed that simple act with more pleasure. I only regret that the quality of the paper on page 91 rather limited the legible expression of my good will, and that I could not show as clearly as I would like my thanks to one who has written so appreciatingly of my hero.

"I might have added 'fellow soldier' to the inscription, but I fear that my year's service against the Indians on the California frontier, when the regular troops were withdrawn to Eastern battlefields, would scarcely justify me in taking that title. But I want you to believe that my knowledge of men and camps enabled me to praise a hero understandingly.

"If you still feel under any obligation to me, you can discharge it very easily. I am anxious to know something about your vicinity, and the prices and quality of accommodations to be found there this summer. My doctor has ordered me to the mountains, for my neuralgia and dyspepsia, and I can procure a leave of absence of three or four weeks. I have thought of going to Switzerland with a member of my family who is studying painting in Düsseldorf, and I should therefore prefer some locality where she can sketch from nature. I want some quiet, pretty place, away from the beaten track of tourists-- some little pension, not too expensive. Can you give me some information regarding prices, localities, etc., etc., and how early in the season it would be advisable to come?

"I shall look forward confidently to your telling me something as soon as you can.

"Yours very truly,
Bret Harte."

This letter gratified me, as I now looked forward to the pleasure of having Mr. Harte with us in Switzerland. He wished a quiet place. Where in all the world was there so quiet and so lovely a spot as our own "Bocken," on the lake, with the green hills about it and its views of snow mountains, and all close to beautiful Zurich. We were to spend our third summer there. So I proposed *"Bocken"* and also "Obstalden," a hamlet we often went to in the higher Alps.

He took up with Bocken, however, and wrote:

"June 19, 1879.

"My Dear Mr. Byers:--Let me thank you for your two welcome letters and your book on Switzerland. You could not have sent me a volume more satisfactory to my present needs, nor one that could give me so strong a desire to know more of the author. My good genius evidently joined hands with the State Department in sending you to Switzerland ten years before me.

"Make the best arrangements you can for me at Bocken for about the 7th of July, the exact date you shall know later. You can, if you think it better, keep some hold on Obstalden. Dr. Van K---- yields his favorite Rigi, and thinks I can get strong at Bocken or Obstalden; such was the power of your letters on the highest medical wisdom of Düsseldorf.

"Nothing could be kinder than your invitation, but I fear that neither my cousin nor myself can permit you to add to our great obligations this suggestion of coming to you as guests. Let us come to Bocken like any other tourists, with the exception that we know we have already friends there to welcome us. My cousin, Miss C----, desires to thank your wife for her good intentions, and hopes to have the pleasure of sketching with her.

"I sent you yesterday the only book of mine that I could lay my hands on, a little volume in return for 'Switzerland.' There is something about mountains in it, but I fear your book is the more reliable and interesting.

"My cousin was greatly pleased with your suggestion of your wife's sketching and aiding her in pursuit of the picturesque.

"Very truly,
Bret Harte."

Delays set in, and he wrote again.

"July 23, 1879.

"MY DEAR BYERS:--Are you losing your patience and beginning to believe that B. H. is 'a light that never was on land or sea.'

"For the last week I have been trying to assist somebody, who has come out from the Custom House in N. Y., duly certified to by the State Department, and is 'wanting to know, you know' all about 'market prices and prices current.' But I think I should have scarcely staid for him, if the weather had not been at its worst, blowing a stiff gale for forty-eight hours at a time, and raining in the intervals.

"My present intention is to leave here Saturday, or Sunday, the 26th, but of course will telegraph you exactly when and how.

"Yours hopefully,
BRET HARTE."

At last, he and his cousin, Miss C----, a charming woman, who soon joined my wife in sketching excursions, reached Bocken. Bocken has enough big rooms for old knights of ye olden time to carouse in, but very few bedrooms for real folks to sleep in. So Mr. Harte and I, for a time, occupied a bedroom together in the annex. I was a gainer by the arrangement, for we sometimes lay awake half the night and more, whilst he related to me reminiscences of his early life in California and his literary and other experiences. They would fill a book, but I forbear. This much only I copy from my diary of the time.

August 8, 1879.--Bret Harte and his cousin reached us some days ago. He seems a sick man. He looks nothing like the pictures I had conjured up of him. He is forty-one years old, of medium height, strongly built, legs like an athlete, weighs about one hundred and seventy-five pounds, has fine head, a big nose, clear-cut features, clear good eyes, hair cropped short and perfectly gray, face full and fine; in short a very handsome man, and an exquisite in dress. He is neatness personified, and he seems to have brought a whole tailor's shop of new clothes with him to this simple place, as he appears in a different suit daily, sometimes semi-daily.

There is little at the pension table that he can eat, for he has dyspepsia. So, as we have our own cook and kitchen, we have of late invited him and his cousin to dine with us. At noon, our table is set under the chestnut trees out on the terrace overlooking the blue lake. He can eat here. It is a wonderful spot to dine at with such a view before us.

We have our breakfast in the corner room of the chateau, where the famous tile stove stands, with its pictures of Swiss history. The walls of the room have massive panels of old oak, and around them are low seats that open like chest lids. From the big, leaded windows of the room the view is as fine as on the terrace. Joining this corner is an immense banquet room-- the knights' hall of the olden times.

While sitting at the old, old table, sipping our coffee, we see the pretty steamers pass on the lake far below us, and towards Glarus we see the snowy Alps reflecting the morning sun.

Plain old Chateau Bocken was built centuries ago as a country home for the Burgomasters of Zurich. Those fellows of the olden time knew where the beautiful spots of earth were. I often think Bocken, in summer, the loveliest spot on earth. I am sure it is, for me. Evenings after supper on the terrace, we sit out there at the table with the lamps burning till bedtime. We have good times in talk and reminiscences. Harte is as fine a conversationalist as I ever knew. He uses the most choice and elegant language possible. This surprises one, on recalling that his famous California stories are so often in the dialect of the gold mines. His voice is fine, his speech extremely taking, and I think he has a good heart. When feeling well, he is a delightful companion--an interesting man--apart from his work and fame.

These evenings out on the terrace, we talk of the poets too. Each expresses his preference. Harte said almost the finest poem in the language is Browning's "Bringing the Good News From Ghent to Aix." He recited it with splendid feeling.

To me, Browning's "Napoleon at Ratisbon" seemed almost equally good--a whole drama in a dozen lines or so.

I spoke of Harte's own poem, the "Reveille." His recital to us of how it was produced in San Francisco was in itself a picture of old war times, exciting in the extreme.

A great mass meeting was to be held in San Francisco one evening. Men were wanted to enlist--to go out and *die* for their country, in fact. Somebody must write a poem, said the Committee, and Thomas Starr King, the patriot orator, suggested the name of a young man employe at the

Government mint. It was Bret Harte. The day of the evening came, and, with fear and doubting, Mr. Harte read his little poem to Mr. King. "I am sure it won't do--It is not good enough," he added deprecatingly, and with self-disappointment. "You don't know," answered Mr. King. "Let *me* read that poem aloud to you once."

In his great, fine voice, he rendered the verses, till Harte himself was astonished with his own lines. Still, the judgment of a friend could be over partial.

Harte was almost afraid to go to the hall that night; but he went and crept up into the gallery. All San Francisco seemed to be present. It was a terribly exciting time. Would California rise up and be true to the Union, or only half true?

"I will read a poem," said the magnificent King, after a while. "It is by Mr. Harte, a young man working in the Government mint."

"Who's Harte?" murmured half the audience. "Who's he?"

The orator commenced, and ere he reached that great line, "For the great heart of the Nation, throbbing, answered, 'Lord, we come,'" the entire audience were on their feet, cheering and in tears.

It was too much for the young poet to stay and witness. He thought he would faint. He slipped down the back stairs and out into the dark street, and walking there alone, wondered at the excitement over verses he had that morning feared to be valueless.

One can imagine a young man out there alone in the dark, for the first time hearing Fame's trumpet sounding to him from the crowded theater.

August 15.--The days were passing in delight at Bocken. I come out from the consulate early in the afternoon. Occasionally I stay here all day, and then with Harte and his cousin we have little excursions in the vicinity.

Yesterday, I helped Mr. Harte read over the proof-sheets of his "Twins of Table Mountain." We lay in hammocks and read. I do not think it approaches some of his former stories.

Miss C---- copies much for him, and he also occasionally dictates to her. I wonder that any one can write in that way.

The other afternoon I took him in to consult Dr. Cloetta, a distinguished professor and physician. The good doctor, who speaks but little English, put him on a lounge, examined him carefully, and said, "Mr. Harte, I think you got *extension* of the stomach." Coming back on the boat, Harte laughed a good deal about this; cursed a little too.

August 18.--Mrs. Senator Sherman, of Washington, and two of her nieces, are stopping for a while in this part of Switzerland. A lieutenant of the navy is also with them. The other day we all took a notion to cross the country in a post diligence, and turn up at the Rigi.

We started from Bocken early in the morning. The driver was jolly and we had much fun. I only fear some of the peasants thought us tipsy, as we passed through their villages singing "Shoo Fly, Don't Bother Me," and like joyous American ditties. We had a big, red umbrella fastened above the diligence, and when we came to a hamlet the driver put his horses on the gallop and blew his bugle. Mrs. Sherman looked a bit serious over it all, but the noisier ones of the party were in command.

The hotel on the Rigi had not a single bed for us that night. "May we sleep on the hall floor?" innocently inquired Mr. Harte. "No," answered the landlord. "Perhaps out on the doorsteps then?" continued Mr. Harte. "Just as you please," said the keeper of the hostelry, crustily. "My beds, I tell you, are taken. I can do nothing for you." "Yes, but--" went on Mr. Harte, with a knowing smile--"it is awfully cold and dark out there--suppose our little party orders a good champagne supper, with lots of chicken and etceteras, and sits at the table here all night. You wouldn't mind that would you?" The landlord coughed a little cough.

The supper was ordered, and before it was half over our host bethought himself. He said he had just got a telegram from Prince ---- and his suite, who had engaged the four finest rooms in the house. The Prince could not come. We could have the Prince's rooms, all of them. "Hurrah for the Prince of ----," we all cried, clinking our glasses to him. The fact was, and we knew it, the telegraph office had not been open since 6 o'clock. All the same, we had the finest rooms and a moderate bill. And the next day one of the nieces was engaged to the young lieutenant. So a good deed prospers.

"You will not mind telling us why you did not give us the rooms in the first place, will you?" said Mr. Harte to the host next morning, as he settled the bill for the party. "We know, you know, that you got no telegram at all from the Prince." "Frankly," said the landlord, "it was because Americans don't often order wine. My *profit's* in my *wine* and if none is ordered, better the rooms remain empty. But you folks are not Americans, I know by the *many bottles*." Nevertheless, it was Mr. Harte's good nature that won the day for us, or rather the night.

We were up too late for the "Sunrise on the Rigi" next morning; but the splendid view of a dozen blue lakes and snow white mountains all around us, repaid the party for the trip.

Mrs. Sherman liked the Rigi for its own lonesome heights. Mr. Harte praised the whole wonderful scene; the Lieutenant looked into the blue eyes of Miss ----, and all were satisfied.

Obstalden.

August 30, 1879.--When we got back from the Rigi to Bocken, Mr. Harte proposed that we go for a week to Obstalden, that picturesque hamlet hung above the Wallensee. We ourselves had spent parts of three summers there. It is indeed a characteristic Alpine village. It is on the side of a mountain. The wonderful little Wallensee, blue as a summer's sky, lies 2,000 feet below it. Behind it rise majestic mountains. It is all green grass up there, even up to the very doors and windows of the brown, hewn log houses. A little white highway winds up to the village from the lake, while the rest of the roads are simple, narrow goat paths. They lead about over the grass from house to house, and from the village up to the higher Alps, where the village boys herd goats and cows from sunrise till evening. The peasant women all weave silk, and this necessitates the great number of long windows in their ham-brown cabins. The men are almost as brown as their houses, and live to be a hundred years old. I never saw so many *very* old people in my life. They live on bread and milk and cheese, with a little sour wine. Some of these centenarians are Alpine guides, and I have had them carry my overcoat and haversack and escort me up high mountains with the nimbleness of a boy of twenty. I was ashamed to have them lug things for me, a member of the Alpine Club, but they insisted.

American tourists don't find Obstalden. The hamlet is kept a close secret among a few Swiss and Germans, who want only picturesque scenes and *very* simple life. It was a great favor that a friend told me about it, and got the little village inn to always give me the refusal of a room or two.

I had learned Mr. Harte's tastes, after his coming to Bocken. They were not for the *utterly* simple life of mountain villages, after all, and my wife and I protested against his going to Obstalden. But go he would and we had to accompany him.

When we got there, the little hotel was overflowing with people. It held but a dozen guests. The keeper of the inn offered to sit up that night, and let Miss C---- and my wife have his room. But at last he thought of the village pastor's wife, and she took in the two ladies. He tried to get a room in a peasant's house for Mr. Harte and me. It was impossible. We could walk about all night, at the imminent risk of falling off a couple of thousand feet or so, or we could sleep in a peasant's hayloft.

Many of Mark Twain's famous "Chamois" were likely to be hopping around in that little hayloft. Mr. Harte hesitated a little --wished he had never heard of Obstalden. He wore one of his newest, swellest suits, and the situation "gave him pause." At last he nimbly climbed up the ladder. I followed, and without much undressing in the dark, we were soon under a big coverlet, where to me, for a novelty, the sweet hay was better than any sheets ever made.

Mr. Harte found it all "mighty tough" and "mighty rough." He had wanted, he said in his letter "a little inexpensive simplicity," but this was too much for anything--a couple of representatives of the *great* United States, and one of them a New York exquisite, tucked away in a hay mow above the goats and cattle. Obviously, he had not been a mountaineer, fine as had been his tales of the rough life in California.

That was something I always wondered at--how Bret Harte could write such splendid touching tales of "hard cases," being himself so much the reverse of all the characters he depicted. It was the genius of his character that had done it all. Some men take in at a glimpse, and can perfectly describe what others must experience for a lifetime, to be able to tell anything about.

We lay awake much of that summer night, in the hay mow, but the "poetry" of the thing was all wasted on Mr. Harte. We heard the solitary watchman of the village, who with his lantern walked about in the darkness, cry to the sleepers: "Twelve o'clock, and all is well." That solitary watchman's occupation did touch Mr. Harte. It is indeed a singular life, going around there alone all the night, the towering pinnacles of the rocks on one hand, the depths of the valley and the lake below on the other, the flash of waterfalls close by, the thunder of distant falling avalanches. Never a night in three hundred years but some watchman has gone about the byways of Obstalden with his lantern, calling aloud the hours.

A tin cup, and a little mountain rill that laughed its way through the village, afforded Mr. Harte and myself our opportunities for morning toilettes. Mr. Harte's new clothes had been *pressed* in the hay-mow, but not always in the right direction. We met the ladies at the breakfast table of the inn. Mr. Harte's narrative to them of the adventures of the night made a hearty laugh. Never did a breakfast of brown bread and butter, with good coffee, hot milk and wild honey, taste better.

The table was set out on the terrace. The blue lake was far, far below us. On its opposite shore, the perpendicular rocks, a mile high, shut in the loveliest water in Switzerland.

Up on top of those walls of rock, on a little green plateau, we could see the town of Amden. Nothing like it in the world. Not a horse nor a carriage up there. It is reached by a stone stairway, zigzagging along the face of the rocks. Everything the people buy or sell is lugged up and down this wonderful stairway on peasants' shoulders.

In the afternoon, Mr. Harte's attention was riveted on a curious procession of row boats, slowly crossing the lake in our direction. One of the boats was entirely covered with garlands and white flowers. It was a village funeral, said our landlord. They don't have ground enough for a graveyard up there in Amden; so they bury their people this side of the lake.

"There is your story," I said to Mr. Harte--"the wonderful stairway--the lake funeral--the town on the high rocks."

"Yes--all right," he answered; "but, somehow, I never have luck with material I don't find out for myself. I must suggest it myself." I recalled Bayard Taylor's saying, "there is no satisfaction in even a pint of hot water which has been heated by somebody else." I am afraid I heated this water, not very hot. The story will never be written.

That evening we visited the "goat village," not far away, and watched hundreds and hundreds of goats, led by a young mountaineer, with a great bunch of Alpine roses tied to his staff, and a wreath of roses on his hat. He was coming down from the grassy slopes of a mountain. He was whistling and singing all the way. It was a picturesque sight. The "goat village" is composed of scores of little huts or pens, each one big enough for a single goat. It was interesting to see how each goat knew its own hut among the many, and hurried into it to be milked.

In a very few days Mr. Harte had had enough of Alpine simplicity, though we had secured a room in the inn.

Far down below us on the lake lay pretty Wesen. It looked more civilized, and he would try it there. When he was shown his room in the Wesen inn, and strolled into the little drawing-room, what was his surprise to notice lying among the books on the table, "the *Works of Bret Harte*."

This was fame--away off in an Alpine village of Switzerland to find his name was known, his books read.

When he told me, I recalled that other first night in San Francisco--the applauding assembly--the unknown poet out in the street in the dark.

Mr. Harte soon came back to us at Bocken, and on the 26th we accompanied him on his way to his home in Germany, as far as the Falls of the Rhine.

But we stopped first in Zurich. As it was his birthday, we had a little good-bye dinner together in the Tonhalle by the lake, and did all we could for his "health" with a bottle of "Mumm's extra dry."

That he might be right over the Rhine Falls by moonlight, the host of the Laufen Castle gave him the room with the balconies above the water. It was beautiful, but the noise of the falls kept Harte awake all night.

In the morning we said good-bye and parted, he for Crefeld via the Black Forest, and we for Bocken.

Yesterday I got this letter from him:

"CREFELD, Aug. 27, 1879.

"MY DEAR MR. BYERS:--We arrived here safely last night. *Of course*, the railways did not connect as you said they would, and *of course*, we did not go where you promised we should, but we got to Düsseldorf within twelve hours of the schedule time set and are thankful. Only let me beg you to post yourself a little on Swiss railroads before you travel *yourself*. Your knowledge does well enough for a guide to old experienced travelers *like us*!!! but it won't do for a simple, guileless, believing nature like your own. And don't let the landlord of the Chateau 'Laufen' cook up a route for you.

"Our ride through the Black Forest was a delicious revelation. I should say it was an overture to Switzerland, had I entered Switzerland from its borders, but coming *from* Switzerland, I could not but think it was really *finer* than the Alps in everything that makes the picturesque, and that Switzerland would have been a disappointment afterwards. It was very like the California 'foothills' in the mountain ranges, and the long dashes of red soil and red road--so unlike the glare and dazzle of the white Swiss turnpikes--were very effective. I wanted much to stop at Freiberg, still more at a certain ruined castle and 'pension' called Hombeck, which was as picturesque as Castle Laufen, minus the noise of 'factory wheels and fulling mills' from these awful rapids. Heidelberg was a sensation, with its castle that quite dwarfs the Rhine River (as all these things do by comparison when one travels) and we could have stayed here two or three days and enjoyed ourselves.

"The weather has changed back to the old wet season that we thought we had left behind us when we turned our faces Southward. It is dull and rainy. Nevertheless as soon as I get some work off my hands that has accumulated here I shall try the seaside for my hoped-for rehabilitation.

"My cousin sends her regards. I suppose she will write or has written to Mrs. Byers. I hope you will not give up your Rhine trip (with a suitable guide) and that we may see you in Düsseldorf soon.

"With my best regards to Mrs. Byers,

"Very truly yours,
BRET HARTE."

September 29, 1879.--We are just home from a ten days' trip up and down the Moselle River, that neglected Cinderella sister of the Rhine. It is more beautiful than the Rhine itself. It has more pretty hills and mountains on its shores; its villages are more picturesque; its ruins of castles more numerous; its wines as good. Parts of our journey we went in a row boat, often we walked along the shores. At Cochem, we visited friends and had a good time. We also went to the magnificent "Elz," the only German castle Louis XIV's invaders failed to find and destroy. It is among the dark wooded hills, miles back from the Moselle River. Nothing like it to-day in Germany. Heidelberg is a ruin. Elz is a perfect castle of the Middle Ages. Portcullis, gate, tower, moat, walls and halls, stone floors, fireplaces, tapestries and furniture, as they were centuries ago. Everything has been left, and the owner of Elz keeps all the surroundings in the spirit of the olden time, even to the troops of hounds.

To wander through this castle is like reading Scott's novels, only here all is old German. No wonder the French never found the castle. Even we, with a guide, blundered right on to it, before we knew we were within miles of it. We heard dogs baying, looked, and there among the rocks and woods saw the lofty walls and towers. We had no passes allowing us to enter, but our guide had a brother among the men in charge, and we were shown across the bridge and moat.

I know no spot, castle, or ruin, in Europe, where one feels himself so absolutely back in the Middle Ages. While in there, I forgot there were such things as gunpowder, railways, gas and cannon. The walls were hung with spears, swords, bows and battle clubs.

Another of the perfect works of olden times visited by us on the Moselle was the ancient gateway at the City of Treves. This "Porta Nigra" impressed me much. I think there is nothing to equal it, even in Rome. Many of the works of the Romans, built in this German town, are in better preservation than anything in the "Eternal City." Some of them are just as grand. The town itself is only a feeble reminder of the great, old times, when seven different Roman Emperors made this town their residence.

There is one church here, the "Liebfrauen Kirche," exquisite in its beauty, that stands as the most perfect specimen of Gothic architecture remaining in the world. It is indeed "a thing of beauty" and a "joy;" if not forever, for at least five hundred years, and it may last a thousand years to come. The "Holy Coat of Christ" is kept here in the Cathedral. It is claimed to have been brought here by Helena, the mother of Constantine. I can see no reason why this may not be true. Relics of a million times' less significance have been preserved by men for ages. Nothing would be so easily traced and cared for, from century to century, as a relic that half mankind revered as holy.

November, 1879.--We are again at our home in Zurich, 7 Centralhof. We are anxious for a long visit to Italy, and I have asked for a leave. Mr. Harte thinks to go along with us.

"November 9, 1879.

"MY DEAR MR. BYERS:--I have your welcome letter of the 7th, and hasten to say that two words by telegraph from Mr. Seward give me my leave of absence. With this in my pocket, I am in no hurry, knowing that I can rush off at any moment, when Crefeld becomes unbearable. When the Rhine fog gathers thickest, and the office lights are lit at 3 P. M. and neuralgia becomes lively, I clutch the telegram and smile a ghostly smile.

"And we may meet, after all, where the sun shines. The doctor here tells me I must go to upper Italy, say Bellagio on the Lake of Como. But there is a time to think of that. Let me know *when* you get your leave. You will get it *of course*.

"My cousin had a dismal voyage home, tempestuous weather and seasickness nearly all the time. She writes rather sadly from New York, where she has found her brother-in-law hopelessly ill, and her sister in great distress. Her quiet life in Düsseldorf makes that busy city seem strange to her, and I hope when she gets to Washington she may shake off her sadness. I have written to her urging her, if she have the slightest feeling of 'homesickness' for Europe again, to start off with her sister Jessie and come back to me at once. I hope she certainly will in the spring, for it is terribly lonely here.

"Tell Mrs. Byers to stop this shooting of Parthian arrows from Obstalden. I am not so very particular, but if we travel in Italy together, we must certainly have more than *one* bedroom for us *three*. I know I am fastidious as to location, but I'd let that go. I'd stick out for *two* bedrooms, if we had to telegraph a week ahead. If Mrs. Byers and myself are to quarrel in this way we must all have separate apartments, and two wash bowls.

"I forgot to ask you to procure me a book of Swiss photographic views for about eight or ten francs. It is for a child's present and I leave the selection entirely to yourself. Will you charge your soul with it, and credit me with the enclosed.

"Yours ever,
B. H."

And later he writes:

"November 23, 1879.

"My Dear Mr. Byers:--A line to thank you for the album. It was a great bargain at 10 R. M. And yet people talk of the impractical, unbusiness-like character of the literary mind.

"I am still here, but knowing that I can go when I can stand things no longer, I put up with an india-ink washed sky, a dismal twilight that lasts eight hours, and stands for 'day' to the Rhenish perception, and find some work. I have just 'turned off' a story longer than the 'Twins,' and did it in spite of neuralgia and *'extension.'*

"I see by a telegram to the Daily London News that Mr. Seward has resigned, and Colonel John Hay takes his place as Assistant Secretary of State. Hay is a good fellow, was in the diplomatic service once, is an accomplished, well-mannered gentleman of whom any American might be proud, and only a few years ago earned his bread by literary labors as editorial writer on the Tribune, besides being the author of 'Jim Bludsoe' and 'Little Breeches,' as you, of course, know. He married a rich wife and is quite independent of the office.

"All this ought to presage some *intellectual discrimination* of the deserts and needs of *certain other literary men in the service*. But we shall see. Certainly you will get your leave of absence now.

"When you have made up your mind to go, let me know. Meantime give my best regards to your wife.

"Yours ever,
BRET HARTE."

*****

July 1, 1879.--The business of the Consulate goes smoothly on. I have good assistants and no little leisure. Besides, Zurich is so centrally located that in a few hours I can travel to the most interesting spots of Europe. Germany, France, Italy are only a little journey off, the first but a couple of hours' ride away. The scenery here is delightful, the climate moderate.

"What would you like if you could choose," said a Swiss to me at my tea table the other night. "Nothing," I replied, "only to stay here forever." "You are content," he answered. "I envy you--you are a happy man--the first one I ever saw!"

CHAPTER XXII
1880–1881

A LITTLE STAY BY THE MEDITERRANEAN--AM OFFERED A POSITION IN CHINA--AN ARTICLE ON THE SWISS RHINE--ALSO ONE ON MY EXPERIENCES IN THE REBEL ARMY--TWO LETTERS FROM GENERAL SHERMAN--GRANT AND THE PRESIDENCY--SAYS THE BARE NARRATIVE OF MY ESCAPE FROM PRISON WOULD BE AN EPIC--BANQUET AT THE LEGATION--I WRITE FOR THE NEW YORK TRIBUNE AN EXPOSE OF HOW CERTAIN EUROPEAN COMMUNITIES SENT PAUPERS TO THE UNITED STATES--AM VIOLENTLY ATTACKED FOR IT BY MANY AMERICAN JOURNALS AND REPRIMANDED BY STATE DEPARTMENT--SWISS GOVERNMENT COMPLAINS--INVESTIGATION FOLLOWS--I AM JUSTIFIED--LETTER FROM SHERMAN AS TO HIS SON TOM--VISIT AMERICA--SECRETARY BLAINE COMPLIMENTS ME--THE PRESS CHANGES ITS TONE AND NEW LAWS ARE ADOPTED AS TO IMMIGRATION IN UNITED STATES AND SWITZERLAND--TRIBUNE SAYS EDITORIALLY, "MR. BYERS DESERVES THE THANKS OF THE AMERICAN PEOPLE"--A LITTLE VISIT TO THE POET LONGFELLOW, AND THE ALCOTTS; ALSO TO THE AUTHOR OF "AMERICA."

March, 1880.--During a recent leave of absence I saw the Italian cities for the second time. We also spent some weeks at San Remo, by the Mediterranean, taking little foot excursions to Monte Carlo and Nice over the celebrated Cornici road. This lofty highway of Napoleon's, above the sea, is the finest foot excursion in Italy.

Olive Trees by the Mediterranean.

Monaco and Monte Carlo.

While at Florence I wrote "Philip," and at Prato I secured the beautiful censer described in the verses. The days now go by quickly enough, as many reports are asked for by the department, and the leisure goes in writing verses or articles for the magazines.

March 30 had this from General Sherman:

"WASHINGTON, D. C., March 17, 1880.

"DEAR BYERS:--I was glad to receive your interesting letter from San Remo, Italy, a place I well remember on our drive from Nice to Genoa. I remarked the same thing that you did, that gorgeous scenery of sea and shore, of sheltered vales and olive-clad hills, with the snow-capped Pyrenees behind, seemed lost on the dirty, beggarly natives. Were it not for the English and American traveler, the Corniche would be poor indeed. All accounts from Europe and California describe the past winter as very severe, whilst here in Washington and indeed in all the country east of the Mississippi there has been no winter at all. January and February were like the same months in Louisiana. We had last week a little spurt of snow, but now the sun shines warm and bright, the grass is green, and the trees begin to show leaves, whilst crocuses and lilacs are almost purple with their buds. I fear we have not had winter enough to make a healthy and profitable summer.

"Elly will be married to Mr. Thackera, of the Navy, in May, and Minnie will come on the first time since her marriage. She now has four children, two boys and two girls, all healthy, strong children. For some years she has occupied a suite of rooms at Windsor Flats in the city of St. Louis, but she has just removed to a house I possess in the suburbs, with five acres of lawn, orchard and garden. She writes that they are very comfortable, and I propose to go out and see for myself about April 1. The rest of our family is here, Tom alone excepted, and we continue about as usual.

"Politics are beginning to buzz. Grant is still in Mexico, but will return via Texas next week. I suppose we may assume that he wants to be President again, and will probably be the Republican candidate. Whom the Democrats will choose, is hard to guess.

"I will look to the article you name in Harper's. Mrs. Sherman always reads your letters.

"Ever your friend,
W. T. SHERMAN."

This month's Harper has my article on "The Swiss Rhine," illustrated by Mrs. Byers, and the May Atlantic will have my "Ten Days in the Rebel Army." This is the story of the time I escaped from the Macon prison, and went into the Rebel Army in disguise. The desperate venture came near costing me my life when I was taken, as our own generals had been executing rebels for similar action in our own army a short time before.

This is my eleventh year in the foreign service. I like the life and the duties, and the country I happen to be stationed in. It is also a gratification to have it said that I stand well with the Department at Washington. This is indicated by my being offered other and better posts than this. A recent letter tells me, if I wish it, I may have my choice of General Consulates in China or Japan. My preferences are for life in Europe; besides, we now have our friends here, and know the people, the language, and the customs.

June 14.--Our anniversary. Celebrate it by going to Bürglen, the birthplace of William Tell. Made sketches and had a good time.

A cottage inn stands on the spot where Tell was born. I asked the young woman who answered the door bell if Mr. Tell were at home. She laughed and answered, "No, but I am Mrs. Tell."

An American friend joined us there, and, with "Mrs. Tell," we all sang songs and waltzed half the night to the music of a cracked piano, played by one of "Mrs. Tell's" sisters.

*****

Received a letter last week from General Sherman. He regrets Grant's having to scramble for the Presidency.

"WASHINGTON, D. C., May 11, 1880.

"DEAR BYERS:--I received in good time your kind letter of April 3, and laid it one side for attention after Elly's wedding. Meantime, the clock came all safe and right, and I acknowledged its receipt of the merchant in New York through whom it came.

"The wedding came off all right at the appointed time, Wednesday, May 5th, and the young couple are now at Niagara, and will return next week via Boston and Philadelphia. Mr. Thackera is a fine young naval officer of excellent reputation, and Elly is the best of my children for such a vagrant life.

"I know that you receive the papers and telegrams and that it would be idle for me to attempt any news of public events. We are, as you well know, in the very throes of a Presidential canvass, which in itself constitutes a revolution. Grant is still a candidate, but instead of being nominated by acclamation, will have to scramble for it, a thing I cannot help but regret, as his career heretofore is so splendid that I cannot help feeling it impaired by common politics. He could so nobly rest on his laurels, but his family and his personal dependents prod him on, and his best friends feel a delicacy about offering advice not asked.

"We are now residing in a rented house--No. 817--Fifteenth Street, in the best possible neighborhood, and at rates better than to purchase. I look on St. Louis as my ultimate home, and don't want to be embarrassed with property here. I own two most excellent houses in St. Louis. One is now occupied by Minnie and her family, and the other is leased to good tenants who will take good care of it till we need it.

"We are all in good health, that is, all my immediate family, but my aide, Colonel Audenreid, whom you must well remember, is at this moment dangerously ill of some liver complaint. The doctor assures me that we ought not to be alarmed, but I cannot help it, for he has been a month in bed, and I discover no signs of reaction.

"My best love to Mrs. Byers and the children. My aide, Colonel Tourtelotte, is now abroad and will see you.

"Yours truly,
W. T. SHERMAN."

August 15.--Another interesting letter from General Sherman came to-day:

"WASHINGTON, D. C., Aug. 1, 1880.

"DEAR BYERS:--I was absent all of July, making a tour to the Northwest as far as Bismarck. On my return I found your two letters. One about Colonel Audenreid's death, which I have put into an envelope along with many others of the same kind for poor Mrs. Audenreid, when she is in a condition to be comforted by the sympathy of friends. The other letter of July 13 is now before me for answer. I really don't know where to look for that pamphlet about the burning of Columbia, when you and I testified, and this being midsummer, everybody is out of town, and I am at a loss whom to consult to hunt it up. Was it the Committee on the Conduct of the War in session as the war closed, or later? I have a faint memory of testifying, but must beg you to write your article absolutely fresh, just as it remains in your mind, or as noted in any memoranda you possess. I am sure you could make a magazine article of infinite interest, painting your individual capture, imprisonment, hopes, fears, numerous escapes, concealment, etc., etc., the arrival of my army in Columbia, and your supreme joy both for yourself and country, at so happy a termination of your imprisonment. The bare narrative would be an epic, but you can dress it up without risking errors or controversy. Contemporaneous documents, of which thousands exist, will always take precedence of magazine articles at this late day, but Homer's Iliad is as fresh to-day as when penned, so of Robinson Crusoe. If I can find what you want I will send, but beg you not to wait. I must go September 1, with the President and a select party, to California, Oregon, etc., to be gone all of October, so I will have little time.

"I don't observe the least possible excitement about the Presidential election, and hope, as you say, one candidate or the other will obtain a decisive majority with as little force or fraud as possible. Hancock's nomination by the Democrats gives assurances that even if the Democrats succeed, the Union will be safe. He is unquestionably patriotic, and has a stronger character and more ability than political enemies concede. Garfield is a man of unquestioned ability and force.

Yours,
W. T. SHERMAN."

October 19, 1880.--Two days ago Mr. Nicholas Fish, our Minister, invited us to a diplomatic dinner at Bern. The Spanish Minister and his wife were present, as also one or two gentlemen of the Swiss Cabinet, and all the Consuls in Switzerland.

The Fish family live in a pretty villa in the outskirts of the capital, with splendid views from their terrace. The Minister is the ideal diplomat, trained by long service, accomplished, cautious and conservative. The standing of the family at the Swiss capital is very high.

Before the banquet, two sweet children came into the drawing-room for awhile, a boy and a girl of the family.6

Spent Sunday also with Mr. Fish's family, and drove about the queer old town with its arcades, its bear pit, its rushing waters and its glorious mountain views from the terrace.

October 24.--For years I have been observing the character of the immigration from Europe to the United States. Much of it is very bad. It came to my certain knowledge, too, that hundreds of paupers, drunkards, criminals and insane people were absolutely being taken out of workhouses and jails at different places on the continent, and shipped across the sea to us at the expense of local authorities, who found it cheaper to send them to America than to provide for them at home. It did not seem possible, but a very little investigation proved its truth. As if by accident, numerous cases happened right within my own district. I protested, and, in some cases, compelled the return of paupers after they had reached the sea coast. But the traffic went right on, and every day's investigation revealed more of the extent of the imposition on the American Government. Our country is rapidly filling up with the off-scourings of Europe. There are plenty of good emigrants, but also an awful population of thriftless beggars and tramps invading the United States. Worst of all, nobody in America seems to believe a word of it. Our Government looks on supinely, our people welcome emigration of course, little dreaming of the chaff and the straw that come with the wheat. Nobody's attention can be secured to what is going on. Some weeks since I determined to make a public statement.

November 30, 1880.--Every mail, these days, brings me marked American newspapers, with articles abusing me for my exposé of pauper immigration, in the New York *Tribune* of November 12, 1880. It seems the larger part of the American press regards me as misrepresenting facts, and as a common disturber.

Dozens of letters filled with violent abuse, also come to me, and from Chicago come letters even threatening my life, should I ever put foot in the United States.

Even the conservative State Department has been influenced to send me what the newspapers call "a severe reprimand" and threatens my removal from office.

Nothing but my past good record saved me. "In a Consul of less meritorious services," says the official dispatch, "it would be considered sufficient cause for removal."

Committees went to the Secretary of State, and demanded my dismissal, anyway. It seems I have brought enmity on my head from every direction.

The Swiss papers have copied the American attacks, and join in the malicious abuse and misrepresentation. My article is misrepresented, and I am regarded an enemy of Switzerland. Some of the German press join in the howl, and even Bismarck has been asked to make representations to our Government.

The Swiss representative at Washington complains to his government about me, and asks investigation. The Swiss government in quick time entered its complaint. This is my chance, for I have only told the truth, and have in my hands a hundred things to prove it, though at the present moment they have made me the most disliked man in Switzerland. There seems simply to be no "let up" to the misrepresentations concerning this article. Those who know the inside facts, are naturally indignant that I have exposed them.

I have gone on accumulating testimony, showing how scandalously our American hospitality has been abused by certain communities shipping their paupers and scoundrels to us.

Yesterday an emigration agent offered to furnish me the names of four hundred paupers whom he alone had been hired to ship to the United States.

In Italy, the other day, a great train load of poverty-stricken and perfectly ignorant immigrants were started off for the United States. They numbered one thousand. There was not a dollar apiece in the whole crowd.

February 9, 1881.--Here and there, a Swiss newspaper has looked into the matter of my *Tribune* letters for itself, and with shame admits that the leading charges in my *exposé are true.*

Our Minister, Mr. Fish, at the request of the Department, also investigates me and my exposé, and a few days ago announced to Washington "that the statements made by Consul Byers, and objected to by the Swiss Government, *are correct.*"

So all this storm of abuse has been unwarranted. Mr. Fish did me the compliment to add in his dispatch "that instead of being unfriendly to the Swiss, he (Mr. Byers) has done much to encourage and cherish good relations between the two countries. He is one of the ablest and most experienced consular officers in the service and has for nearly twelve years performed his duties with integrity, ability and faithfulness."

This report of me from a superior officer is a little set-off to the "reprimand" and to the five hundred howling newspapers in the United States.

I am now getting letters of thanks from many people who appreciate my trying to do my country an honest service. Many of the newspapers, too, both at home and abroad, have commenced seeing "a new light," now that overwhelming evidence as to the facts is printed in pamphlet form by Minister Fish, and submitted to Congress.

Many that attacked me a month or so ago, now praise. The New York *Tribune* has stood by me through it all, and now editorially says: "He deserves the thanks of the American people."7 What a change from a few weeks ago!

January 17.--General Sherman writes me an interesting letter about his son Tom, and regrets that he is not in an active career.

"WASHINGTON, D. C., Jan. 2, 1881.

"DEAR BYERS:--I was very glad to receive yours of November 25, for it assured me of your general well-being, that your family enjoyed health and a fair share of this world's blessings, and that your thoughts and feelings turned toward this, your native land. Our newspapers are so full of current news and gossip, and the telegraph so swift, and steamers so regular that letters are stripped of the interest they once possessed. I cannot hope to tell you of anything public, and in private everything seems to me so commonplace that I imagine you can, without being told, know that I and my family continue pretty much as when you were last with us. My daughter Elly is married to Lieutenant Thackera, of the Navy, now on duty in Boston, supervising the construction of modern guns. I was there last week to visit her, and instead of the child I am wont to consider her, I found her a full developed woman. Minnie is at St. Louis with four children, one of them staying with us here in Washington, and all my girls are grown. The youngest boy, now fourteen, is tall, slender, red haired, and is said to resemble me in form and quality. My oldest son, Tom, is also here with us on a New Year's visit. He is some sort of a Catholic divine, not a priest, but employed in one of the Catholic educational establishments near Baltimore. This is all directly antagonistic to my ideas of right. He ought to be in some career to assist us, and to take part in the great future of America. I feel as though his life were lost, and am simply amazed he does not see it as I do. Mrs. Sherman and the rest are as well as usual, and we are drifting along with public events toward that end which we now can foresee. If you come back I hope to see you often, and hope you, too, will sooner or later embark in the live questions of the future. Anything which comes from you I always read with interest, whether a letter or magazine article. Give my best love to Mrs. Byers, and believe me always,

"Affectionately, your friend,
"W. T. SHERMAN."

March, 1881.--On the 11th of last month, we left Zurich for Liverpool, and sailed to New York on the 15th. Reached Washington in time to see the inauguration of President Garfield. It snowed on the night of the 3d, and the Washington streets were cold and miserable on the evening of the 4th. There were great crowds of people at the East front of the Capitol, and everybody was touched when the oath was taken, as Garfield turned around and kissed his aged mother.

The street parade was fine, but the weather cold. Thousands probably died from diseases contracted while viewing the ceremonies.

*****

Yesterday evening, was taken to see Mr. Blaine, the new Secretary of State. His selection is regarded as adding great power to the administration.

I went with General Sherman to Blaine's home on Fifteenth Street. He entered the dooryard just as we came, and greeted us on the steps. I was in great doubt as to how he would receive me, knowing the attacks on me in the press, and the "reprimand" from his own department.

"You have been giving our country some information on the emigration question," he said to me, as he hung his overcoat up in the hall.

This was followed by an ominous silence, and we all walked into the drawing-room, and were presented to Mrs. Blaine, who was just leaving. The Secretary walked to the open fireplace, turned his back to it, and, addressing me, said: "Mr. Byers, I want you to understand that I consider that in this pauper emigration matter you have done a good thing--and I am going to support you in it."

"You can give me the information I want," he continued, later in the conversation, and invited me to come and see him on the following Monday.

I think the conversation helped Mr. Blaine to make up his mind to send a certain strong letter abroad.

*****

May, 1881.--When at Washington, I was invited to prepare the Decoration Day poem. I wrote "The Nation's Dead." The President and many distinguished people were present at its recital.

As I could not be present to read my poem personally, some one suggested that the distinguished Robert Ingersoll should be invited to read it. General Sherman, in a letter to me, objected in strong language. Ingersoll was a friend of his, but he regarded it manifestly improper for an infidel to be delivering poems over the graves of American soldiers.

*****

Before sailing, I visited at the Allen home and school, West Newton. James T. Allen had been one of my best friends in Europe. The school was somewhat on the plan of the celebrated Beust school at Zurich; that is, fewer textbooks and better teachers.

I had a letter to the poet Longfellow, and Mr. Allen suggested that we go over to Cambridge on Sunday afternoon. My letter was from Mr. Longfellow's nephew.

The poet came into the little drawing-room with a full blown red rose in his buttonhole. He took me by the hand and welcomed me very kindly. I commenced to apologize for coming on Sunday. "Tut--tut," said he, "no apology; I hope we are not so puritanical as not to want to see our friends on a Sunday." And then we sat down and talked about his nephew who had been in Switzerland. His language was vivacious, his eye clear, his cheeks rosy, his hair perfectly white. I was surprised to see how small was his figure, for I had always thought of Longfellow as a tall man with a great Leonine head; his pictures make him so.

Vecchio Palace, Florence.

I could not wholly help a glance around the famous room. I am sure he saw it, for he offered to show me some of the things that he knew I had read about. They were not bought bric-a-brac, but souvenirs, or else things his poetry and life had immortalized. Somehow he seemed to me a man to love-- simple, pure and beautiful as his verses.

I also had letters to Mr. Bronson Alcott, the transcendentalist philosopher. He received me one morning in a very cordial manner. It was in his library. We talked of books and something of his life. I had just been out to the battlefield of Lexington, looked at the bronze monument of the "Minute Man" there, and was so struck with the verse on it as to commit it to memory. "And Mr. Emerson wrote it," I said, somewhat uncertain as to my memory. "Certainly, certainly," said Mr. Alcott. "Of course, that is Mr. Emerson's. We Americans don't half know what a poet we have in Mr. Emerson." He went to the book shelves and brought a volume of Emerson's poems, presented to him, with this particular poem marked in it, and showed it with evident pride.

By the rude bridge that arched the flood,
Their flag to April's breeze unfurled,
Here once the embattled farmers stood,
And fired the shot heard round the world.

Shortly, he proposed to take a walk. He would show me the town, the old elms, the old, old graveyard and the famous Lecture Hall, "and then," said he, "we will swing around and call on Mr. Emerson."

He showed me all about, talking, as only Mr. Alcott could talk. When we reached the unpretentious frame building called the

Lecture Hall, in the edge of the bushes, I reflected what great things had been said there, what ideas given wing, and now I felt sure I was about to be overwhelmed with deep philosophy. Nothing of the kind. He spent a full half hour telling me about the cost of the wooden structure and its course of building, from the underpinning to the top of the chimney. I was anxious to move on and be sure to have our call on Mr. Emerson. We really started once, but immediately Mr. Alcott recalled something about the wonderful "Hall" he had not shown me, and we went back.

At last we started in earnest, and reached the white frame house that neighbors and friends of Mr. Emerson had built in place of the one destroyed by fire.

"Mr. Emerson is at home, I suppose," said Mr. Alcott to the girl who answered the door bell. "Yes," said she, "that is, he has just this moment left for Boston." I was a bit disappointed, and I think Mr. Alcott was, but he made up for it in fine and kindly talk, and we went back to the library. There was an invitation to stay to lunch, but the hour for my train back to Newton interfered. He gave me a fine photograph of himself. Mr. Alcott was a great and powerful looking man. He had an immense head and face, shaggy eyebrows, and clear deep eyes. He was tall and large in body. His voice was gentle and his manners were delightful and simple.

"Now, is there nothing I can do for you?" he said, as I was about to take my leave. "Thank you, Mr. Alcott," I answered, "and yet it would be a pleasure if I could have the honor of meeting your daughter."

"Bless me," he cried, jumping up; "don't you know Louise? Louise!" he called out at the top of his voice, "Louise, come in here." There was no answer. "Come on," he said; "we'll hunt her up," and away we started through the rooms of the house on a chase for the famous woman.

We found her in morning gown, with carpet sweeper in hand, dusting one of the chambers. She was as kindly and simple as her father. She could not hear well, but she was very vivacious and full of fun. She asked me to go with her all about the house, looking at this souvenir and that, as if she herself were not at that moment the greatest sight of all. She dwelt especially on some pictures on the wall that a sister had painted in Paris. My stay abroad must have fitted me to know about paintings, she insisted. These were indeed interesting and good.

As we were talking, two young fellows ran over the stile and out into the street. Mr. Alcott gleefully nudged me on the arm, and said, "Look, the 'little men.'" We all looked. Miss Alcott smiled and said, "Yes, they are the boys."

The train was just starting as I reached it at the station, and there I had a glimpse of a tall, intellectual-looking man crossing the platform, apparently looking for some other train. He carried a little hand bag. I heard a passenger next me say, "There is Mr. Emerson."

*****

Mr. Allen took me to Newton Center, to see the famous Dr. Smith, author of the song "America." It was dark when we called. His daughter went to fetch matches, and was no little surprised on coming back to find the gas burning brightly. Mr. A. had lighted a match on his shoe and found the gas lamp. Shortly, Dr. Smith came in. Though old and partially deaf, his face was kind and his eyes bright. He liked to talk with us about his past, and told us much concerning the origin of his famous song. I thought his home old and dingy for so famous a man. The people of America could well afford to give him a palace. His song has done more to preserve the American Union than any army ever did. He was interested about music in Switzerland, and asked me to tell him what effect the mountains have on the Swiss character. I told him to judge by their songs. No country in the world has so many music festivals, so many singing clubs. "And the songs they sing?" inquired the doctor. "They are mostly about their country, their mountains, their lakes, their rivers," I answered. At a great musical contest last year, attended by ten thousand people, forty-six songs were sung in chorus. Nineteen of these were about the Alps, or hymns to nature. Seven were about Switzerland, two or three about the Rhine, and ten were love songs.

It was a Sunday evening and we feared to prolong our visit.

*****

After I had reached my post at Zurich, a New Yorker wrote me to send him a book printed in the Swiss language. I had seen but few. There is a Swiss language, all the uneducated speak it; so do many of the cultivated, when among themselves, but not among strangers. It is also spoken much in the family circle. It has many dialects, and some of them are older than the German language itself. An occasional newspaper is printed in these dialects, but books rarely.

CHAPTER XXIII
1881

ELM AND ALL ITS PEOPLE DESTROYED BY AN AVALANCHE--A FOOT TRIP IN IRELAND--FENIANS --REDCOATS--POVERTY--THE QUEEN HOOTED--OUT OF JAIL AND A HERO--MUCKROSS ABBEY BY MOONLIGHT--AN IRISH FUNERAL--A DUPLICATE BLARNEY STONE-LETTERS FROM GENERAL SHERMAN--THE DUKE OF WELLINGTON--THE ASSASSINATION OF PRESIDENT GARFIELD.

September, 1881.--It is a year now since pretty Elm and all its people were buried in an avalanche.

Only a few days before, we had climbed over one of the obscure bridle paths from the Rhine valley to Elm. The path led over a glacier and was 9,000 feet high. All that summer night in Elm we heard the avalanches fall in the neighborhood, for we were in the higher Alps; lofty and awful pyramids of eternal rock and snow were all about us.

Right behind the little inn, where we staid that night, frowned a threatening, almost perpendicular mountain, 12,000 feet high. What if that dark pile should tumble over on the village, we thought, as we looked out into the moonlight. How little we dreamed what was about to happen. We were hardly back in our home in Zurich, when a telegram announced that the mountain had fallen, that Elm and all the people had been destroyed.

Shortly, Consul Mason, of Basel, and myself hurried by rail to Schwanden, and in a little wagonette went up the comparatively easy valley road to what was once Elm. The sight was terrific. A part of the mountain overhanging the village slipped off on Sunday, just as the people had returned from afternoon church services. The mighty debris of rock and earth overwhelmed and buried the pretty village. It filled the valley for half a mile. Mason and I climbed over granite boulders and broken rocks as big as a house. Nothing of the town was to be seen, the houses had been torn to pieces and buried fifty feet below. Nearly everybody had been killed. There were no funerals, for till this day the peasants of Elm sleep under the mountain that overwhelmed them. The few who had escaped, by being on hillsides or out looking at their herds on the higher fields, wandered about as if dazed. They shed no tears. To them, the end of the world had come. Some of them told me, without a tremor in their voices, how they stood on some high place and saw their wives, their fathers or their children first thrown into the air by the awful concussion and then buried with their houses. The keeper of the little inn where we stopped that night had been spared, and told us how he saw the big iron bridge across the river Sernf tossed a hundred feet into the air, twisted like a straw, and thrown against a hillside.

The river bed had been dammed up by the falling rock, and the waters now wandered aimlessly over the ocean of debris above the people's homes. It is all silent now, up there in the Alps where Elm stood, silent save where the winds from the mountain peaks on moonlight nights moan a requiem to the sleeping dead.

September 20.--President Garfield died yesterday at 5 A. M. (Swiss time), and all the world went into mourning. I draped the flag here, and put it out at the consulate. Many people called to express their sorrow. A more unprovoked murder of a ruler never occurred. The President's agony since July 2d has been terrible, and his courage to bear it has been tremendous.

Early this month, I made a little foot tour in Ireland. Everybody said, "Don't go!" Even in Dublin, a friend warned me, saying: "It is a terrible time in Ireland. Landlords are being murdered and farmers locked up in prison. You are a stranger here. The English soldiers, on the watch everywhere, will take you for an American Fenian. The Irish will take you for an English spy."

It was all a mistake, as to myself at least. I went everywhere unmolested. True, the tourists were frightened out of the country. British redcoats were being sent up and down the island looking for "boycotters" and assassins. The people everywhere were sullen, and ominous silence reigned in many places. The country seemed to be sitting on a volcano. I often walked miles on country roads without meeting a soul, and nobody at all dared to be abroad at night. At little country inns where I stopped, people did not talk about the situation. I suppose they dared not.

By accident I picked up a newspaper one day and read a warning signed by New York Fenians against any one's traveling to Europe on an English steamer. "They would blow them all up." To my horror another item told how an "infernal machine" was believed to have been put on board the "Adriatic," that had sailed on the 8th. This might go off in mid-ocean and destroy the ship. My wife and two children were on board that vessel, and the ship had sailed. There was nothing to do but wait, and fear. Besides, it did not seem possible to me that the friends of Ireland could resort to such crimes. In Ireland itself, however, there was little respect for law, and for England none at all.

Once I was on a railroad train near Mallow. I was in the third class, because there I could see the common people. A Fenian, out of jail that very morning, sat next to me. He would not talk about the government, but constantly asked me to "look out at the green fields"--they were so beautiful to him after months of imprisonment.

Many redcoat soldiers, in charge of prisoners wearing handcuffs, were on the train. The prisoners yelled: "Down with England! Hurrah for free Ireland!" and sang the "Wearing of the Green." The soldiers could not help themselves and simply laughed.

The train stopped at a little country village and I saw a great mass of people running towards us. The soldiers said they were coming to stone the train. I wished now that I had listened to the "warnings." Instead of stoning us, however, the mob rushed into the car where I was, seized the man by my side and bore him out on their shoulders. The men hugged him, the women kissed him, and everybody cried for "free Ireland." It was his welcome home from prison. The redcoats said nothing and did nothing. As the train moved on, I could see the mob still carrying the man up the street, while the village band marched at their head.

I wanted to go to Limerick for the races next day, but I saw a train with three hundred armed and uniformed policemen going to the same place, so I stayed away, and took to the quiet and safer country roads.

I passed lovely scenes in the neighborhood of Killarney. The lakes equal the Swiss lakes in beauty; there are bright waterfalls there, groves, grand estates, ruined castles, and wretched poverty.

Saw Muckross Abbey by moonlight--nothing more romantic conceivable. The grand old trees, the broken arches, the ivy-covered walls, the graveyard with its bones of long-dead Irish kings, all silent and lone under the soft light of a summer moon, impressed me.

A young Irishman and his newly wedded wife, stopping at the inn, had joined me in the wish to see Muckross by moonlight. We walked down the road to the entrance of the ground. The care taker at the gate was upstairs in the lodge in bed. When we called to him to unlock the gate, he poked his head out of a window and ordered us away instantly. We offered him good pay to come down and let us into the grounds. "Not for a dozen pounds would I come down there," he yelled back at us. "How do I know what you are or who you be, tramping around the roads this time of night. You might be going to blow the top of the head off of me. I tell you go along wid you." We went along further down the road, climbed over into the enclosure, and without blowing off tops of heads of anybody, had a good time. We knew the man would not venture from his lodge. His fear showed the kind of times Ireland was living in.

The next day I saw an Irish funeral at Muckross Abbey. The coffin was borne on men's shoulders, at first. When they passed out of Killarney village, they put it on top of an immense hearse, the shape of an omnibus, and behind it capered along a company of old women and girls, groaning, bawling and shrieking by turns. Occasionally, on seeing a friend at the roadside, these hired mourners rested themselves a moment and greeted the friend with a grin. It seemed a hideous performance. The grave was not dug when the procession reached the abbey, and there was nothing to do but wait till some one came with shovel and spade. In the meantime I slipped away.

I had many long walks through the country as I footed it off towards Cork. Most of the peasants seemed sticking close to their wretched little hovels, called houses. Excepting an occasional magnificent estate that I saw walled in at the country roadside, all seemed wretchedness. In a hundred miles I did not see a farmhouse that an American would regard as anything more than a barn or pig sty. These huts are of stone, one or one and a half stories high, covered with straw, and no floor but the ground.

Wherever I talked, pitiable tales were told of bad living, high rents, extortionate landlords. In the midst of all the wretchedness and the present danger (and danger there is, for arrests and murders and crimes are going on all the time), the peasants seem rather jovial and cheery, though not contented. It is amazing where they get the money to pay the landlords. One man told me he paid thirty dollars a year for a dirty little hut without a foot of ground or garden. It was all the house would sell for. "Yes," said the man, "and I would be tumbled into the road in six minutes if my rent were not paid; that's what all them constables are hanging around for." I went into many of the little dark farmhouses. All I saw was wretchedness --a pig or two, a few chickens--maybe a cow staked outside-- some dirty children--a woman, cheery in spite of it all.

At one little hut a peasant woman asked me to stay and see what her dinner was. Shortly she gave a call and the "brats" came running in. She took a pot from the fire and gave to each a few potatoes, some salt and a piece of bread, nothing more. The boys took their dinners in their caps.

I was affected to tears, when the good woman put some potatoes on a plate and offered to divide with me, as I stood looking on in the doorway. "Oh, sir," she said, and even cheerfully, "there are many worse off than we. We cannot complain." The husband was off at the coast at work. On Sundays, he brought home a part of his wages to pay the rent and part of the wages he spent for drink. He brought a little coarse fish with him, too.

In some houses no meals were had. The potato pot hung by the fire, and each helped himself out of it, whenever he felt hungry.

And that was peasant life in Ireland.

Potatoes and bread, with a bit of meat or fish on Sundays, seem to be the regular rations of the family. What would have happened had Sir Walter Raleigh never introduced the potato there? And what did the people live on before they had potatoes?

The Irish are full of hope, and all the people look to the new "Land Bill" to save them. But it won't do it!

One day I overtook two Americans who, like myself, were wandering about Ireland on foot. We went together to Blarney Castle. We did not see the herd of white cows that rise up out of Blarney Lake at night, but we climbed to the top of the castle tower (120 feet), where the youngest of the party caught hold of an iron bar at a window and let himself down outside the tower until he could reach the Blarney stone. Few ever venture so foolhardy a feat, or have the muscle to hang on by one hand at so perilous a height. The rest of us thought him a dead man. No wonder the ancient Irish firmly believed that if one could kiss this stone it would give him eloquence, because they knew it *could not* be kissed, not by one mortal in a million.

The old poet was safe in saying:

"There is a stone there
That whoever kisses,
Oh, he never misses
To grow eloquent."

There is a kind of duplicate "Blarney stone" placed at a convenient and easy spot on the castle for kissing, and the old woman in charge smiles as she pockets the tourist's shilling, turns the key in the door and says to herself: "Lord, what fools these mortals be!"

At Queenstown I met my wife and two little ones returning from America, the little girl suffering with a pain that shortly took her sweet life away from us.

*****

At the request of the Harper's Magazine editor for something of the kind, I have written an article called "My Farm in Switzerland." My wife has illustrated it, as well as the one on "The Swiss Rhine."

The farmers here seem to be doing as well on ten acres as our people do on quarter sections. There is the same complaint about mortgages and all that, of course; but with it all, at the end of the year, the Swiss peasant, like the American farmer, has made a living.

The investigation necessary for this paper showed me two things. First, the Swiss are better farmers than the Americans. Second, they are ten times as economical, else they would starve to death. Economy is a fine art here. There is no other way to explain how it is a Swiss lives, even poorly, on ten acres, while the Yankee requires one hundred and sixty. Grass land here costs $200 an acre, grape land $1,000. Big farms are impossible at such prices.

Suppose the Swiss has five acres of grape and garden land and ten of pasture and meadow. His investment is $7,000. He lives from it with less hard work than the American has, who owns one hundred and sixty acres, worth $60 an acre or $9,600. The American's investment is much more than that of the Swiss, his labor must be double, his income the same--a *living*. What is the matter? It is this. The one *saves*; the other *wastes*. Expensive farm machinery does not lie around the fields rusting to pieces in Switzerland. Horses and cattle are not thinned down and killed off by exposure to bad weather. Care for what you have earned, is the Swiss peasant's motto. Waste everything you get, is the practice of the American. After a while, careful foreigners will own all the farms in America, and the American farmer will be loafing around village stores, starving. Swiss economy applied to American land culture, would enrich every farmer in America. Economy is the thing that keeps the Swiss farmer from the poor-house.

*****

I give two letters from General Sherman; the first, with something about the Duke of Wellington, and the science of war; the second, about President Garfield's assassination. The little girl, referred to in the first letter, was our little Helen, now drifting away from us, although we did not think it.

"WASHINGTON, D. C., October 4, 1881.

"DEAR BYERS:--I have your good letter of September 21, with the slip from the London *Times*, which I have read with profit. The English cannot discuss any proposition without bringing in the Duke of Wellington. No man, if living, would be quicker to avail himself of improved transportation and communication than the Duke, but it would astonish the old gentleman to wake up and read in the *Times* of all events in America and Asia the same day of their occurrence.

"The science of war, like that of natural philosophy, chemistry, must recognize new truths and new inventions as they arise, and that is all there is of change in the science of war since 1815. Man remains pretty much the same, and will dodge all the risks of war and danger if by electricity and nitroglycerine he can blow up his enemy ten miles off. Nevertheless, manhood and courage will in future wars be of as much use as in the past, and those who comprehend the object and come to close quarters will win now as before.

"I am very sorry to hear that your little girl is in such precarious health, and hope with you that the complete change in surroundings may bring her back to her wonted health. All my flock is about as well as usual, but now scattered. I expect Rachel home from Europe by the Celtic, which leaves Queenstown October 21. My aide McCook lost his wife at Salt Lake City and Bacon lost both his children, boys, this summer.

"We all feel the effect of Garfield's death yet, but next week the called session of the Senate will meet, and then the political pot will begin to boil and bubble. The telegraph keeps you so well advised that it seems useless to attempt anything by letter.

"Give my best love to your wife and family and believe me as always,

"Your friend,
W. T. SHERMAN."

*****

"WASHINGTON, D. C., Dec. 14, 1881.

"DEAR BYERS:--I have owed you a letter for a long while, and though we have had enough in all conscience here to furnish fit topics for letters, I have known that the telegraph would be a long way ahead. In Europe you know as much of the tragedy of Garfield's shooting and death as our own people in the interior, and many returned travelers describe the intense interest of all classes in Garfield's fate, as long as he clung to life. The patient submission of our people, and their continued endurance of the brutal Guiteau till he shall have had a fair trial, is most honorable to us as a law-abiding people, but even I am sometimes impatient at the law's dallying, as this trial draws its slow length along. I think the court means to make the trial so full, and so perfect, that all the world will be convinced of the justice of the sentence of death. So intense is public feeling that if the fellow was turned loose, he would be stoned to death by the boys.

"The transition of power from Garfield to Arthur has been so regular, so unattended by shock, that it proves the stability of the Government. I have never known a time when there was so little political excitement, or when the machinery of government worked more smoothly than now. There is the same outward pressure for place, but President Arthur fends it off with the skill of an old experienced hand. So I infer there will be as few changes as possible. Blaine goes out to-day and Frelinghuysen in, but it makes no more noise than a change of bank presidents. In the army the same general composure prevails, and we believe Congress will give us our 30,000 men, which will increase the strength of companies and thereby increase the efficiency of the establishment.

"All my family continues *statu quo*, reasonably well, in our house on Fifteenth Street. Our season also seems mild for December, for this far we have had no signs of winter.

"With my best love to all your folks, I am as ever,

"Your friend,
W. T. SHERMAN."

On Sunday, as often happens after church here, the people were at the polls, voting as to the adoption or rejection of a batch of laws that had been adopted by the parliament. This is the "Referendum" in action. Absolute order and decency prevailed, and there were no intriguing ward politicians hanging around the polls, to buttonhole voters. Voting is a responsible, dignified act with the Swiss. A majority of the people seem to think the "Referendum" operates well enough with a people so intelligent and patriotic as themselves, and in so small a country. Yet, thousands here ridicule the idea of submitting great questions of state to be voted on by the intelligent and ignorant alike. In great cities, the world over, the ignorant and vicious are in the majority, and the laws would all be bad if such citizens had the decision of them. My own observation is that even the Swiss misuse this Referendum and adopt just as many bad laws as they do good ones.

CHAPTER XXIV
1882–1883

VISIT NORTHERN ITALY--AMERICAN INDIANS IN ZURICH--DEATH OF THE POET KINKEL--LETTERS FROM CARL SCHURZ AND THE POET'S WIFE--LETTER FROM SHERMAN AS TO THE BOUNTEOUS MISSISSIPPI VALLEY--A SECOND LETTER FROM SHERMAN--THE PRESIDENCY--CONVERSATIONS WITH SCHERR, THE WRITER--THE POET KINKEL'S SON--HIS POWERFUL MEMORY--WE VISIT BERLIN--MINISTER SARGENT'S TROUBLE WITH PRINCE BISMARCK OVER AMERICAN PORK--SARGENT IS APPOINTED TO ST. PETERSBURG--INDIANS AGAIN--BABY LIONS--VISIT AMERICA AGAIN--FUNERAL OF THE AUTHOR OF "HOME, SWEET HOME"--SWISS NATIONAL EXHIBITION--THE SWISS WAR MINISTER VISITS ME--WE HAD BEEN COMRADES IN LIBBY PRISON--TROUBLE WITH FRAUDULENT INVOICES--ORIGIN OF EXPERT SYSTEM AT CONSULATE--I SUCCEED IN STOPPING THE FRAUDS--MY ACTION IS REPORTED AT WASHINGTON AS SAVING A MILLION DOLLARS TO THE GOVERNMENT--ANOTHER LETTER FROM GENERAL SHERMAN--HIS COMING RETIREMENT FROM THE ARMY.

January, 1882.--The lake and the mountains and the white city do not seem so beautiful to us to-day, for the little girl who loved them most of all, lies in the next room covered with flowers.

Juliet's Tomb, Verona.

*****

All was changed to us this past summer. In October we made a fourth trip to Italy; this time to the lake regions at the foot of the Alps. There is something about life in Northern Italy that seems to make a stay there almost more desirable than in other places in the world. The scenery is still Alpine, but it is the Alps with perpetual sunshine on them, and warm laughing lakes about them. I think the peasants more picturesque here than elsewhere. They carry red umbrellas, and the peasant women wear short skirts, showing bright stockings of red or white or blue. The low, white wooden sandals, with the red leather band over the instep, worn by the women, are very pretty, too. Only one wonders how they keep them on their feet. With every step the sandals go click, clack, up and down, at the heels. The headgear of the girls is a bit of black lace thrown over the head and hanging down behind. The whole outfit, with the pretty black eyes of the girls, the bright faces, and the merry demeanor, make one think that here, in the sunshine of North Italy, is a happy peasantry. The men also wear bright colors; the poorest has at least a cravat of blue and a red band on his roguish soft felt hat.

The soft Italian language, and the singers with their guitars in the moonlight by the lakes, add to the real romance of the scene.

The people of the lake regions are rather poor, spite of the rich productiveness of the soil. There are too many of them, and too many rocky heights, and mountains and lakes. The little stone-built villages cling to some of these heights like crow nests on tree tops, but somewhere, near to every height, on some spot of land beautiful as Eden, we see the gardens and villas of the rich. These are the summer homes of the aristocrats of Milan and cities farther south.

Villa Carlotta on Lake Como, sitting among the lemon trees, its gardens washed by the blue waters, its halls and salons filled with the works of genius, could tempt one to want to live there always.

And Villa Giulia, on that fair promontory running out into Lake Lecco at Bellagio, seen of a summer evening with the deep blue waters on either side, the snow white Alps in front of it, and groves of citron and boxwood and lemon behind it, wakes the feeling in one that here indeed is the fairest scene of all; here one could be happy.

*****

The other morning the staid old city of Zurich was suddenly awakened by the whoop of a band of American Indians. Had a cloud fallen, some of the people could not have been more stirred up. The wild men were the genuine article, in war paint and feathers. Not one Swiss in a thousand had ever seen a real Indian before. It was part of a band of Chippewas, being carried around Europe for exhibition. The show was a great success. Everybody went to see it, and even followed the strangers about the streets in crowds. The Indians had their difficulties, however. An occasional one with too much "fire water" lay prone on the sidewalk or rested in the lockup. They also had quarrels with their manager, and daily for a time this painted band of my fellow countrymen came to the consulate and held pow wows on the floor of the office. They were a helpless lot of human beings there alone, knowing nothing of the language, with a manager supposed to be robbing them. I got them out of the lockup, and out of their other many difficulties as best I could, and won their esteem and gratitude.

November 16, 1882.--Three days ago the great Gottfried Kinkel was carried to the graveyard out by the foot of the mountains. He had been a warm friend since the day we came to Zurich.

He was passionately fond of the Swiss mountains, and we have had delightful little excursions together. His death was sudden. One day he was stricken with apoplexy and could not speak. He motioned his wife to help him to the window, where he could once more look out at the beautiful mountains. He looked long and wistfully at them and then waving them a farewell with his hand went to his bed and died. Poetry and art and all things beautiful wept when Kinkel died. His funeral was the greatest ever seen in Zurich. He was buried by torchlight by the students of the University. When the grave was closed and the great procession of uniformed corps students with badges, flags and torches came back into the city, they marched to a public square, formed an immense circle and, casting their torches into a great funeral pile in the center, watched them burn to ashes.

December 14.--Our American statesman, Carl Schurz, had been a friend of the poet, patriot Kinkel in the revolutionary times, and had also rescued him from prison and death.

I wrote him a description of the funeral and received his reply to-day.

"Dec. 4, 1882.

"MY DEAR SIR:--I have just received your very kind letter of November 21st in which you describe Kinkel's funeral, and I thank you most sincerely for it. His sudden death had been reported by cable, but your letter gave me the first information about the last days of his life, the circumstances of his death and the touching demonstration of popular feeling at his funeral. The letter will appear as a special correspondence in the Evening *Post* to-morrow.

"I enclose a letter of condolence to Mrs. Kinkel, which I shall be greatly obliged to you for delivering or forwarding. I venture to ask this favor of you as I do not know whether, after Kinkel's death, Mrs. Kinkel remained at Zurich or not. I have no doubt you know where she is, and where the letter will reach her.

"Believe me, dear sir,

"Very truly yours,
C. SCHURZ."

The sweet singer had now gone to be absorbed into the beautiful nature of which he had talked to me when his daughter died. They were to be one with the flowers and the sunshine, but without identity.

Mrs. Kinkel, a woman bright and talented, had ideas not greatly different from her husband about this mystery called death. Once, later, I sent her my poem of "Baby Helene," and this was her answer:

"UNTERSTRASSE, DEN 25, 1858.

"GEEHRTER HERR CUNSUL:--Meine Freude beim Empfang Ihres Buches war wirklich aufrichtig, und ich hatte Ihnen so gleich meinen Dank dafür gesagt, wenn ich nicht von einem und dem andern Gedicht so angezogen worden wäre, dass ich über das Lesen das Schreiben zurücksetze. Die Gedichte an das liebe Helenchen haben mich tief gerührt. Nur wer einen gleichen Verlust hatte, fühlt so ganz den wehen Schmerz, der sich darin ausspricht mit Ihnen.

"Wie beneide ich Sie um die Hoffnung sie dereinst wiederzusehen. Mein Trost allein ist, einstmals ewig vergessen zu können.

"'Auf Wiedersehen' hebe ich nur noch hervor von den vielen, die mir besonders noch gefielen. Erst durch Sie bin ich darauf aufmerksam gemacht dass das in englischer Sprache fehlt. Wie viel Gutes verdanke ich nicht schon den Dichtern.

"Hoffentlich ist Ihnen die Ausfahrt mit Lawrence am Sonnabend gut bekommen. Ich erkannte Sie leider erst im letzen Augenblick, als das Schiff schon in Bewegung war.

"Grüssen Sie Mrs. Byers und Lawrence sehr von mir, und seien Sie ueberzeugt, dass Sie mir mit dem Buch eine grosse Freude gemacht haben.

"Mit vorzüglichster Hochachtung

"ergebenst
M. KINKEL."

*****

November, 1882.--Have an interesting letter from General Sherman on politics and farming.

"WASHINGTON, D. C., Nov. 7, 1882.

"DEAR BYERS:--Time and distance seemingly do dull the edge of correspondence, if not of friendship. Your letter of October 22d is received, has been seen by Mrs. Sherman, and shows that too long an interval has passed since we have written you, but you may rest assured that our friendly interest in you and yours is in no way lessened, and that news from you is always most welcome to me and mine. We still remain in Washington, except Minnie at St. Louis, Elly at Philadelphia and Tom at Woodstock, but all reasonably well. Last Summer Minnie lost two of her children, both girls, one two years and eight months old, the other an infant in arms. Both came East for health and change, though all were as healthy as kittens. Mrs. Sherman had taken a furnished house at Oakland on the very top of the Alleghanies, where all the family was assembled, but the cold nights and warm days were too much for the little ones, caused congestion of the stomach, followed quickly by dysentery and death. I have recently been to St. Louis and found Minnie well, and her three remaining children, two boys and one girl, in strong vigorous health.

"I am now beginning to think of my own course of action when the law compulsorily retires me at 64 years, viz.: Feb. 8, 1884. We have all agreed to return to our old home at St. Louis, and as February is a bad month for moving, I will in all probability anticipate the time by a couple of months--move the family in October and follow myself in November or December. So the probability is, if you give up the Consulate and turn your attention to your Iowa farm, I will be your neighbor and rival, for I too own a farm in Illinois nineteen miles out from St. Louis.

"The present has been probably the most fruitful year ever experienced in America, all parts alike sharing the general abundance. Of all this you are probably as well informed as I am, but when I remember that the gold crop of California at its best only equaled sixty-five millions a year, I am amazed to think of a wheat crop valued at five hundred millions, and a corn crop of eighteen hundred millions of bushels at 65 cents a bushel; other crops in like proportion, and cotton estimated at six millions of bales of 450 pounds each at 12 cents a pound. I am especially glad of this, for some years, as you well know, land was held at a discount, all persons having money preferring to buy stocks or bonds which promised an income.

Now the farming class is so comfortable, with bounteous crops, and good homes, that the country will draw from the crowded cities and towns the redundant population. The farming class never give the trouble which the manufacturing and mercantile are always threatening.

"To-day is the great election day of the country, more excited than usual by reasons of feuds and dissenters among the Republicans, which will enable the Democrats to elect their candidates. Apprehension is felt that the next Congress will be Democratic, but long heads say that success now, means defeat next time, when another President is to be elected. Washington goes right along improving and embellishing all the time, and I really believe we now have the cleanest, if not the handsomest city in the world, not excepting Paris. Of course we have no Alps or lakes like yours at Zurich, but the Potomac when walled in and its marshy banks converted into clean grass plots and parks will approximate in beauty even the Rhine. But the old Mississippi and Missouri, dirty and foul, will ever be the land of bounteous plenty, and will in time hold the population and political control of this continent. We will have plenty to eat and can afford to travel to see beautiful mountains and lakes.

"Accept this in its length, not substance, as a measure of my love and respect, and believe me always,

"Truly yours,
W. T. SHERMAN."

One of our interesting visitors and friends these evenings is young Dr. Kinkel, son of the great poet. He is renowned in the city for his marvelous learning and memory. All that he has ever read, and he is a high classical scholar, he seems to know by heart. He is writing a history of the Byzantine Empire, and his studies for this are enormous.

I tested his memory a little last night by questions on the Life of Washington. He answered as if the book had been open before him. Every detail and date that he has accidentally learned as to the lives of his friends, he can instantly recall. What was said of Macaulay could be said of him, "He is a book in breeches."

December 23.--To-day I have a letter from General Sherman. He speaks of the Presidency. Mrs. Sherman, I know, is just as much opposed to his entering politics as is he himself.

"WASHINGTON, D. C., Dec. 12, 1882.

"DEAR BYERS:--I have just received your letter enclosing your lines to your daughter Helen, composed to the same measure as 'Sherman's March to the Sea,' and have sent both to Mrs. Sherman for perusal.

"Congress is now in session, and the effect of the last election is manifest. Though the Democrats have gained a large majority for the next Congress, they recognize that their victory is a dangerous one, for it seems to be more a rebuke to the Republicans for the very sins of political government, which the Democrats long since inaugurated and will carry into practice the moment they gain power, than a victory to the Democrats. No single man can handle the affairs of this country without the agency of a strong well organized party, and all political parties are about the same.

"As to my ever consenting to the use of my name as a Presidential candidate, that is entirely out of the question. I recall too well the personal experience of Generals Jackson, Harrison, Taylor, Grant, Hayes and Garfield to be tempted by the siren voice of flattery. It is too like the case of the girl who marries a drunken lover in the hopes to reform him. It never has succeeded and never will; the same of any individual trying to reform the government, he will be carried along and involved in its scandals and unavoidable sins. No, I am going back next fall to St. Louis to spend the remainder of my days in comparative peace and comfort.

"Wishing you and yours all the happiness possible in your sphere of action,

"I am as always your friend,
W. T. SHERMAN."

*****

Was with Professor Scherr and others last night at the Orsini again. Scherr is not only a literary man, he is an educated German thinker. I was interested in some things he said about human existence. "Nine men," said he, "were born to serve a tenth. It never was otherwise; it never would be otherwise; it never could be otherwise." "Education of the masses is all a mistake," he continued. "Education only makes them discontented, and humanity is not bettered." I wondered to myself if this were true. In America, I reflected, the masses are educated. They are, too, the most discontented people on earth. Nobody ever saw an American quite satisfied with his condition. I observed to Prof. Scherr that in certain Italian districts where the people were wholly illiterate and poor, I had noticed many signs of happiness. "Exactly," replied the Professor. "They don't hear constantly of what somebody else has got, and so believe they have got it all. This belief satisfies them, they want nothing more; their ignorance is their greatest blessing."

"The Swiss, though," I said, "are all educated and are happy." "Not a bit of it," he answered, "they are growing more discontented every day. They were happy till they got free schools and education, and till they saw your rich American and English tourists living in luxury and scattering gold like French compliments. No, education without talent, is a curse. The first social revolution in Europe will be here within a gun shot of where we are sitting, here in so-called educated Switzerland."

January, 1883.--Spent the holidays at Berlin visiting in the home of Mr. Sargent, our American Minister.

Mr. Sargent had for weeks been in a stew with the German Government on account of their prohibiting our American meats. The same kind of trouble was had in Switzerland; but when it happened that I was able to prove that the American hams in which trichina were *officially found*, were *Antwerp* hams "fixed up" and stamped "American," the ban on American meats to Switzerland was raised.

Germany, however, for her own reasons, intended fight, and press and Government opposed Mr. Sargent and the American exporters' rights. In the train on our way to Berlin, a German newspaper happened to fall into my hands that told, not intending it, the whole story of Bismarck's opposition to Mr. Sargent and the American pig. On his great estates he had pigs himself to sell, so said the newspaper. I translated this article and put it in Mr. Sargent's hands at once.

In a secret official dispatch to Washington, he quoted this German newspaper as to Bismarck's pigs, and put it in quotation marks. By some means the dispatch was given to the public by the Department, and the quotation marks of Mr. Sargent left out. The newspapers printed it as an official declaration by the American Minister at Berlin. Bismarck and his followers naturally were soon furious, and a course of action was adopted that should be as offensive as possible to Americans.

We reached the capital one morning before daylight. Mr. Sargent met us, sent us to his house in his carriage, and hurried off to report our names to the Chief of Police. We had a great laugh over it all at the breakfast table, when he came back. There is a fine of many marks for taking people to one's house in the German capital, without letting the police know who they are. It is by such means that Germany keeps track of everybody.

Kaiser Wilhelm.

Our Minister's home was close to the Thiergarten, and there we saw the old Emperor William, the Crown Prince Frederick and others of the royal family, walking or driving daily. They were simple enough and were not run after in their walks. I was told that every time the Emperor leaves the palace for a drive, the fact is telephoned to every police station in the city, and that extra officials and detectives in civilian dress are abroad everywhere in parks and public places. It seemed to me that on all occasions in Berlin half the people we met were soldiers or policemen.

The history of the German capital is of more interest than the city itself. One wonders that the Germans had courage to build a city on this great ugly sand plain, nor can one think of comparing Berlin for beauty with Paris or Florence, Vienna, Dresden or Washington. But Berlin is a great city and its collections and museums are among the greatest in the world.

At one of these museums we saw the golden necklaces, and rich headgear of Helen of Troy. Dr. Schliemann, the explorer, had presented them to the German Government. They are of immense interest and enormous value. Every night the case containing them is let down into a great vault under the museum. The elaborate gold work of Helen's arm bands is as fresh and bright as if made yesterday.

At Potsdam nothing interested us so much as "Sans Souci," and especially the chair that Frederick the Great was sitting in when he died. We also stood by Frederick's coffin under the pulpit of the old Garrison Church.

Our conductor let me have a candle that burned above the coffin. I thought of the time when Napoleon stood in this little dark chamber by the body of one as great in Germany as he himself was in France. But both the great men did their countries more harm than good.

Mr. Sargent gave one or two large dinners while we were at his house. There was little talk of interest, but plenty of good music, and plenty of good wine, which in a German company, might have stimulated to notable sayings. Perhaps there were too many American teetotalers present for a good time. I notice a few turn their glasses upside down, in a sort of "I am better than you" fashion. Had they quietly allowed their glasses to be filled, nobody would have asked why they did not empty them. I have noticed always at German and Swiss dinners how the talk sparkled with the wine, and how the witty things said were in some way a test of the quality of the stuff in the decanter.

We went with the Sargents to the circus and saw the Crown Prince Frederick and his boys and girls in a box. The Prince had a singular and delicate way of applauding softly, with the palm of one gloved hand on the back of the other. His children were all glee at the antics of the performers, and expressed their joy in a much more boisterous way.

An enormous closed cage of wild lions was hauled into the arena, and when the boards were let down and they saw the blinding lights and the crowds of people their roaring was terrific.

A big African armed with a shotgun was let into the cage from an iron hood suspended against the doors. There was the greatest excitement. Many people instantly rose and left, fearing to see the man killed before their eyes. We kept our seats. There was no performing with the lions; it was simply a dare-devil venture to go among them, for they were absolutely untamed. The African had serious difficulty in getting back into his hood. It was his last act but one; the next night he was torn in pieces.

In one of the public halls of Berlin, we recognized to our surprise a party of American Indians performing war dances. They were the same Indians who had been at Zurich and whom I had helped out of serious difficulties, as their manager, it was claimed, had broken his contract and left the poor barbarians stranded. They said then they would never forget me. On seeing my wife and myself in the Berlin hall, they suddenly stopped their dancing and to the astonishment of the assembled spectators leaped from the platform, grasped me by the hand and called to each other: "It is Mr. Byers! It is Mr. Byers!" They were overjoyed at seeing some one in all Europe who had been kind to them.

A little later, in March, these Indians took passage home on the steamer from Bremen. The vessel was wrecked, still in sight of land, and every soul of them drowned. I, too, had engaged passage on the steamer, but business detained me in Zurich till the next boat.

On Sunday morning we went to the Zoölogical Gardens, where one of the keepers pleased my wife by raking a baby tiger and a baby lion out of their cages and giving them to her to hold in her arms. The lion was a chubby, woolly little fellow, the size of a cat and very cunning. While we had it in our hands, the mother stood perfectly quiet and glared at us as much as to say: "Hurt it, and these iron bars won't hold me a moment." She manifested great joy when the little fellow was passed back into the cage. The action of the tiger mother was not different, except that she gave a revengeful growl when she got her baby back.

Several times in going to the city, I passed the home of Bismarck. It was an unpretentious place, but armed sentinels walked up and down the pavement in front of it.

At noon one day, I noticed hundreds of people standing in front of the Emperor's palace. I stopped to see what was the matter. The increasing crowd stood there in the rain. "There he is," I heard some one cry out, and there was a doffing of hats. "There's who?" I asked of a man near me. "Why, don't you see him at the window?" he answered. It was the old Emperor standing there, smiling.

Once a day all Berlin can look on their Kaiser, and once a day the Kaiser interrupts his Cabinet council, steps to the front window and looks upon his people. It is much better than the crazy hand-shaking of the mob at the White House.

On our way back to Switzerland, we stopped at beautiful Dresden. One night at the opera we saw a white-haired old gentleman in a box, closely following the libretto and the singers, whose face seemed familiar to my wife. It was the King of Saxony--kind old Albert who, incognito, had played with our children that day in the mountains, and to whom our little girl had cried as he left, "Good-bye Mr. Albert."

*****

Our Minister's difficulties at Berlin increased. The matter of American pig, or no pig, became a battle between German and American newspapers. Correcting the false statement and the misrepresentations as to Mr. Sargent's Washington letter, helped none at all. The German newspapers simply did not want American meat. To American farmers and shippers, it meant hundreds of millions of dollars. Mr. Sargent stuck to his post and did his duty, and in a way, our Government supported him. One night Bismarck gave a grand diplomatic dinner. How could he receive Sargent socially when turning the cold shoulder to him officially? The press wondered what would happen. Of course our Minister had to be invited, and of course he had to go, or else show the white feather. Mr. Sargent was not the white feather kind, and he went. "Things went smoothly enough," he wrote me, "and the newspapers got no sensation to report. It was a very quiet and rather tame party. Of course Bismarck and I did not spend the entire evening talking together. He didn't effuse and I didn't effuse. That was all there was of it."8

Our Government approved his course at Berlin by appointing him Minister to St. Petersburg, but he declined.

Sargent, on coming home, was talked of for the Presidency. An abler man, a purer patriot, a clearer headed statesman, is not often thought of for that exalted post.

June 30, 1883.--On the 29th of March I went to America on the "Wieland." Had thirteen days at sea and twelve of them storm and hurricane. The ship was an old rat trap, on her last voyage before repairs. I did not know this until we were in the middle of the ocean.

A young German, a gilded youth, the son of Prince ----, was on board with me, proposing to try gay life a few years in America. One day he asked me if the American shop girls were all "fast," as in certain continental cities, and if young men were interfered with for ruining them. I observed that there was a difficulty; these girls mostly had brothers who would shoot such a scoundrel on sight. The princelet became pensive all at once, and seemed to be reflecting that his visions of fun in the United States were turning all to fog.

*****

Just before my return to Switzerland, I happened to be in Washington again. It was the day set for the public funeral of the author of "Home, Sweet Home." Corcoran, the Washington banker, was paying all the expenses, and a warship had brought the poet's remains home from Africa. The President and the Cabinet and all the dignitaries in Washington, as well as many invited guests, took part. Howard Payne had been a consul at the time of his death. I was asked to participate in the ceremony, and went as one of the staff of General Hancock. The ceremonies commenced in the Corcoran Art Gallery. It was an impressive occasion. I felt very strange, standing there close by the little white coffin that contained all that was left of the sweet singer. President Arthur was one of the pall bearers. At the cemetery there were long rows of elevated seats for the participants. I recall sitting beside General Hancock and looking with interest on the magnificent figure of the Gettysburg hero. He certainly was the most splendid looking military man I ever saw anywhere. A statue of Payne was unveiled at the grave, and a chorus of five hundred voices sang "Home, Sweet Home." A storm was threatening and black clouds hung over the scene. Just as the flag was being drawn aside from the marble face, the sun suddenly came out through a rift in the clouds, while at the very same instant a myriad of yellow butterflies fluttered and clustered about the poet's face. The vast multitude present saw it, and were moved to exclamations of delight.

I visited my home out West, and returned on the "Hammonia." My old school-fellow, J. D. Edmundson, went along. We had then, and more than once afterward, good times together, excursioning among the Swiss Alps.

His was a case of American pluck. When we left school neither of us had a penny. I soon went to the war, and he to a Western town to earn a fortune. Not twenty years went by when the penniless youth, a banker now, traveled the world over, with his check good for half a million, and his mind stored from books and travel.

September, 1883.--The Swiss National Exhibition is open all this summer. Though small, the finest in detail I ever saw anywhere. Never saw so much of real beauty arranged together. The location, too, in a great park between two rapid running rivers, is romantic. It is in view of the Alps and the beautiful lake.

On "Newspaper Day" I had the honor, for the want of a better, to reply to the toast, "The American Press."

I also wrote reports of the successful exhibition to our Government.

The Hon. Emil Frey, Swiss Cabinet Minister, now visited us out on the lake. Col. Frey had been a soldier in our army, was captured and suffered, with me, many horrid months in Libby prison. Our reunion under such different scenes will never be forgotten. He is a great big, generous man in body, mind, and heart. Because of his deserts, there is no post in Switzerland he can not have for the asking. In fact, he don't have to ask. He is one of Shakespeare's men who achieve honor and also have honor thrust upon them.

He was later elected President of Switzerland.

January, 1884.--These were the days when certain unscrupulous silk shippers were robbing the United States Treasury of almost millions yearly by undervaluation of invoiced goods. Honest importers were nearly driven out of the market. There was a constant warfare between the consul and the undervaluer. At last I succeeded in my own district, by employing (at my own expense) trained silk experts. The plan worked well, and Uncle Sam soon employed experts at many of the leading consulates. There was tremendous profit in it for the Government. For my zeal in stopping the frauds, and because of my long service, President Arthur promoted me. A little later, an Assistant Secretary of the Treasury reported officially that Consul Byers had saved the Government in his own district not less than a million dollars, or enough to support the whole consular service for years. He urged a recognition of these services. General Sherman, too, had joined in asking my advancement. One day, later, I saw this little note among the Department files:

"22nd January, 1881.

"DEAR MR. SECRETARY:--I commend Mr. Byers to the President's most favorable notice. He was one of my soldier boys, whom I released from prison at Columbia. He is now at Zurich, is a real poet, a good writer, and is one of the most modest, unselfish, and zealous men I ever knew. His promotion would be a beautiful recognition of past services.

W. T. SHERMAN."

November 10.--Yesterday I received the following letter from General Sherman:

"WASHINGTON, D. C, Oct. 24, 1883.

"DEAR BYERS:--I received in due season your valued letter of September 30th, enclosing the editorial of the London *Times*, which I had seen, but am none the less obliged for the thought which suggested your action. The time is now near at hand when I shall return to St. Louis, where my family is already happily domiciled. I have never known Mrs. Sherman more content, for she never regarded Washington as a home, but she recognizes her present house as a real home. The girls seem equally satisfied. The actual date of my retirement is Feb. 8, 1884, but I thought it right to allow Sheridan to come in at an earlier date so as to make any recommendations he chose for the action of the next Congress, and I asked of the President an order to authorize me to turn over the command on the first day of November, which he did in a very complimentary way on that day. I will turn over my office to Sheridan with as little fuss or ceremony as a Colonel would do in transferring his Regt. to the Lt. Col.

"I will then pay a visit to Elly at Philadelphia, afterward New York and then St. Louis. My address there will be Number 912 Garrison Avenue, a house you must remember. I have had it fitted up nicely. We are all very well, and I am especially so.

"I do not feel the least slighted in this whole business, for Congress has acted most liberally with me.

"I am constantly asked how I shall occupy my active mind and body. I postpone all thought of this till the time come, but I am resolved not to be tempted into politics, or to enter into any employment which could bring money liability.

"I hope you also will get your promotion, and then come home and settle on your Iowa farm. We should then be neighbors. Love to Mrs. Byers and the family.

"Your friend,
W. T. SHERMAN."

CHAPTER XXV
1884

SOME INTERESTING LETTERS FROM GENERAL SHERMAN--REQUESTS FOR SOUVENIRS--HIS "FLAMING SWORD"--ONE ON THE PRESIDENCY--I AM APPOINTED CONSUL GENERAL FOR ITALY--AN AMERICAN FOURTH OF JULY PICNIC ON LAKE ZURICH--LORD BYRON'S HOME IN SWITZERLAND--SOME OLD LETTERS ABOUT HIS LIFE THERE--THE LAKE DWELLINGS OF SWITZERLAND--KELLER, THE ANTIQUARIAN--POWER OF SWISS TORRENTS.

In a recent volume of my poems, some little change had been made in the stanzas of "The March to the Sea." General Sherman did not like these changes, and wrote me that in his opinion "no writer, having once given a thing to the public, had any right to change it."

He refers again to his preference in the following letter:

"ST. LOUIS, MO., Feb. 24, 1884.

"DEAR BYERS:--Yours of Feb. 6th is received. I had previously noticed that in the printed volumes there were variations, especially in the 'March to the Sea.' And I had simply noted on the margin of my copy that I liked the old version the best. Indeed, I think that Minnie has the original which was handed me at Columbia, which you remember was beautifully written. I have no doubt you will have occasion to enlarge your volume in time, and the last edition will always be accepted as the standard.

"We have had universally a hard winter, with storms and flood, of which you have doubtless heard as much at Zurich as if you were living in Iowa. The winter now begins to break, we have more sunshine, the grass begins to grow a green tint, and even the bark of the trees shows signs of a change. A hard winter makes a good summer, and I shall expect a pleasant summer.

"I find not the least trouble in putting in my time. Everybody supposes that I have nothing to do, and writes to me for tokens of remembrance, from a baby whistle for a namesake, to the 'flaming sword' I carried aloft at the South, to decorate his or her library. To comply with their kind messages, I would need a fortune and an arsenal. In fact and truth, we have a good comfortable home, and by economy we can live out our appointed time, and I do aim to manage so that my children will not have to beg of Government some pitiable office. I will build a neat cottage on my Illinois farm, and two good dwelling houses for rent on some lots we have around here for a long time, on which we have been paying taxes.

"In August, I will go to Minnetonka, to attend the meeting of the Army of the Tennessee.

"We are all reasonably well and are always glad to hear from you. Give my best love to Mrs. Byers, and congratulate her on the development of that boy of yours.

"Ever yours,
W. T. SHERMAN."

July 3.--Received a most interesting letter from General Sherman telling of his opposition to the use of his name for the Presidency.

"ST. LOUIS, MO., June 21, 1884.

"DEAR BYERS:--I received your letter of June 1st some days ago, and would have answered earlier, but had to go down to Carthage, Joplin, etc., in Southwest Missouri, to see a district of country settled up in great part by our old soldiers, who have made it a real garden, with nice farms, pretty houses, with churches, schools, etc., resembling New England, North Ohio, etc., rather than old Missouri, for which the Creator has done so much and man so little. So after all, we at St. Louis must look for civilization and refinement to come as a reflex wave from the West.

"We are now established in the very house in which you found us in 1875–6, in good condition, and with employment sufficient for recreation, diversion, etc.

"Last night I had to make a sort of an address to the Grand Army, in presenting the portrait of Brig. Gen. T. E. G. Ransom, after whom the post is named, and if printed, I may send you a copy. I do all that I can to keep out of the newspapers, but they keep paid spies to catch one's chance expressions, to circulate over the earth as substantial news. Recently I was informed by parties of National fame that in the Chicago Republican Convention, in case of a dead-lock between Blaine and Arthur, my name would be used. I begged to be spared the nomination but was answered that no man *dared* refuse a call of the people. I took issue that a political party convention was not the people of the U. S., and that I was not a bit afraid and would decline a nomination in such language as would do both myself and the convention harm. Fortunately Blaine and Logan were nominated, and they are fair representatives of the Republican party. Next month another set of fellows will meet at Chicago and will nominate Jeff Davis, Ben Butler, Tilden, Cleveland or some other fellow --no matter whom--and the two parties can fight it out. Fortunately, and thanks to the brave volunteer soldiers and sailors, the ship of state is now anchored in a safe harbor, and it makes little difference who is the captain. Our best Presidents have been accidents, and it is demonstrated by experience that men of prominent qualities cannot be elected. Therefore I will take little part, sure that whoever occupies the White House the next four years, will have a hard time of it, and be turned out to grass by a new and impatient, disappointed set. Meantime all the fertile spots of a vast domain are being occupied by an industrious class, who will produce all the food needed by our own population and the rest of the world, and will buy what they need, including the silks of France and Switzerland. Of course you do right in watching the invoices to see that the revenues of Uncle Sam are not defrauded, but if you expect to attract the notice of the State Department or the country, I fear you will be disappointed.

"I will go up to Minnesota about the middle of July to attend an encampment of the Grand Army of the Republic, and will wait over at Minnetonka till the middle of August, for a meeting of the society of the Army of the Tennessee, after which I will return to St. Louis till mid-winter, when I will go East for social engagements and the meetings of the Regents of the Smithsonian of which I retain membership. Marriages and deaths and the hundreds of incidents in every community, occupy my time so that thus far I have not been oppressed by ennui. I recall perfectly the house in Bocken in which I saw you in 1873, and sometimes doubt if you will be able to content yourself equally well in Iowa when the time forces itself on you; but the world moves right along, and we must conform.

"I am as always your friend,
W. T. SHERMAN."

July 4.--To-day, joined by all the Americans we could muster, and a few Swiss and English friends, we chartered a pretty steamer and went to the Island of Ufenau. It was a nice sight to see the boat sailing along the Zurich waters, covered with American flags. The Swiss band could play none of our American airs, but "God Save the Queen" did just as well.

"She's nothing but an old granny, though, and everybody laughs at her, privately," exclaimed an English lady to me as the band struck up the tune. This want of respect for the Queen is not so uncommon among English living on the continent as one would imagine.

Gladstone, too, whose name I honor, comes in for any amount of bullying and abusing among traveling Englishmen. "He simply ought to be hung, that's what ought to happen to him," I heard one Englishman bawl out to another Englishman once. I was not so especially surprised. For some reason or other, most of the English we meet shake their heads, when we praise the great Christian statesman. I wonder if only the jingo English are rich enough to travel. Gladstone's friends, if any abroad, are dreadfully silent.

We had a fine picnic on the island to-day, with the blue waters of the lake about us and white Alps right in front of us. One American signalized himself by getting drunk. We left him in a farmhouse on the island.

Came home with a glorious sunset turning the Alps into crimson and gold. One view like this evening would repay for a journey over the ocean, and we have had it almost daily for fifteen years.

On reaching Bocken I found a cablegram from Senator Wilson saying I had been promoted to be Consul General at Rome. I was happier that the news came on this particular day. When I went out on the terrace though, and looked at the beautiful and familiar scenes around me that I must leave forever, the pleasure over my promotion was almost turned into a pang.

*****

A few weeks ago, Cupples, Upham & Co., in Boston, printed the first edition of my volume of poems called "The Happy Isles." They are now sending me reviews and notices of the book. They are as good as I could wish. It was pleasant to-day, too, to receive a warm letter commending my poems from Oliver Wendell Holmes. Some of them "had brought the tears to his eyes." To me this was sweeter praise than anything the reviewers could possibly say. Whittier, too, wrote a pretty little Quaker letter, full of kind praise. One of the poems, "The Marriage of the Flowers," he had picked out as the best of all. I hear it is being much copied. "If You Want a Kiss, Why Take It" also seems to please the editors. A friend writes "they are copying it, everywhere."

*****

Recently we went to see Byron's home, villa "Diadati," a few miles out from Geneva. It is a handsome house with windows and balconies opening on to the lake. Here he wrote "Manfred," "The Dream," parts of "Childe Harold" and "Darkness."

Byron's Home on Lake Geneva.

I could not help thinking of him and Shelley and Shelley's wife, sitting out there on the veranda nights, telling ghost stories. I came across some letters the other day, long out of print, written by a Swiss, who also was whiling his days away on this lake in 1816. The first one says, "Last night I met Lord Byron at Madame de Stael's. I can compare no creature to him. His tones are music, and his features the features of an angel. One sees, though, a little Satan shining in his eyes which, however, is itself half pious. The ladies are mad after him. They surround him like little bacchantes, and nearly tear him to pieces. I hold him as the greatest living poet. Every stormy passion is witnessed in his glance. One sees the corsair in his look, which, though, often is good, tender, and even melancholy."

I also have followed Byron's footsteps in his trips in the higher Alps. He went up into the Simmenthal to Thun, to Interlacken, and the heights near to the Jungfrau. "These scenes," he wrote, "are beyond all description or previous conception."

My boy made a picture of the old ruin of a tower near Interlacken, pointed out as the scene where the "Manfred" of the poem struggled with the spirits. Manfred was Byron's best work, but the printers left the best line of it out, by accident. What would Tennyson nowadays say to a publisher's leaving the best line out of his best poem?

Byron liked the Jungfrau better than Mt. Blanc, and the scenes about the upper end of Lake Geneva inspired him. "All about here," he exclaimed once, "is a sense of existence of love in its most extended and sublime capacity, and of our participation of its good and its glory."

His trip among the grandeur of the higher Alps did not tear him away from his wretched self. He could not forget that he was Byron, and his "Manfred," arguing with ghosts in the old ruin by Lake Thun, might have been a photograph of himself. That's what Goethe believed it to be, anyway.

Last week, Professor Ferdinand Keller, the Swiss antiquarian, asked me to visit the Lake Dwelling excavations at Robenhausen. This is an excavated village of the stone age, 5,000 years old, the experts think--maybe older still. The famous Keller himself is a marvel, and might be out of some other age. He is eighty or ninety years old, a little, short man, with white hair standing straight on end, shaggy eyebrows, perfectly immense in their projection above a pair of eyes that burn like stars. Spite of his many years, he is bright, cheery and active, and capable of labor as a boy of thirty. His face is as well known in Zurich as one of the city monuments. The young people think he has walked the streets always, and nobody expects him ever to die.

His antiquarian rooms look out over the lake. Indeed the old stone Helmhouse is built in the lake, and it contains the greatest curiosities of the world. One day Keller was looking out of his window and observed some queer shadows of things down in the water. Investigation proved these "things" to be piles, on which in some remote age, houses and towers had been built. Shortly, the shallow inlets of half the lakes of the country were found to have once been the abode of peoples. The oldest of all, like Robenhausen, were of the age of stone. I was glad of a chance to go, and excavate a little for myself in these towns that were old and forgotten a thousand years before Pompeii was even born. This particular village has been perhaps twelve hundred feet square and stood on a platform supported by 100,000 piles. It was three hundred feet from the shore and was once connected with the mainland by a bridge. In some of the villages once lived a people possibly as much civilized as the Mexican of to-day. This is proved by the relics found in the later ones of looms and cloth, and swords and jewelry of lovely patterns. At Robenhausen life had been simple, but I myself dug out specimens of good cloth. There is nothing to see at Robenhausen save the myriad of rotting piles where the turf bed that took the place of what was once a lake has been removed. All the belongings of the village are buried in mud and water. The cedar and beech poles on which the town once stood had been sharpened by fire before driving. They were twelve feet long and eighteen inches around and stood in regular rows. The huts on the platform (two or three complete ones have been found) were one story high, twenty-two feet wide and twenty-seven feet long, built of upright poles matted together with willows and plastered with clay inside and out. The floors, too, were plastered and the roofs were made of rushes. The remains of grinding stones and mills have been found in every cabin. Not the sign of a hieroglyphic or an alphabet has ever been found, to show who those people were.

I prepared for Harper's Magazine a paper called "The Swiss Lake Dwellers," describing the excavations at all the Swiss lakes up to the present time. A Swiss artist illustrated it for me.9

*****

We hear much of the awful force of Swiss mountain torrents. The other day I saw what is ordinarily a brook suddenly rise and sweep thousands of tons of huge rocks on to farms in the valley. The debris of rock and granite was from three to ten feet deep for a mile. The force of these streams is simply tremendous beyond belief--the fall is so great; even the wide river Reuss falls 5,000 feet in thirty miles.

It is a constant wonder why people build homes and hamlets in the way of these awful torrents when their destruction some day is almost certain. However, it is on a par with their building villages on mountain crags and on almost unapproachable slopes when there is plenty of level land in the word.

*****

Yesterday Koller, the animal painter, asked us to take tea in his studio. Congressman Lacey and his wife went with us. Koller is pronounced, by the Swiss at least, to be the greatest animal painter living. He had a splendid harvest scene on the easel--storm coming up, peasants hurrying to get the hay on the wagon, the threatening sky, the uneasy horses, their tails and manes, like the dresses of the girls, blown aside with the wind. It seemed to me I never saw so much action in a picture. Koller was threatened with blindness not long ago, when the prices of his pictures went sky high. Agents were sent out of Germany to buy them up at whatever figure. His great painting of the St. Gothard diligence crossing the Alps is famous. Nothing finer in the way of galloping horses and mountain pass scenery can be imagined. His home and studio are on a little horn of land running out into the lake. He keeps a herd of his own cattle for painting, and every day these beautiful dumb helpers of his are seen in the shallow water of the lake. Mrs. Koller poured the tea for us. She looks like an artist's wife. Koller is a big, full-bearded German-looking Swiss, seventy years old, who is beloved all over the little republic for his supreme art. Switzerland has four great names in art: Calame, Stückelberg, Böcklin, Koller.

CHAPTER XXVI
1884

START FOR ITALY--THE CHOLERA--TEN DAYS IN QUARANTINE ON LAKE MAGGIORE--A HEROIC KING--WE ARE PRESENTED TO QUEEN MARGARET --AMERICAN ARTISTS IN ROME--THE ROYAL BALLS --RECEPTIONS AND PARTIES--MEET MANY PEOPLE OF NOTE--THE HILLS OF ROME--MINISTER ASTOR AND HIS HOME--HUGH CONWAY--IBSEN--MARION CRAWFORD--ONE OF THE BONAPARTES--KEAT'S ROOM--THE CARDINALS--ISCHIA DESTROYED--CHRISTMAS IN ROME--LETTER FROM GENERAL SHERMAN--HIS VIEWS OF ROME--CLEVELAND'S ELECTION--FRANZ LISZT AGAIN.

August 4.--Sunday evening I walked from Bocken to Zurich to take the train for my new post at Rome. Walked along the Albis hills above the lake, ten miles. It was a delightful summer evening and the view of mountains and lake seemed finer than ever before. I could not help stopping many times to turn round and drink in the glorious scene, possibly for the last time. It was the only time I ever shed tears on leaving a scene of beauty. Besides I was leaving Switzerland, where I had had fifteen happy years.

It was a dangerous time to go to Italy. The cholera was raging in Spezia not less than in Marseilles and Toulon. Many Italians were flying home from the scourge-stricken districts, and at the last moment I learned that a quarantine had been established on the Italian frontier. I hoped, however, to get through at a little village on Lake Maggiore. To my surprise all the lake region was filled with guards and I was soon arrested and cooped up with a thousand others at an old sawmill by the lake.

For ten long days I walked alone up and down the upper floor of that big sawmill, every hour expecting the cholera to break out among the crowd of refugees down in the yard. Once a day a guard was sent to conduct me down to the lake, where I could go in and swim. What a treat that was for me! The guard stood on the shore with fixed bayonet, watching that I did not swim out too far and get away. Mrs. Terry, our good American friend, happened to be spending the summer in the mountains near by. She heard of me and, like a good Samaritan, brought me grapes and other delicacies. We could only stand and talk to each other at a distance with the line of guards between us.

One morning I received a great big document, it looked like a college diploma, saying that I had finished with the quarantine and could proceed on my way.

In the early morning twilight I crossed beautiful Lake Maggiore in a row boat, and like a bird let loose from its cage flew away to Rome.

Once on a time when my wife and I had been in Rome visiting, a lady friend said to us just as we were about leaving: "Come first with me to the fountain of Trevi, throw a penny into the water, and you will return to Rome." We went one beautiful moonlight night and tossed our coins into the fountain. And now, sure enough, here I was again in the Eternal City.

The officials of the consulate met me at the train. I went through another terrible fumigation for the cholera, and was soon settled down to live in Italy. The office was at once moved to Palazzo Mariani, 30 Via Venti Settembre, and there later we made our home, when it was safe for my family to follow me.

My friends, Congressman Lacey and wife, who seemed to be about the only strangers in Rome, also met me. We stopped at the great, big, empty "Hotel di Roma." We had it all to ourselves, and we had much amusement with the waiter, who understood none of our lingo, nor we his, further than the word "ancora" (more). The little mugs of milk he brought us for our figs, were but spoonfuls, so we constantly cried "ancora!" He smiled, and the mugs came almost by the dozen. I was no little surprised to see on my bill a long list of repeated charges, sometimes written out, sometimes dotted down, for half a yard. It was the word "ancora," at a half a franc apiece.

The Laceys left Rome, after taking one long, last look at me at the station, for they believed they were leaving me there to die of the cholera.

Rome was as silent as a grave that summer. Everybody seemed seized with a panic, and fled to the sea or the mountains. I was indeed lonesome, and with just half of an attack of cholera would have probably succumbed. I saw little but closed shop windows, silent streets, and men going about the alleys and corners scattering lime and disinfectants. Everybody I knew or met carried a bottle of "cholera cure" in his coat pocket for there was danger any moment of tumbling over in the street. Away from the office I scarcely met a soul I could talk with. Suddenly I bethought myself of my friend Frank Simmons, the sculptor, and was at once ensconced with him in the rooms above his studio. When not busy at the consulate I could spend my time watching him turn his live models into clay and marble, and in the beautiful summer nights we sat up in his rooms and talked of art, and America, till midnight.

Mr. Hooker, the banker, (what American that ever went to Rome in the last twenty-five years did not know him?) invited Mr. Simmons and myself to supper. He lived in the palace once owned by Madame Bonaparte, the mother of Napoleon. Here she died. The chambers were still filled with paintings and sculpture and other souvenirs of the Napoleon family. That night Mr. Hooker, Mr. Simmons and myself sat till towards the morning round the little table in the very room where Napoleon's mother spent her evenings thinking of her eight children, seven of whom were kings.

In a few weeks, the scare over, the people commenced returning. Then the cholera broke out in Italy sure enough. It was at Naples now, and with horrible fatality.

The brave King Humbert took train and went there to help and to encourage the afflicted. He went into the hospitals everywhere, took the sick by the hand, and possibly helped many a dying one to take courage and live. He took his own provisions with him, even drinking water, from Rome, and whenever he went among the sick he smoked constantly. His staff complained he was leading them all to death, but they had to follow into dens and holes and hospitals more dangerous than a battle field.

King Humbert.

Queen Margherita.

September.--My family have come, and now we are all living at the Consulate, Via Venti Settembre 30.

The King came back to Rome from cholera-stricken Naples a day or two ago. He has become the greatest hero in Italy. I never saw such a reception. The main streets of Rome were packed solid with human beings, trying to touch the King's extended hand, his horses, the wheels of the carriage. The beautiful Queen Margaret sat at his side smiling and bowing right and left. The young Crown Prince sat on the front seat. I did not know a King could be loved so by his people. But this King was a hero.

The Van Marters had asked me to view the procession from their balcony on the Via Nazionale. They had hung out American flags. The King saw the colors, took off his hat and profoundly greeted them as he passed.

I never saw a President receive half the ovation that this King did, riding through Rome with his Queen and son, and without any escort or signs of royalty whatever. The vast crowd were simply mad with pride, enthusiasm and love for their King and Queen Margaret.

October.--It is easy enough to get acquainted in Rome, at least for an official; besides, there are many of one's countrymen living here, and parties and receptions are the order of the day and night through the entire social season. The members of the consular and diplomatic corps we soon met, and then there are so many American artists here worth knowing whose studios are open to all lovers of the beautiful. We made immediately the acquaintance of U. S. Minister and Mrs. W. W. Astor at their home in the Rospigliosi palace. There we met many interesting people.

Mrs. Astor is a young and very beautiful woman, and very charming in her manners. They have two pretty children. Mr. W. Waldorf Astor, though a multi-millionaire, personally leads a simple life in Rome. He is a close student. Every bright morning sees him riding with an antiquarian among the outskirts and ruins of the city. He is an acknowledged authority in kindred matters and his papers on the discoveries in Yucatan and elsewhere, read before one of the learned societies here, attracted attention. He is not playing ambassador as an amusement. His legation business is as closely attended to as if he were a poor, hard-working clerk in need of a salary. There is no ostentation about him personally. Officially, he attends to it that the social position of the United States Minister is what it should be.

One night at a dinner party he was relating the incident of a Union soldier who had donned a gray uniform once and entered the Rebel army at Atlanta. He had read a description of this soldier's experiences and hairbreadth escapes in the

Atlantic Monthly, and had been extraordinarily impressed. The soldier's name, as he remembered it, was the same as my own. Could we be related? I astonished him by saying that I was more than related, that I was the soldier myself, and the article in the Atlantic was my own. Mr. Astor grasped my hand, saying he had thought of that soldier's action a hundred times. My narrative had made Mr. Astor a friend. He rarely introduced me to a friend after that without adding: "He is the man who went into Atlanta."

The palace where Mr. Astor lives is the same that our Minister Marsh occupied when I was here some years ago. It is built on the ruins of the Baths of Constantine.

I have looked everywhere trying to find the "hills" of Rome, but almost in vain. They can barely be located, and are not half as defined as the hills of Boston.

*****

Yesterday I went to look at the apartment where the consulate used to be by the Spanish stairway. The consul's little back room is where the Poet Keats died. I could think I saw him lying there waiting for beautiful death to come, and I seemed to hear him say to his friend Severn: "I already feel the flowers growing over me." And I saw Severn too, forgetting his easel, to sweep and cook and wait and watch all the nights alone, till the beautiful soul of Keats should take its flight. The room is a poorly lighted common little bedroom where the poet died, but it will be visited many a day in memory of one who lived, not between brick walls, but in high imaginations. We also went to the poet's simple grave, as we had often done before, and looked at the green sod above one who

Had loved her with a love that was his doom.

It was the love for Fannie Brawn and not the bitter pens of the Quarterlies, that killed John Keats after all. Severn found that out only six short years ago, when the love letters from Keats to Fannie Brawn were placed in the now old man's hands.

December 28.--Spite of bad weather we are having some wonderful sunsets lately, and strangers in Rome linger long on the Spanish stairway to enjoy a scene they have so often heard of--a sunset by the Tiber.

Last night Madame Bompiani invited us to tea with her. She lives at the Hilda's tower palace, celebrated by Hawthorne, in the "Marble Faun." Her husband is a well-known Roman lawyer, and she herself writes interesting letters to the Chicago *Interior*. We learned much about things in Rome direct from him, and after the supper we were taken up to the tower.

One of the guests was Madame Guyani, a sister of the hostess. She was a fine conversationalist and interested us much. Only a few months ago she was a sufferer in the terrible earthquake at Ischia. She is still lame as a result of the experiences of that fearful night. She told us all about the earthquake. The night of the disaster she wandered or crept about the fields till morning. The parts of the island which were nothing short of an earthly paradise in the evening were only piles of ruins and dead people in the morning. It was as if Eden had been struck by a thunderbolt, only here there was a happy, unsuspecting people to be suddenly hurled out of existence.

Sunday.--Instead of going to church I stay in Mr. Franklin Simmons' studio and watch him making a bust of Marion Crawford, the novelist. He has a good subject, for Marion Crawford is a large, handsome man with a fine figure and a genial face. There was a joking dialogue going on as to whether it is the great novelist now sitting to the sculptor Simmons or the great sculptor Simmons doing the face of a novelist, each modestly insisting the other only had claims on immortality. I liked Crawford and his genial ways. I had just finished reading his "Roman Singer."

Frank Simmons seems to me to be the best sculptor in Rome, though he is not yet the most celebrated. He does not seem to try to seek fame; but lets it seek him, which it is doing. Marion Crawford, too, I know, regarded Simmons as the best sculptor living, and some day he will make him the hero of a great novel.

Italy is called the land of art and yet curiously there are few great Italian artists. Its galleries sometimes seem to me like opened coffins, where one beholds among the bones the jewel work of some dead age. I feel here much as I felt in Berlin when looking on the golden necklaces of Helen of Troy, dug up by Schliemann. All the fine paintings and marbles here in Rome seem like the ruins, relics of another time. Foreign artists by the hundred, live and work here for the inspiration they get from the fragments of the past. They taste the wine made good with age and mix some of it in the bottles of new wine of their own making. There are more imitators in Rome than anywhere else in the world.

*****

The duties of the consulate here are nothing compared with Zurich or with any other commercial consulate. The office is often full of callers, but their errands are visits of courtesy or to have passports issued and the like. The trade of Rome with America is insignificant.

There are two regular consular clerks here, burdened with nothing to do. The laws provide for some thirteen of these "regulars" in the consular service, who hold their places for life. They are rarely promoted, and grow gray doing little. One good, hired clerk whose staying in depends on his zeal and fitness and not on his self-importance, is worth a dozen of them. They should be made responsible to somebody. The salary of the Consul General does not pay his expenses in Rome.

Palazzo Mariani, where we live, is a very magnificent structure outside, with great white marble stairways within, leading from floor to floor. But it is cold as a sepulcher. No stoves and no fire-places save one little niche in the wall, where a few burning fagots scarcely change the temperature.

At night we come home (very late, as parties only begin at nine or so), and go to bed in a big cold bedroom with a brick floor. Our so-called cook stove is a little iron box heated with charcoal, in a kitchen about five feet square, but Antoinette seems to know how to broil a kid on it every day.

Our drawing-room is heated (?) by the fagots in the niche in the wall; but even this is *too warm* for our Italian friends, who, when they call, apologize and go and sit in the back end of the room as far from the so-called fire as possible.

We have our furniture here from Switzerland, and to us that is a comfort. Occasionally a couple of priests come into our house without asking and walk about through all the rooms, sprinkling holy water on the beds as is a custom here. On going out, they indicate their willingness for a fee, which is not surprising in a land where feeing is universal.

Like most modern houses in Rome, our big palace is built on top of a series of old arches that once supported the houses of ancient Rome. From our cellar we can prowl around unknown distances through these mysterious chambers.

The water for the house is still conducted from the Alban hills in one of the old Roman aqueducts. It is a queer combination, this old and new in Rome.

*****

Mr. Astor had written me that last night my wife and I were to be presented at court. At ten we were climbing the magnificent stairs of the Quirinal palace to be presented to Queen Margaret. Gorgeously uniformed sentinels stood on the stairway left and right. We were shortly escorted to one of the great drawing-rooms of the palace, where we found other ladies and gentlemen also waiting to be presented. In a little while we were all directed to stand in line around the walls of the drawing-room. A dead silence ensued, and then the Queen of Italy entered at our right, escorted by the Marchesa Villa Marina, who had in her hand a list of all of our names. A few moments before she had passed along the line whispering to each of us and confirming the correctness of her list. Queen Margaret turned to her left as she passed in and very graciously greeted a young Italian lady, whom she seemed to know personally. She extended her hand to the young lady, who, greatly honored, blushed and looked very pretty. This was the only instance where the Queen gave her hand that evening. As she started along the line toward us she halted before each one. The Marchesa promptly made the presentation, when the Queen bowed very sweetly and made some remarks. I noticed that in each case she spoke the language of the lady or gentleman presented. I could hear her speaking German, Italian, French. Certainly she cannot speak English, I meditated, but in a moment our turn came. Our names were pronounced, and the Queen commenced in very agreeable English. Her manner was extremely winning, kind and simple. She "knew we would like Rome," she said. "Everybody did, and she hoped our stay would be long and very happy." She wore an elegant gown, cut extremely low, revealing a fine form. Around her neck was the famous pearl necklace, to which the King adds a string of pearls every birthday. She carried an enormous white fan of ostrich plumes which she constantly waved while she talked with us. She looked the queen, and I thought more German than Italian. Her whole bearing was graciousness. Her smile seemed as sincere as beautiful, and no one but would call her a happy, beautiful woman.

The presentation over, we will now be entitled to invitations to the palace balls and other public functions. There is an American lady here at court whom we knew in Switzerland. It is the Countess Ginotti, formerly Miss Kinney, of Washington. Her husband is a court official and is entrusted with important duties.

Last night we went to our second court ball at the Quirinal. A week following our presentation we had had the customary invitation to the first. We go at ten at night, ascend the same brilliantly lighted stairway as at the presentation, and even more gorgeously uniformed sentinels line the way on left and right.

The dress is prescribed; gentlemen in evening attire of course--there is nothing else a man can do but dress himself in mourning and call it festive; but so many ladies, in their elegant, light gowns and extremely low bodices, with swan white necks and shining diamonds, made a lovely scene. We shortly found ourselves seated among five hundred other guests in a brilliant ballroom of the palace. A raised dais and a royal chair stood at the end in front of us. There was a little gossip with each other, a little wondering at the gorgeous gowns, when suddenly the music from a lofty gallery proclaimed the coming of the court. Instantly, side doors unfolded, and King Humbert with Queen Margaret on his arm, marched toward the raised platform, followed by the court officials and all the Ambassadors in Rome in gala attire. We all rise, the ladies courtesying and the men bowing, as the King gracefully swings Queen Margaret into her seat and takes his place, standing beside her chair. There is some more bowing and smiling and courtesying. The music changes for the dance and the guests look on while the Queen and the Ambassadors and their wives dance the royal cotillon. The Ambassador of Germany, the head of the diplomatic corps, dances with Queen Margaret. It is all very lovely, though some of us guests feel we could beat the dancing all to pieces. In a few moments the Queen is back on the dais talking with the ladies privileged to surround her. The music has changed and some of the five hundred present are swinging in the waltz.

All has been simple and beautiful. Such a ball might take place in the extremest republic in the world. Some formality, some etiquette, there must be everywhere. While the others dance, the Queen and the King talk with the ladies, with the Ministers, and the Ambassadors. I was close to the King at different times in the evening. He was as unpretending as any other gentleman in the room. He seemed to have a bad cough, and his great eyes sometimes glanced around in a strange way. His mustache is almost as big and bristling as was his father's, Victor Emmanuel. He has a kindly, earnest look, and Italy has in him a patriotic King. At midnight everybody repaired to little marble tables in an adjoining room, where most expensive refreshments were served. Every one seemed to have a bottle of champagne to himself. I never saw such a flowing of wines, yet all managed to keep sober. The ball souvenirs presented to every guest were all made in Paris and of every conceivable and lovely design.

*****

We are not far from the "Porta Pia," and often go out walking or driving on the Campagna. Much of this barren land was a graveyard once, and splendid broken marble tombs still stretch away for miles. One can guess at the enormous wealth of the old city by walking for hours among the fallen columns and broken tombs of the rich out here on the Campagna. It is as if a wilderness of marble trees had at some past time been torn down by a whirlwind, and only the debris left behind.

The most impressive scene about Rome is the great aqueducts by moonlight, as they stretch across this waste of the Campagna. They are one hundred feet high and built on immense arches. One gets an idea of what the population of Rome must have been, on reflecting that at one time there were twenty-four of these canals through the air for carrying water into the city, and that fifty million cubic feet of water a day flowed into Rome through them. I was surprised to learn that hundreds of miles, too, of these aqueducts were built under ground. A tunnel a few thousand feet long we regard as a wonder at home, but some of these aqueducts were thirty-six miles at a stretch, under ground.

The Campagna was honeycombed in all directions by these strange canals, and the miles of arches above ground to-day impress one more than does the Coliseum.

However desolate the Campagna to-day, in the olden time it must have been a wonder with its catacombs and canals under ground and its magnificent tombs, pillars and aqueducts above ground.

Evenings when the weather is fine we see the Cardinals with their cassocks and hats of flaming red, taking the air. They drive over from the Vatican in closed carriages and when once on the Campagna get out and walk about.

Next to the Cardinals, these Campagna shepherds are picturesque and interesting. They wear leather leggings, sheepskin jackets, goatskin breeches with the long hair outside, a red sash and a rakish hat. They look very much like stage villains, which they are not. When they ride into town, two or three on the same donkey, they make a remarkable figure; but a very miserable one, when the one behind is seen jabbing the donkey with an awl to make him go faster with his load of vagabonds.

January, 1885.--Christmas Day we went to see the magnificent ceremonies in the church called the Santa Maria Maggiore. Its forest of vast marble columns was wrapped in hangings of crimson and gold. The priests, bishops, cardinals and other dignitaries wore the most gorgeous regalia of the church.

At the height of the ceremony a part of the Holy Manger in a crystal chest was borne up and down the aisles, among the kneeling, praying multitudes. Whatever the history of this relic, I think it was regarded that day by every one present as very sacred. I never saw a multitude so impressed with one thought. To many present, death itself could not, I think, have caused deeper emotion.

Great church ceremonies are all the time going on in Rome, and as there are more than three hundred church buildings, one can go to a different place every day in the year. Not at the Sistine Chapel alone, with its "Last Judgment" scenes, its moving music and officiating Pope, need one be interested; in dozens of churches great things are always going on.

*****

A few evenings ago we were invited to a party at the Danish consul's. Met a number of interesting people, but the lion of the evening was Ibsen, the great dramatic writer. He is a little short man with a big head, a great shock of white hair, and twinkling eyes. I talked with him some in English. Famous as his dramas are, I knew little about them, and our few minutes' talk was on indifferent subjects, not worth remembering or jotting down; only he talked like a very genial, open-hearted man.

The next day there was an afternoon reception at our own home, and among our guests was Hugh Conway, the author of "Called Back." He went with me to a little corner in the dining-room, where we had a chat about his famous story, his own past, and his future hopes. He had been an auctioneer in England, and on trying his hand at stories was astonished to find himself suddenly famous. He was simple, kind and communicative as a child. Shortly his wife joined us, agreeable as himself, and they were promising much to themselves from another season, which they intended spending in Rome. And we were going to be friends. He told me of their children in England. We emptied a glass to the children's health, and the next day they started for Nice. He took a cold on the way, and a little later came the sad news that the lovable man was dead.

Almost every day, afternoon or evening, we go to receptions. Half the Americans living here give them, to say nothing of those given by the English, French and other foreign residents whom one happens to know. One meets a sprinkling of Italians at all of them, but this is by no means Roman society. That is something that few foreigners know very much about. The receptions are all about alike, though differing in interest of course, according to the personality of the entertainers. People come to them and stand up and gossip a little; some pretty girls pour tea, and occasionally there is a song by some visiting celebrity. Getting a "celebrity" to be at one's receptions and parties, by the way, is a part of a society woman's bounden duty in Rome. What lions have we not met at these delightful afternoon and evening affairs--Liszt, Crawford, Ibsen, Rogers, Fargus, Bonaparte, Houghton, the Trollopes, Wallace, and how many others less great. One meets most of them just long enough for a cup of tea together, or a glass of wine, a hand shake, a few words, and then "au revoir." Yet the memory of it all remains.

Rome is always full of great people and they all seem to like to be lionized. Then there are the distinguished artists of many countries who live here by the hundred, and who honor the hostess and sometimes themselves, by dropping in at these receptions for a stand-up cup of tea and a general hand shake.

We have attended three, four, even half a dozen receptions the same day. If ever I go into business in Rome it will be to sell tea to people who give receptions. A man of war could float in the tea poured out here by pretty girls every afternoon.

Some of the artists also, like Ezekiel, the sculptor, give unique little receptions in their picturesque studios. These are almost the best of all.

*****

Had an interesting letter from General Sherman yesterday.

"ST. LOUIS, MO., Nov. 14, 1884.

"DEAR BYERS:--I was very glad to receive your letter of October 28, from Rome, telling us that you are now fairly established in the Eternal City. Somehow that renowned city did not make the impression on me that its fame warranted, but I was told that it grew upon every man who dwelt there long enough. I hope you will experience that result, and realize not only contentment, but gather much material for future literary work, because I fear your diplomatic career is drawing to a close. It now seems almost certain that all the little petty causes of discontent and opposition inside the Republican party have united with the Democrats and elected Cleveland President. When installed next spring he will be a stronger man that he has credit for, if he can resist the pressure sure to be brought on him, and consulships will be in great demand, for distance lends enchantment, and exaggerates the value of such offices. I have no fear of violence, and believe that Cleveland will not allow the solid South to dictate to him. If he does, and the old Rebels show the cloven foot, the reaction four years hence will be overwhelming.

"We are all very well in St. Louis, and the autumn has been beautiful, crops good and bountiful, general business dull by reason of apprehended change of tariff, but the country growing steadily all the time. My daughter Rachel is in Maine on a visit to the Blaines, at this critical period. Mrs. Sherman is at Philadelphia on a short visit to our daughter Elly, so that the family here is small. I expect to make a short visit to New York and Washington about Christmas, with which exception I propose to remain quiet. Time, with me, glides along smoothly and I am amply convinced that I was wise in retiring just when I did. I don't believe the Democrats will materially hurt the army, but they will make Sheridan's place uncomfortable. I visited Des Moines in September and found it a prosperous, fine city. I should suppose you might make it your home, devote your time to literature, and give general supervision to your farm. I'm afraid, however, that you have been so long abroad that it will be hard to break yourself and family into the habits of Iowa farmers. Give to Mrs. Byers and son the assurance of our best love.

"Your friend,
W. T. SHERMAN."

The other night we were at a private musicale, next door to one of the hotels. Some girls, and a certain princess, played and sang extremely well. In the midst of the evening the door opened and who should walk in? It was Franz Liszt. He was in his slippers just as he had been in his room next door. He had heard the music and had just dropped in. Quite a little emotion was created among us all, when after standing and listening a little bit, he went straight over to the young girl at the piano and put a rousing kiss on her forehead. She blushed, and was stamped for immortality. To her last hour she will remember that approving kiss of the master.

After the musicale I was presented and was glad he remembered me so well from Zurich. He recalled a kissing scene that I had witnessed there as well, and laughed heartily about it.

But Liszt is getting old. He has had his day of great life. What genius and a great deal of work can do for a man in this world anyway! Liszt, with his genius, worked too at the piano like a galley slave, years before any soul applauded.

*****

Yesterday, one of the Bonapartes came to the office on some business. It was Napoleon Charles. He owns the villa Bonaparte and is a rich man, for his villa grounds are to be sold off at great prices for the new Rome rapidly building. I observed him closely because I had been told that his is the real Bonaparte face. He is taller than was the First Consul. His family name is still a power in Rome. It interested me to see one who is closely connected with the Great Napoleon. He wrote me a pretty French note of thanks, and that is pasted in among my autograph letters from interesting people.

CHAPTER XXVII
1885

STILL IN ROME--PRESENTED TO POPE LEO XIII--STORY, THE POET SCULPTOR--RANDOLPH ROGERS--TILTON--ELIHU VEDDER--ASTOR RESIGNS--SECRETARY OF LEGATION DIES WITH ROMAN FEVER--I AM PUT IN CHARGE OF LEGATION--CAPRI--GOVERNOR PIERPONT--THINGS SUPERNATURAL--TALK AGAINST GLADSTONE--SHAKESPEARE WOOD--SENATOR MOLESCHOTT, A REMARKABLE MAN--INTERESTING LETTERS FROM GENERAL SHERMAN--PARTY STRONGER THAN PATRIOTISM; MY RECALL--MONEY LENDING AND TAXES--KEEP OUT OF DEBT.

February, 1885.--On Sunday morning we (myself, wife and son) together with others, were presented to the Pope, Leo XIII. The card of notification told us how we should dress. Full evening suit, with black cravat and black gloves for the gentlemen; black silk dress for the ladies, with black lace veils over the head, instead of bonnets. Our carriage entered the court yard at a private entrance, where dismounting we entered at a side door and went up the Bernini stairway. The Swiss guards, glad to hear their own tongue spoken, were very polite to us. Colonel Schmidt, their commander, is also a personal friend, who had visited us in Switzerland. He soon turned us over to the Pope's personal body guard. These are young Roman nobles. We were led through a labyrinth of apartments, and put in charge of some of the court officers at the reception room.

Pope Leo XIII.

"The reception will take place in just thirty minutes," said one of the officials, and this gave us time to look out of the window, and wonder what part of the enormous pile called the Vatican, we were in.

Outside, the four thousand room building, with its two hundred stairways, looks like an ugly collection of big yellow factories. Inside, it is all magnificence. We were standing in rooms where the Popes ruled Rome, at a time when Rome ruled the world. The history of a thousand years was made and written under this roof. The genius of many ages found a resting place here. Here for centuries God, himself, was supposed to have his only agent on earth.

Just as we were meditating on all this, a rustle of officers entering the room is heard. We are placed in a line, single file, around the walls of the apartment. "You will all kneel," whispers an official, "as his Holiness enters." That moment the door opened, and Leo XIII, robed in scarlet, entered the room. Everybody knelt. As he passes the door an attendant draws the scarlet robe away, and he stands before us in white and gold. He is a very old man, tall and thin, colorless in face, and with silvery hair; there is a soft, sad smile on his lips; his clear, steady eyes look out of a kindly face. He motions us all to rise, and then slowly walks around the room, speaking a gracious word to each as presented. An official walks with him carrying a list of our names. The Pope's half-gloved hand with the signet ring, is held forward for us to kiss. His words are kindness itself. I never saw so saintly a face before. I do not wonder that many in the room are weeping. They are faithful Catholics and this moment is the event of their lives. Some have traveled ten thousand miles to have that white hand placed on their heads with a blessing. To them, the doors of paradise are this moment visibly opening.

Everybody, Catholic or not, was affected. Shortly the kindly voice comes to us, "And you are from America--America--good, far off America," he says in English, and then changes to French, and Italian. He placed his hand on our heads and blessed us--and, believing or disbelieving--a feeling of a holy presence moved us.

Shortly, a signal indicated that all should come to the center of the room and kneel, and then a blessing was asked on the lands from which we came. It was an impressive moment. Numbers kneel down and kiss the gold cross on his embroidered slipper. An attendant enters, throws the scarlet robe gently over his shoulders again. There are some kindly smiles, a bow, and the Pope leaves the room. Our reception at the Vatican was over.

*****

Last evening visited Mrs. Greenough, wife of the celebrated sculptor. They have lived here many years. She is an interesting woman, but delicate as a lily. She talked much of Margaret Fuller, whom she had known well for many years.

We find many self-expatriated Americans here, first-class snobs, mostly a rich and terribly stuck-up gentry, hanging around the edge of Italian society, watching opportunity to pick up an alliance with somebody with some sort of a title. They are usually ashamed of their own countrymen, even those of them who are here, and regard themselves entirely too good to be Americans. It is a great pity in their minds that they were born in the United States at all, where, likely as anyway, their fathers made their fortunes selling hides and hominy.

*****

March 21.--Spent last evening till very late, sitting on the steps of Frank Simmons' studio, talking with W. W. Story, sculptor and poet. He is the finest talker I ever heard. Of course, he knows everything about Italy; he has lived here most of his life, and his "Roba di Roma" tells more worth knowing about Rome than any similar book ever written. We talked, too, of

America. He lamented that he had never achieved distinction in the United States as a poet. That, not sculpture, had been his first ambition. I told him he did not know how many loved his name at home for the poetry he had written. On my last trip over the sea, a young and discriminating newspaper man had envied me that I was going where I would know Story, the *poet*. He had committed "Antony and Cleopatra" to memory, repeated it to me walking on the ship deck one evening, and said it was the "best American poem." The incident gratified Mr. Story very much, as it should.

We spoke of the Washington monument at the capital. "It is nothing but a great, high smoke stack," he said. "There was a design offered, for a monument, that had some taste, art, grandeur about it, but the mullet-headed politicians, knowing nothing, and thinking they knew everything, naturally threw that aside."

There was but little outlook, he said, for any immediate realization of true art in America. "There was but one god there --money getting."

I liked Mr. Story's generosity of speech concerning other sculptors less famous than himself, and for poets with less renown than he believed he had. He is altogether one of the most agreeable men I ever knew. His studio is full of fine work that brings great prices, but it does not seem to me greater than the work of Frank Simmons, or even some of the statues of Ives and Rogers. There is a sea nymph at Ives' studio more beautiful than anything else I ever saw in marble.

We often go to the studio and the home of Randolph Rogers. He is an invalid, has been paralyzed, and sits most of his time in his chair; but he has a great, big, joyous heart, and is happy at seeing his friends. His fame is very wide. His "Blind Nydia" is one of the great things in marble. Very many copies of it have been made. They are everywhere. "Nydia" and his bronze doors at the Capitol in Washington, more than all else, made his reputation.

I have met no one in Rome who seemed to retain his real, joyous, bluff Americanism as Mr. Rogers does. He knows his art, but he has not forgotten his country.

His home is one of the most delightful here. He is justly proud of his wife, as she is proud of his art. "She must have been very beautiful in her youth," said an American innocently. "Yes," replied Mr. Rogers, "my wife is beautiful now."

The other morning occurred the wedding of his daughter to a worthy and handsome officer of the Italian army. Every hour he is expecting orders to go to Africa to help avenge the massacre of a lot of his countrymen.

Mr. Tilton, the American painter, showed us a Venetian scene yesterday of supreme loveliness, as most of his water scenes are. I never saw so much delicious coloring as is always in his pictures of the Adriatic.

He sells mostly to the English, and at great prices. He showed me his selling book, and I was astounded at what he got. It was pounds, where others of our artist friends got dollars.

Went to Elihu Vedder's studio. He received me very coolly at first, because he thought I mispronounced his name; a very important matter. Afterward, he took some pains to show me his work. It is certainly characteristic, at least, and original, and nobody ever misses guessing whose picture it is, if it should be from his brush.

March 25.--Mr. Pierpont, the Secretary of Legation, is down with the Roman fever. Strong and young and handsome as he was, constant late hours and cold stone floors were too much for him. He may never recover.

His coming here was almost a sensation, and no one ever got into "good society" in Rome so promptly. His handsome face, genial ways, good family and fine talents have made him welcome everywhere. He is a son of Attorney General Edwards Pierpont, of New York, once Minister to England.

They have taken him to the German hospital up by the Capitol. What makes his illness worse just now is that Mr. Astor, the Minister, has sent in his resignation and will go home at once.

April, 1884.--Went to the Island of Capri, only a couple of hours' sail from the most beautiful bay in the world. This is the spot where the Garden of Eden ought to have been.

Went to the Blue Grotto--wonderful! While floating about there in a little boat, I thought of T. Buchanan Read's lines:

Oh, happy ship to rise and dip
With the blue crystal at your lip

Just mere common existence ought to be a delight on Capri. The combination of romantic scene, delicious air, blue sky, and almost bluer sea, make it adorable.

One should need little to live on here, and I think the peasants indeed have little aside from fruits and olive oil and wine. The young women are strikingly beautiful.

Tiberius, when he built his palace up on top of this wonderful Isle of the Sea, at least knew where to find the beautiful.

Ischia, even more beautiful, if possible, is close by, and we look over and think of the terrible fate of its people only a few months ago.

In front of us is Naples, and, in sight, Vesuvius sullenly smokes away as if to remind us of the eternal peril to all who stay among these loveliest scenes of earth.

Naples.

We visited Pompeii, with its lifted mantle of ashes and cinder, that have helped mankind to patch out history. I was impressed by the extreme smallness of the Pompeiian houses. They look like little stone kitchens. Everything in the excavated city seems in miniature. One could think of a toy town built of stone, but supplied with everything wonderful of art and luxury.

I fail to see anything wonderful in unearthing Pompeii. It was easy to dig it out of its ashes. There is no lava there. And it would seem a question if two dozen people ever lost their lives in the disaster. It simply snowed ashes for a day or so, and why should people deliberately sit there and smother!

Paestum.

From the top of Capri we fancied we could almost see the temples of Paestum by the other bay, those temples without a history--those grandest ruins on the earth.

They want no history--their's a voice
Forever speaking to the heart of man.

And we thought of the Paestum roses, too, of indescribable fragrance, that bloom twice a year, and that have flourished there on the sickly desert a thousand years. No story like this in all the floral world.

*****

One time lately my wife admired very much a little water color of Mr. Tilton's. This morning he carried it up to her as a present from the artist. It will long be treasured as a remembrance of one of the most genial men in Rome, and of a delightful artist.

April 19.--Young Mr. Pierpont died two days ago, and that before his father and mother could reach him. They are still at sea. Yesterday afternoon he was buried from St. Paul's church in the Via Nazionale. The sorrow for his premature death was very sincere. Dr. Nevin read the service, assisted by the Master of Rugby School, and the pall bearers were the ambassadors of Austria, Germany and Belgium, with myself representing the United States. King Humbert was represented by the Duke of Fiano. The Italian Foreign Minister was also a pall bearer. There were many beautiful flowers by the casket. It was a sad burial, this putting into the grave a youth to whom the future had beckoned with such golden hand.

*****

Mr. Pierpont's death, and the resignation of Mr. Astor, put the affairs of the Legation into my care. The archives have been moved to the Consulate General, on Via Venti Settembre.

*****

April 25.--Governor and Mrs. Pierpont came yesterday, and I took them out to the Protestant Cemetery to look at the casket containing their son. It stood in a receiving vault covered with roses. It was a sad day!

This afternoon Governor Pierpont talked with me about supernatural things. He doubted them himself, and yet, he said that when he was Minister to London he rarely was at a dinner in England when some one at the table did not relate of something supernatural that had occurred to himself or else to some trustworthy friend. This fact must put people to thinking. Possibly there was something in it after all. Get it out of the hands of charlatans, and possibly we could lift the veil a little more than we imagine. If there is another world, spiritual, it need not be very far away.

*****

April 20.--The parties and the receptions and the balls go on this winter, just as if all Rome had nothing to do but have a good time.

The Journalists' ball the other night was most striking for its elegance, its diamonds, gowns, and its beautiful bejeweled women.

The German artists' masquerade ball was also beautiful. We went to both the same night.

The Roman theater is good, and spectacular opera is given this winter with great effect. "Excelsior" is the most gorgeously gotten up spectacle of dance and scenery I ever beheld. Its ballet possibly has never been approached.

A funny story is told here of Joaquin Miller. One afternoon he attended a reception at Miss B.'s. Two old maids, Italians, asked to be seated next the lion of the Sierras. They listened in utter astonishment, but with perfect gullibility, while he wickedly regaled them with immense stories of how he had galloped over the plains of his native country on the backs of wild buffaloes, how he had fought prairie fires, slain Indians and rescued maidens from captivity. The women were amazed, and with grateful hearts thanked their hostess for introducing them to so great a hero. The party over, all are gone, and Miss B. looks about the house. To her astonishment, the wild-eyed poet is there yet, standing alone by the dining-room table. She gently draws the portiere aside to look. He holds a glass of wine in his hand, and, as he balances it, and looks upon its color, he smiles and exclaims to himself, but in tones heard behind the curtain, "Holy Moses, how I did lie to those women."

*****

April 22.--Went to a party at Shakespeare Wood's the other night. He is correspondent of the London *Times*, and is an important man among foreigners in Rome. They say his salary is as good as a Minister's. I fear that is a mistake. Saw many noted people at his house--Lord Houghton, the poet and critic, the Trollopes and others.

Heard much talk against Gladstone. One English gentleman said, with apparent approval of a little group of English listeners, "The man ought to be shot for the good of England." It seemed inexplicable, impossible--so much hatred of the world's best Christian statesman.

Lord Houghton is a good, gray, old man, full of vivacity and with opinions of his own. He has renown in Italy, for he has been a great friend in the country's struggle for liberty, and his life of literature has had great reward.

Shakespeare Wood knows more about Rome and Italy than half the Italians themselves, and is besides an artist and an antiquarian.

Last evening I was invited to dine at the home of the celebrated Professor Moleschott. He is a distinguished author and a Roman Senator, though a born German. My invitation came as a result of a letter to him from my friend Johannes Scherr, the German author. Moleschott had once lived in Zurich.

This was an "evening" for certain delegates to a World's Congress of scientific and medical men. Dr. Sternberg, of Washington, was there. Few of the guests understood Italian. Moleschott seemed able to speak with each in his own tongue. Scherr's letter caused him to pay me no little attention, and he chatted with me considerably. He is the most remarkable looking man I ever saw. Has a head like a lion. He is short, stout, broad faced, and has big eyes, and low side whiskers. I asked him how on earth he could learn so many languages in addition to his enormous duties as a scientific writer, a constant lecturer, and an Italian Senator. "I don't learn them," he said; "I must absorb them. I have no time to learn them." "But you must have studied *English*," I replied. "You are too much of a master there, to be merely an absorber." "Well, yes, a little bit," he answered. "That is, I laid your English grammar on my dressing case mornings for a few weeks, and while I walked up and down the room putting on my clothes I got hold of your language."

He was one of the rare men we meet who seem to know everything. Observation great, memory powerful. What would the world be, if all men had Moleschott's intellect. Like Goethe, he has universal knowledge.

He passes our door daily in an open cab, and is always sitting with an open volume in his lap, and yet he sees and greets people and goes on with his reading.

House of Gold, Venice.

May 1, 1885.--I have this entry in my diary: "This day I resigned my post as Consul General of Italy and will soon leave the service, after many years of constant and faithful duty. These last weeks I have also had charge of the diplomatic affairs of our country here, and it is gratifying to receive, by the same mail that brings a letter asking my resignation, another letter expressing appreciation of some of my recent services."

On my arrival home in America, I found the following letter waiting me from General Sherman:

"ST. LOUIS, MO., June 29, 1885.

"DEAR BYERS:--I have your letter written at sea, in which you give me the first information I had received that you had been displaced at Rome. I knew, of course, it was bound to come, for party allegiance with us is stronger than patriotism, and the pendulum of time was bound to swing against us, and we will be lucky if we are not indicted for horse stealing and for the murder of men who resorted to arms to destroy the very Government of which now they are the main supporters. Of course, in due time the pendulum will swing back, but meantime, we must lie low, else history will record Jeff Davis the patriot, and Mr. Lincoln the usurper.

"I am glad to know that you propose to settle at Des Moines. It is a beautiful and seemingly prosperous place, and if you can engage in any business there, you will soon have reason to feel a sense of security in not being the slave of the State Department.

"We are all here now, but in a short time Mrs. Sherman and all the family will go to Lake Minnetonka for the summer. I have some business which will detain me here a while, when I will follow, but I have a positive engagement at Mansfield, Ohio, August 15; New York, August 20, and Chicago, September 9 and 10. So you see I am kept busy. I have long experience and declare that it is harder for me to maintain a modern family with fifty dependents and a thousand old soldiers claiming of right all I possess, than to command a hundred thousand men in battle. Still I expect to worry along a few years, till summoned to a final rest. I now merely write to welcome you back to your native land, and to express the hope that Mrs. Byers will soon regain her wonted health, and that you, too, will settle down with as much contentment as you can command, after your long sojourn abroad. Hoping you will notify me of your arrival at Oskaloosa and Des Moines, I venture to send you this to New Wilmington, Pa.

"Sincerely your friend,
W. T. SHERMAN."

Another letter of interest came from him:

"ST. LOUIS, MO., Sept. 30, 1885.

"DEAR BYERS:--Now I shall know where to find you. You are fully competent to manage your own interests, and I shall not commit the foolish mistake of proffering advice where it is not asked. I remember when money was worth 3 per cent a month (in California). It broke both lender and borrower, for the borrower simply gave up the houses and land mortgaged, and the lenders themselves became borrowers for the taxes. To-day money in the United States is worth 3 per cent per annum, and all over that rate is 'risk,' *not* interest. If I had money to lend, which I have not, I would not lend it on an Iowa farm at 8 per cent, but on a Government bond at 3 per cent, because I would conclude sooner or later I would have to take the Iowa farm, which would be an elephant. A farm is a good thing for a farmer, but a bad thing for an owner. Still I have good faith in the ultimate value of good farm land, because it yields annual crops, whereas mines and manufactories play out. My heavy expenses still go on. In St. Louis, we pay as taxes, full rent, and have to pay the objects of taxation direct. Thus our taxes are $2.50 on a full valuation, and we must in addition pay for watering the streets, for street-paving and improvements, for special police, for the militia and for schools. I can manage to make ends meet, but I wonder how a man can, in business, make profit enough to cover his family expenses. These economic questions will become the questions of the future.

"Mrs. Sherman is absent at the East, to visit Elly and Minnie. The rest of us are here. Love to all.

"Your friend,
W. T. SHERMAN."

In October he writes again:

"ST. LOUIS, MO., Oct 23, 1885.

"DEAR BYERS:--I feel easier on your account, since you tell me that you find the business in which you were about to embark, overdone. Nearly all the calamities which have overtaken families in America, can be traced to the credit system, which necessarily prevails. I had enough experience in it to put me on my guard, and I am firm in my faith in Shakespeare's 'Neither a borrower nor a lender be.' And the consequence is that to-day I owe no man a cent, and have no incidental obligations as indorser or bondsman. All my children know this, and while I give them liberally of what I have, they never dream of asking me to borrow or indorse.

"There is a great deal of wisdom in Dickens' character of Micawber. 'Income, £100; expenses, £99.19.6--result, happiness. Income, £100; expenses, £101.4.3--result, misery.' I quote from memory.

"If you and Mrs. Byers will be content with what you have, and live within your income, whether $1,800 or $6,000, your days will be long in the land of the living. Now, surely, even in Des Moines, you can supplement your income by the sale of occasional articles from your pen, which will add to your frugal fund most of the luxuries of life.

"In any and every event, I beg you will keep me advised of your progress, so long as I travel in this world of woe and mystery.

"Mrs. Sherman is now back from her visit to our married children at the East and I think we shall remain unchanged all winter. I have numerous calls, but generally answer that I am entitled to rest and mean to claim it.

"My best compliments to your good wife and son.

"Your friend,
W. T. SHERMAN."

CHAPTER XXVIII
1886

THE NORTH AMERICAN REVIEW ENGAGES ME TO EDIT SEVERAL CHAPTERS OF THE SHERMAN CORRESPONDENCE--SHERMAN WRITES AS TO MAGAZINES AND HIS BOOK--THE GENERAL INVITES ME TO COME AND STAY AT HIS HOME IN ST. LOUIS--HE OFFERS ME THE USE OF ALL HIS PAPERS--I PUBLISH ALSO IN THE REVIEW A PROSE NARRATIVE OF THE MARCH TO THE SEA--MRS. SHERMAN READS IT TO THE GENERAL--BUFFALO BILL--GENERAL GIVES ME HIS ARMY BADGE--NIGHTS IN SHERMAN'S OFFICE--CONVERSATIONS WITH HIM--LIFE IN THE SHERMAN HOME--THE GENERAL'S COMPLETE RECONCILIATION WITH HIS SON "TOM"--INTERESTING LETTERS FROM SHERMAN AS TO MAGAZINES--HIS FORTHCOMING BOOK--FARMS AND TAXES--WAR HISTORIES--GRANT'S BOOK--NEWSPAPERS--CHRISTMAS LETTER.

The interval between my resignation at Rome and my reappointment as Consul General for Switzerland was spent in my home in Iowa.

Early in 1886, the North American Review asked me to prepare and edit a series of General Sherman's letters for the magazine.

I received an interesting letter from the General about the tempting offers made to him by the magazines. They make offers of that kind to one man in a million, and only one man in a million could decline them. He mentions his forthcoming book.

"WASHINGTON, D. C., Feb. 3, 1886.

"DEAR BYERS:--I was glad to receive your letter of the 1st inst. It indicates a purpose to join in the throng now publishing articles about the war. Last year Rice, of the N. A. Review, offered me $1,000 for an article on Grant, which I declined and he obtained that of March for nothing. I hate controversy, but could not escape this with F----, who is an army officer, retired, and usually very accurate, but his denial to furnish me the source of his extract from one of my private letters led up to my reply in the March number. If you have read from the magazine itself, all right, but if you have only seen the newspaper extracts, I would like to have you get the Review itself and read the whole. The Century Magazine is also a very respectable vehicle for war stories and has tempted me with high offers in money, but I have resolved to keep out of the newspapers and magazines as far as they will let me, confining myself to the memoirs revised, which will be issued by the Appletons by May next. I have gone over all the proof and will now stand by it. The first and last chapters are new--as well as the index, maps and illustrations.

"We are all very well here and I shall regret to give up my own home here for a hotel in New York, but I shall never consent to housekeeping in New York.

"My best love to Mrs. Byers and the children.

"Truly your friend,
W. T. SHERMAN."

At the General's invitation I went to St. Louis, and for a time was a guest in his home as I had been before in Washington.

A few notes of the great commander's life at this time may not be amiss here.

General Sherman was now a retired officer. After a great life on the military stage, he had himself rung down the curtain. He was living in a comfortable, brown, two-story brick house, at 912 Garrison Avenue.

His simple little office, where he spent most of his time, was down in the basement, just as it had been in Washington. The same little sign bearing the simple words:

"Office of General Sherman"

was on one of the basement windows. In this room, on shelves and in cases, were all the records of his life--his memoranda of the war, military maps, correspondence. There were letters on file in that little room from eminent men all over the country. A magazine editor once offered $40,000 for permission to go down into that basement and pick out the letters he would like to print in his magazine. The editor even offered a thousand dollars for one certain, single letter there. It was never printed till its importance was gone.

One evening he came down into the basement where I was sitting, and taking his keys out of his pocket threw them on the table beside me, saying: "There, I trust you with everything; unlock everything; use what you want." The complete confidence thus placed in me, I recall with pride and affection. I recall, too, the responsibility I felt.

Night after night, day after day, I read among the letters, picking out only those that seemed of interest to the public, and to be perfectly proper to print.

At that time I edited for the North American Review six chapters of them. Nothing went without General Sherman's approval. He allowed his clerk, Mr. Barrett, to copy for me. Hundreds of the most entertaining letters I regarded it indiscreet to print at that time, and they have never been printed yet.

The General and myself sat there in the basement by the little open fire many a time till twelve or one o'clock at night; I looking through the almost thousands of letters and papers, he smoking a cigar and reading. The poems of Burns lay there on his desk all the time, because Burns was his favorite poet. Dickens and Scott, he read time and again; some of the stories once a year, he said.

When I would find something of especial interest among the letters, I would speak of it. He would stop reading and, for an hour, tell me all about it, and add interesting things concerning the writer. What would I not now give could my memory recall faithfully his talks to me in the silence of those nights. He suffered some with asthma, and it was always easier for him to sit up far into the night and talk, than to go to bed. Sometimes a wee drop from a black bottle in the back room refreshed us both, without harming either.

About this time, a few over-zealous friends of Grant, not satisfied with the world's recognition of his genius, were claiming for him the impossible merit of everything that happened in the war, even the origin of the March to the Sea. The claim was ridiculous, and I do not believe that General

Grant personally had anything to do with it. But I am sure that Sherman felt that Grant ought to have spoken at this juncture.

One evening I came across an autograph letter from Grant to Sherman, congratulating him on the achievement of the March to the Sea, "a campaign," in Grant's words, "the like of which has not been read of in past history." There was not a thought of claiming any of the glory for himself. Right beside it lay a letter from Robert E. Lee, telling how this movement of Sherman's resulted eventually in the fall of Richmond. Reading these, determined me, while with General Sherman in his home, to write, myself, an account of the March to the Sea, for the North American Review. My article was printed in the Review, September, 1887.

When it was finished I asked the General to listen to it. He sent upstairs one morning for Mrs. Sherman to come down and hear it also. "Let me read it aloud," said Mrs. Sherman. It was one of the delightful hours of my life, to sit there and hear the wife of the great soldier read to him my story of his March to the Sea. I watched his face while she read, and could see that his mind was again afire with the thought of the campaign. He made no important changes, and a note to the editor of the Review showed that he approved my paper fully.

Life went on in the General's family very much as at Washington. It was a happy, hospitable home. "Tom," the father now being reconciled to the idea of his being a priest, came up often from the college down town, and many were the interesting conversations I heard between the great soldier and his intellectual son. It seemed to me the same fire of intellect was in each, only it was all different in flame and purpose. Mrs. Sherman had a little office of her own upstairs, just as at her Washington home, where she devoted her energy to planning for the poor. She was a noble, unselfish woman, and her charities, unheralded to the world, did much to soften the hard lines of the unfortunate.

The General's health was not the very best. He was often taking such severe colds as even threatened his life. The doctors were uneasy, and Mrs. Sherman was on one or two occasions much alarmed. "Should such a misfortune occur," she said to me one morning after the breakfast, "should I survive him, I want you to undertake the publication of all my husband's papers and correspondence. He has told me of his affection for you many times, and you know my own." I was greatly touched by this new proof of confidence in me, but I could not but think that General Sherman had many years to live.

The General, simple in public life, was still simpler in his home. He came to breakfast mornings in his comfortable old slippers and wearing a shiny little morning coat that was more comfortable than decorative. After lunch at noon, he usually took an hour's nap and then went down in the basement to his work of answering letters. He answered everybody, and gave himself as much labor in this imposed letter writing as if he were well paid for it. Hundreds and hundreds of people asked him to help them get office, and hundreds asked him for money. He gave a great deal, and the giving helped to keep him a comparatively poor man. Mrs. Sherman told me how he kept accounts at certain Washington stores, and sent needy men there almost daily with orders for hats, coats, etc. His daughter Lizzie was one of the kindest and sweetest spirits I ever knew. She was almost a constant companion of her father in his many travels.

We had pleasant chats every morning at the breakfast table, though it was nearly impossible to get the General away from the basement and his newspaper, till Mrs. S. had the papers put on the table with the coffee. Then the General would read and comment. He regarded the press almost as a necessary evil. Few of his comments were complimentary to it. He had a horror of reporters.

A great railroad strike was going on. Some sensational newspapers in St. Louis were helping to keep it up by encouraging the strikers. A month before, the same journals had been obsequious to the railroads. "Some day," said the General one morning, throwing down the newspaper, "these pusillanimous scoundrels of editors will be for calling on me and on the country to save them from the very ruin they are now encouraging. They are pulling the house down on their own heads. If it could fall on them, only! But little newspapers care for the sorrow they carry to human breasts, if they can only start a sensation."

He hated professional politicians even as much as such editors, but he discriminated between a man going to Congress for bread and butter, and a man who tried to labor for his country.

Even Blaine, whom he so cordially honored, he thought a spoilsman at times, not always a statesman.

In the home here, Mrs. Sherman called him "Cump," and that was the title he liked to hear. The name conveyed something dearer and better to him than titles and rank. He had no love for any of these empty sounding baubles, anyway, and never sought a promotion in his life.

One evening he was to address the Ransom Grand Army Post at St. Louis, and in the name of some patriotic man present a flag. He asked me to go along. After supper I came down and found him dressed and waiting for me in the drawing-room. "Where is your Grand Army badge?" he asked, observing I had none. I explained that mine was at home in Iowa. "You must have one," he said, "I'll give you this," and taking the emblem from his breast he fastened it on my coat. I treasure it still. It is an heirloom for my son.

He took me to see Buffalo Bill, the Indian fighter, one day. It was at the Fair Ground. The scout came to the General's box with all the fair manner of a high-born gentleman, saluted, bowed, advanced, took the extended hand and met a genuine soldier's greeting. Sherman had known him on the plains, and respected him as a man of worth. "That man's a genius," he said, when Cody went down to the ring, "and he believes in himself. That's half the battle of life." Sherman, like Buffalo Bill, believed in himself. He knew what he could do, and did it, and asked neither praise nor pay.

That evening, one of Sherman's daughters and a girl friend visiting in the family, danced with Buffalo Bill at a great ball. "He was the best dancer of them all," said one of the girls on coming home. "*Just too lovely for anything*," added the other. And this was the man of the prairies, the hunter, the scout. Environment doesn't count for anything, after all.

One day while at the Shermans, a friend, Mr. Haydock, asked me to go with him to see Grant's log house. It is on the old Dent farm in the woods, seven miles southwest of the city. This now neglected land was given to Mrs. Grant by her father, at her marriage. When Grant was thirty-two, he saw no prospects ahead of him in the army; so he resigned and went out here in the woods to live. "I had no means to stock the farm," he wrote later, "and a house had to be built. I worked very hard, never losing a day because of bad weather. If nothing else could be done, I would put a load of wood on the wagon and take it to the city for sale." For four years, Grant and his family lived this obscure life here in a little log cabin he built with his own hands.

The cabin is now hard to find. The road is deserted, the yard is overgrown with tall grass, straggling rose bushes bloom in what was once a garden; the windows of the cabin are gone, the doors stand open.

Grant cut the trees, prepared and hauled the logs for the cabin himself, and a hired hand helped him to put them up. It is a typical Southern log house, one and a half stories high, two rooms below, separated by an open hall, two rooms above. There is no history of Grant's life, during the years he struggled to make a living on this lonesome backwoods farm. Grant seldom alluded to it himself.

While walking over the deserted cabin and yard, I saw in my mind its whilom owner, the guest of peoples and potentates.

Sherman had an extravagant opinion of General Grant's abilities. "Grant was the one level-headed man among us all," he said to me one night, down in the basement of his home. Sherman went to the opera because he was fond of music, though he could not sing a note. If he kissed the pretty women behind the scenes sometimes, or more likely in front of the scenes, it was because the pretty women kissed him. I never saw a man so run after by womankind in my life. It was a great honor to have him touch their hands, their lips. Once in Switzerland, when he was leaving Bern on a train, the whole crowd of American women at the depot, old and young, pretty and ugly, children and all, kissed him.

When I was leaving his home at St. Louis, Miss Lizzie said I should have something to remember my visit by. "Then I want something from the little basement," I said, "there is where I have spent most of my time." "Papa, why not give him your paper weight." It was a little bronze bust of General Grant that he had used on his desk for many years. It has been mine since that evening, though I needed nothing to remind me forever of the hours spent far into the night down in the basement of the Sherman home.

In April, I received an interesting letter from him on taxation:

"St. Louis, Mo., April 25, 1886.

"Dear Byers:--I have your letter of the 18th, and though I have nothing to tell you, will answer. I understand that your article on the March to the Sea will be in the North American Review for May, and I will look for it. It might have been better had you applied to the Century Magazine, which seems to invite contributions illustrative of the war, though it seems partial to our adversaries. The absence of Mr. Rice in Europe, too, may be one cause of a relaxed interest in such articles as you could supply. J. R. is rather the workman than the editor, and is governed chiefly by the notoriety of the contribution rather than by the merit of the article.

"Hold on to your farm. This removal to the cheaper land of Dakota will not last long, as that is devoid of wood, and cold in the extreme. As soon as the few inviting places west are filled up, the tide will set back to Iowa. But I really do fear now an internal cause of the diminished value of land. Instead of supporting one government as in Europe, we have to support five--National, State, County, Township and Municipal--each of which expects for its support enough taxes for the whole. We are merely the nominal owners. The aggregate taxes here and with you, I infer, are equal to rent, and the question is: Who owns the farm? I infer the State does, and the nominal owner is merely the tenant at will. This fact, with the labor organizations, may bring about conflicts such as desolated Asia, hundreds, if not thousands of years ago.

"I will be in Chicago Decoration Day, Indianapolis June 2d, San Francisco Aug. 3–6, in Washington Territory and British Columbia till September, when I must come to Rock Island for the annual meeting of the Army of the Tennessee, Sept. 15–16, then for New York.

"Mrs. Sherman will go East about July 1st, and we will all meet in New York about Sept. 20th. I shall expect to see you at Rock Island.

"With best compliments to Mrs. Byers, and best wishes for your health and success.

"Truly your friend,
W. T. Sherman."

Later, he wrote me his views on newspapers and war books:

"St. Louis, Mo., June 11, 1886.

"Dear Byers:--I have your letter of the 8th, and note that you are now in correspondence with two of the best monthlies of the country. I feel assured that you will get along, though the speculation of buying young cattle and feeding them on your own land is a better business. The newspapers of our country have been as the morning mist, absolutely lost or dissipated by the noonday sun. The monthlies may hang on a little longer. And only printed volumes with indexes, collected in libraries, will be accepted as approximate truth.

"Grant's book will of course survive all time. Mine, Sheridan's and a few others will be auxiliary, but the great mass of books purporting to give the history of especial corps, regiments and even individuals, will be swept aside, because the world now demands condensation, and probably in fifty years, one hundred pages will be all that the world will allow for the history of the Civil War. Meantime, you can interest and entertain your readers, for which the journals can pay you what you need, money.

"But I would not advise you to attempt any material change of the public judgment, as recorded by Grant. I prefer, when you use any letter of mine, or any of Grant's to me, that you insist on their being used with your text, not theirs. If you consent to their expurgating any special letter, the editor will use it with his own introduction, to justify himself in some conclusion heretofore published. I have experienced this and could not find fault, as it was explained by the usual motives for human action. I would insist on the publication of your articles as you made them, with literal or immaterial corrections, when convinced of their necessity.

"We are now pretty well packed up, and no doubt we will be ready for breaking up here July 1st, after which my address will be Palace Hotel, San Francisco. Present us all kindly to Mrs. Byers and the boy, and believe me that I shall always feel a personal interest in your welfare.

"Your friend,
W. T. Sherman."

On Christmas, he sent me this kindly note:

"NEW YORK, Dec. 24, 1886.

"DEAR BYERS:--I was very glad to receive your kind letter of the 20th, and assure you of my continued interest and affection, wishing you and yours all earthly happiness.

"The task on which you have entered, 'Iowa in War Times,' will afford you full employment for a year and more, and I trust with reasonable profit. Remember that 'brevity is the soul of wit,' and condensation is now the true aim of history. Each regiment will expect you to include a diary of its life, but I know you have industry and patience enough to generalize.

"I shall look out for your article in the North American. I was tempted only yesterday by the Century Magazine to furnish an article on that very subject, which I declined in a letter at some length, claiming that my Memoirs were as full as I can reproduce, and preferring that others like yourself should present the facts in a more agreeable form. To ward off other applicants I have consented to the publication of that letter.

"Truly your friend,
W. T. SHERMAN."

The General had now given up his beautiful home in St. Louis, and was about to move to New York. It turned out to be, as he hoped it would, his last change of residence. Again he wrote me. It was his last letter to me from St. Louis, and again he touched on the troubles he had had with American newspapers. In fact his experiences with newspaper correspondents during the war had been such as to make him hate the entire fraternity. There were times when he had unceremoniously driven them away from his army, as mischief makers and traitors.

"ST. LOUIS, MO., June 29, 1886.

"DEAR BYERS:--I have your letter of the 22d, with copy of yours to R. * * *

"I am willing to risk B.'s preface to any of your articles. He has been always most friendly to me, and I should always fear his *over* praise, rather than his adverse criticisms. Nevertheless, you are right in claiming that your 'articles' should be published as written by you. The editor has the privilege of calling attention to the subject-matter of his special 'articles,' but the article itself should not be 'coupled' with matter written by any outsider before publication and after preparation.

"The chief trouble of my life has been in dealing with newspapers and periodicals. They want something 'sensational,' which will sell as an article of commerce, and their self-interest blinds them to the personal consequences of the publications. To sell 50, 500 or 5,000 of this paper or magazine, is their business. If they make sad a hundred or a million of hearts, it is to them of no consequence. Lizzie and I will be off for California July 1st. Mrs. Sherman and Cump for Marietta, Lancaster Co., Pa., July 2d. You may not hear of or from me till I reach Rock Island, Sept. 15–16. On my arrival at San Francisco, I can buy the North American Review, so you need not send me a copy. We are all now at the Lindell Hotel, and will scatter as I have indicated, in two more days. An excellent family has taken our home for three years, with the privilege of three more--in fact beyond our lives, at $1,500 a year, enough to pay taxes and repairs. I think we have made a fatal mistake, but if our youngest son can thereby be made a real lawyer and man, I will be content. My career is ended.

"Wishing you and yours all the happiness possible,

"I am sincerely your friend,
W. T. SHERMAN."

CHAPTER XXIX
1887–90

AN INTERESTING LETTER FROM GENERAL GRANT--SHERMAN LIVING IN NEW YORK--HIS IMMENSE POPULARITY WITH ALL AMERICANS--LETTERS FROM HIM--EXHIBITED LIKE A CIRCUS--NO UNION MAN LEFT IN FOREIGN SERVICE BY CLEVELAND--HE WRITES FOR THE MAGAZINES--MAGAZINES AGAIN--APPROVES MY ARTICLE IN THE NORTH AMERICAN REVIEW ON THE MARCH TO THE SEA--HUMBLEST UNION MAN BETTER PATRIOT THAN THE PROUDEST SOUTH CAROLINA REBEL--SHERIDAN DYING--CONGRESS SHOULD MAKE RANK OF LIEUTENANT GENERAL PERMANENT--HIS RECEPTION AT COLUMBUS--DEATH OF MRS. SHERMAN--ABOUT HIS MEMOIRS--NO PROFIT--THE ARMY OF THE TENNESSEE AT CINCINNATI--MY POEM THERE--AN ODD INTERVIEW AT THE WHITE HOUSE--CONVERSATIONS WITH SECRETARY BLAINE--DEATH OF THE GREAT GENERAL--SPEECHES ABOUT HIM IN THE SENATE--I AM AGAIN APPOINTED TO SWITZERLAND.

I was now in the West working on my "Iowa in War Times" and sometimes writing an article for the magazines.

Many documents and important autograph letters were put in my hands from all over the country. One of the most interesting of these was from General Grant. It has never been printed and I give it here because it was possibly the only letter he ever wrote during a battle. It was at Black River bridge, Grant was sitting on his horse, Lawler's brigade had just made a successful charge on the intrenchments. An officer from the Headquarters at Washington rides up to the General with an important order. It is for him to abandon his Vicksburg campaign, and join Banks with his army. "Do you see that charge?" said the General. "You are too late." He wrote this letter sitting there on his saddle, and the Vicksburg battles and successes followed. Had Grant gone to Banks, the latter would have been chief in command. Grant's great career would not have had even a beginning. This very minute was the great crisis in General Grant's life!

May 17th, 10:30 A. M.

Dear Gen.:

Lawler's brigade stormed the enemy's works a few minutes since, carried it, capturing from 2,000 to 3,000 prisoners, 10 guns so far as heard from, and probably more will be found. The enemy have fired both bridges.

A. J. Smith captured 10 guns this morning, with teams, men and ammunition.

I send you a note from Col. Wright.

Yours,
U. S. Grant,
Maj. Gen.

Maj. Gen. Sherman,
Com'd'g 17th Army Corps.

I still received an occasional letter from General Sherman. As these were often strong, characteristic and interesting, I copy a number.

He was now living in the Fifth Avenue Hotel, New York, so far as it could be said that he was living anywhere, for his presence was in such demand at public occasions, all over the country, as to make any lengthy stay at home an impossibility. He was beyond all doubt the most loved man at this time in the United States. No American knew so many people by face, and by name. No face was so familiar to almost everybody as was the face of "Uncle Billy Sherman." The soldiers of the Civil War, of whom a million were still alive, absolutely adored their leader. There was no place so high, no post so honored, that his people would not have pressed it upon him, had he been willing to accept it. To no other living American was the Presidency ever offered without the seeking. No other American was ever great enough to turn aside from the proffered gift.

With all this great place in the hearts of a whole people, he went about his daily life with a simplicity that astonished all; a simplicity of which only true greatness is capable. In the great army processions at the reunions, where he might have led the van, borne on the shoulders of his victorious veterans, he marched afoot in the dust, along with the boys he had led from Atlanta to the sea.

Political glory had no charm for him, and the huzzahs of the multitude he measured for what they were worth. It was my good fortune to know him in his real heart, his inside life, and a man less moved by hopes of applause it seemed to me could not be imagined. He constantly saw before him the vanity of human greatness. To him, a modest life of simple things, well done, was as great as a life glowing with renown. The glory that comes from achievement counted as little. The good that follows doing right for right's sake, to him was everything. Everything he ever did, or said, or wrote, confirmed this.

He was an American, too, all over, and a loyal one. When an English General attempted to belittle the North, and to foist Lee onto the top of the victor's column, Sherman answered him.

The following letters refer to this and to his article on "The Grand Strategy of the War:"

"NEW YORK, May 1, 1887.

"DEAR BYERS:--I received your letter of April 24th some days ago, and kept it for Sunday's answering. Of course I could not go to Dubuque on the occasion of the meeting of the G. A. R. and of the remnant of the 13th Infantry. To them, it may seem a neglect, but were I to accept one invitation in the hundred, I would have to abandon family, friends and all peace, to become a vagrant. I am now advertised like Barnum's circus, at Cincinnati, May 4; at Philadelphia *same day*, and at Washington May 11–12, for the dedication of the Garfield statue, all *a la* Pickwick, at my own expense. As soon as I had become domiciled in New York, I was assailed by all the magazines and newspapers to become a regular contributor, at a compensation represented by the algebraic expression $x/2$, but of course I declined with thanks. Yet when General Lord Wolseley's article in Macmillan's March number was published, claiming for Lee the maximum honors, to tower high above every man of this country, I could not resist the temptation to reply, and this is in the May number of the North

American. I suppose you are a subscriber, or can obtain a copy. I would like to have your judgment. Also the Century Magazine wanted an article on 'The Grand Strategy of the War,' which I prepared with some care, and they may publish in the June number, or may withhold as a kind of preface to their intended publication of all the military publications of the past four years. In the multitude of counsels there may be wisdom, at all events we had better put forth all we have, lest the Rebels succeed in their claims to have been the simon pure patriots and 'Union Men' of our day and generation. They have partially succeeded, and may completely succeed, for to-day not a single Union man represents the United States in foreign lands, and the logical conclusion is that we were wrong, and our opponents right. So Lord Wolseley is not to be blamed for assuming Lee as the great hero of the Civil War in America. The war of muskets long since subsided, now the war of the pen must begin, else the remnant of the Union Army must pass down to history as barbarians.

"Your friend,
W. T. SHERMAN."

*****

"ARMY BUILDING, NEW YORK, May 21, 1887.

"DEAR BYERS:--I have received your letter of May 5th, and have seen Thorndike Rice about your articles, but did not tell him all you wrote. I think Rice is too much engrossed with social life to give much of his personal attention to the North American. All that I could extricate out of him was that your article would appear as early as possible. I sometimes pity these magazine men who have to read cords of manuscript, and out of the mass choose that which will pay. The great mass of work devolves on subordinates, and the editor finally indicates what shall be 'set up.' Even after that, articles are kept hanging fire. You had better let what you have done stand, and in future watch the current of the public thought, prepare your papers, and deal with that magazine which you consider fairest.

"Now as to my May number, it was suggested by Thorndike Rice in a telegram from Washington. I at first positively declined, but when I got the full text of Wolseley's article in Macmillan's Magazine, I saw somebody must answer, and all turned to me. I wrote it one Sunday, and gave it to Rice for $500. If I had charged a thousand, he would have paid it. In like manner my article on the Grand Strategy of the War is longer, better, and I charged the Century Magazine $1,000 for it. It was designed to comprehend the whole series of War Articles to be bound in a volume.10 It may appear in the August number of the Century.

"I am besieged by the magazines, but shall reserve myself for chance shots like this of Wolseley's. I am not willing to rake among old embers for new fire.

"Mrs. Sherman and Rachel are now at Detroit, on a visit to Tom. Lizzie and I are at the Fifth Avenue Hotel. All go to Lake Hotel, Lake George, N. Y., early in June. I will retain my room, and circulate generally. I ordered the Appletons to send you my second edition, in the theory that Mrs. S. had not done so. Please inscribe it to your son, on the blank page. You can substitute therefor at some time one of my letters, which will answer for an autograph. It is a good deal of trouble to go to the Appletons to do this in person.

"Love to all

"Yours truly,
W. T. SHERMAN."

Shortly, I was gratified to receive from him a letter complimentary to my article in the North American Review, describing his great campaign.

"NEW YORK, Aug. 26, 1887.

"DEAR BYERS:--In coming from my office in the Army Building, I stopped at the office of the North American Review, to see Thorndike Rice, but he was away at Newport, and his partner, Redpath, gave me an advance copy of the September number, which contains your article, 'March to the Sea.' It reads to me very well, condensed, strong and well sustained by proofs. I think it will command large attention, and I trust it will lead to profitable employment for your pen. The leading events of the war are now accepted, are crystallizing into pages, and even paragraphs. The public is tired of minute details, especially to bolster up this or that man. You have, in the compress of six or eight pages, given all that the memory of the ordinary reader can retain. I have already put it in a sealed envelope, addressed to my daughter Lizzie, who reads and appreciates everything from you. She, with her mamma, Rachel and Cump, has been up at Lake George since June. I have been up three times. Spent last week there, but am now here preparing for the Detroit meeting, Sept. 14–15, as also the G. A. R. Encampment at St. Louis, Sept. 25–28. If you come to St. Louis then, you will find me at Henry Hitchcock's, corner of Fifteenth and Lucas Place.

"As always your friend,
W. T. SHERMAN."

In February of 1888, General Sherman wrote me some very decided views he had, as to the difference between loyal men and disloyal men.

"NEW YORK, Feb. 10, 1888.

"DEAR BYERS:--I have your letter of the 5th, and as I have staid indoors to-day for the express purpose of answering a batch of kind messages sent me on my sixty-eighth birthday, I answer yours in its turn.

"Of course I am pleased to know that you approve my Century article. It would have seemed more opportune had it been printed a year in advance, as it was written at the same time as my Wolseley article. But the editors paid me for it, and could use it for their interests, and at their own time. It looks to me as if the Southern men will succeed, not only in controlling the history of the war, but in achieving the government of this country, notwithstanding we won the battles. Our Northern people split up on questions of minor interest, whereas they have skilled leaders who control 'their people,' and by throwing their vote into one or other of the Northern factions, actually govern both. This is none of my business, and I cannot help it. So long as I live, I will hold the most humble Union man as a better patriot than the proudest Carolinian of South Carolina. Wade Hampton is out in another blast against me for cruelty and inhumanity during the 'March.' The people of Georgia bore their affliction with some manliness, but in South Carolina from the Savannah River to the State line, the people whined like Curs, and Wade Hampton's resistance was so feeble as to excite our contempt. I shall not notice his paper, meant for home consumption, but if he attempt to enlarge his sphere, I will give him a blast of the truth, as you and hundreds know it.

"I shall be glad if you come East, and it may be you can secure a better audience here than from Iowa. The time will come when the Mississippi Valley States will assert their supremacy in literature, as now in the products of the soil, but the time is not yet, and may not be in my day.

"We are all reasonably well except Mrs. Sherman. Wishing you and yours all the happiness possible, I am truly

"Your friend,
W. T. SHERMAN."

In June, General Sheridan was dying, and his great comrade in arms sent me this little note. My book, "Iowa in War Times," had just appeared, and a copy was sent to him.

"NEW YORK, June 2, 1888.

"DEAR BYERS:--I received by due course of mail your letter of May 27th and yesterday came to me at the Fifth Avenue Hotel the volume, 'Iowa in War Times.' I have cast my eye over it, and recognize most of the illustrations. The print, paper, etc., all seem good, and I know the text will be even better. It is hardly possible that I can read this volume in the whole, but I will have occasion to refer to parts, to compare with other accounts of the same general events.

"General Sheridan's extreme illness has caused universal grief. I hear daily by telegraph from his brother, Colonel Sheridan, and have just sent a message of congratulations at his promotion to the full rank of 'General.' But honestly I feel that it was too late to carry with it much compliment. All hope of his recovery seems to be abandoned, and every morning I wake, expecting to find the papers in mourning.

"Congress ought to make the rank of Lieutenant General permanent. It is simply dishonest for the country to compel a Major General to do the work of a Lieutenant General, just as in the war hundreds of Colonels had to command brigades and divisions.

"Mrs. Sherman is not so well, but went yesterday to make a month's visit to our daughter Elly near Philadelphia. Rachel and Lizzie are with me at the Fifth Avenue Hotel.

"Give my best love to Mrs. Byers and the family.

"Always your friend,
W. T. SHERMAN."

By September the Shermans were in their new home in New York, at Seventy-first Street. After all, they were keeping house again. The General had had enough of expensive and fashionable hotels. He had been homeless longer than he cared to be. He describes this house in his letter of the 16th. I was also glad to have his approval of my "Iowa in War Times."

"No. 75 West 71st St.
"NEW YORK, Sept. 16, 1888.

"DEAR BYERS:--When at Columbus, your letter of Sept. 1st was handed me by Maj. Loring, at a time when I was chased from corner to corner as though I had just escaped the penitentiary. I fear the Major thought me neglectful of him and his letter. Let him put himself in my place. Forty thousand ex-soldiers and sixty thousand strangers were added to the resident population, all bent on seeing the sights, of which I was one. Instead of dying out, the interest in the war and its actors seems to grow with time. I was not allowed time to eat or sleep, much less read and write letters, but I escaped alive and should be grateful.

"I am now in our new house, not as large as that in St. Louis, but better located, near Central Park and near the Sixth Avenue Elevated R.R. Four full stories and basement, in which I have my office with all my books and papers. Not divided as they were when I was at the Fifth Avenue Hotel.

"The interior arrangements are not yet complete, so the family is away, but by the middle of next week it will be all ready and the family will come. I hope this is my last change on earth.

"I have at intervals found time to read your volume, 'Iowa in War Times,' and congratulate you in having succeeded in giving to each regiment and organization a fair measure of space, and yet preserved the general authenticity of events. I hope the book pays you proportionately to your labor and expense. As now established with Mr. Barrett I can always supply you dates, facts and figures, should you still pursue your literary labors.

"With love to the family, I am, etc.,

W. T. SHERMAN."

Mrs. Sherman's health had been failing somewhat for months, but nothing absolutely serious was anticipated till, unexpectedly, she was worse in the mid-winter. Then the end came so suddenly that some of her children could not reach New York in time to see her passing away.

I was in California, and shortly received this reply to my letter of sympathy:

"NEW YORK, Dec. 19, 1888.

"MY DEAR BYERS:--Your letter of sympathy is here. Mrs. Sherman had long been ailing from heart trouble and general disability, and everything that could be done for her relief was willingly offered by me and the children. I did not realize any danger until the day before her death, when she began to fail very perceptibly, and I at once telegraphed to the absent members of the family to join us at once. Neither Mrs. Fitch, Mrs. Thackera, or Tom reached home in time to see their mother alive. The remainder of us were at the death-bed, and were witnesses of a painless and peaceful end. We had learned that there was no possibility of her ever fully recovering, and as she therefore must have contended with much pain and suffering, our anguish at her demise was somewhat assuaged.

"Every courtesy was extended the funeral party on its sorrowful journey to and from St. Louis, Mr. Roberts, President of the Penn. R. R., excelling in his kind and accepted offer of his private car. At St. Louis, all preliminaries had been carefully attended to by Messrs. Jas. Yeatman and Geo. D. Capen, so that we were enabled to start on the return trip the same evening.

"I well know the respect and honor with which Mrs. Sherman held you at all times, and in which we all shared, and I beg you now to be assured of our continued affection and deep interest in all that concerns you and yours.

"Sincerely your friend,
W. T. SHERMAN."

In September of 1889 the Army of the Tennessee was to hold its reunion and banquet at Cincinnati. I was elected to deliver an original poem for the occasion. As General Sherman was president of the Association, I sent a copy of my poem to him in advance. It was called "The Tramp of Sherman's Army." I was greatly interested to receive the copy back from him, with marginal notes and suggestions for changes written over it, and even a couple of new lines of his *own composition*. Possibly, it was the only time General Sherman ever indulged in *writing poetry*.

When the reunion took place, many great characters sat upon the stage--Cox, Logan, Dodge, Howard, Sherman and many others of the great war heroes. At the tables sat hundreds whose names had been known in the Civil War.

The toasts consisted of stanzas from "Sherman's March to the Sea." They were elegantly painted by hand on white satin, on which also was traced in gold the route of that famous March. Each toast was responded to by the particular General who had commanded at the point described in the verse. General Sherman, as president, made the first speech.

He then introduced me to the audience, and I recited my poem, "The Tramp of Sherman's Army," with bugle strain accompaniment. Its reception showed that the enthusiasm for war ballads had not died out. Each morning of the reunion the officers of the Army of the Tennessee, preceded by a drum corps or a band, walked in line from the Burnett House over to the hall where they held their meetings. Though Sherman was there, and many other distinguished men, it was almost a sad and pathetic sight as they walked together in the middle of the street, death had so thinned the line and reduced the number! Some of the onlookers did not realize what men were marching there, what names for history, or that among that peaceful looking little band were veterans who had led great armies to battle.

*****

March, 1888.--With Mr. Harrison's installation at the White House, I resolved to again, if possible, enter the service abroad. In the meantime, my military book of Iowa had not been a source of profit. One large edition sold, that was all. It seemed I was not alone in receiving no great income from war books. General Sherman, speaking of his own experience, wrote the following letter:

"NEW YORK, June 14, 1890.

"DEAR BYERS:--I have just received your letter, enclosing the programme of exercises for the 18th. I see so many boys nowadays, who were born after the war, that I am hardened. It so happens that my youngest, Cump, born at St. Louis, since the war, is being examined to-day for admission to the bar. I am also just back from West Point, where I saw the corps of cadets, about three hundred, strong, brawny boys, all born since the war, who now look up to me as a stray souvenir of a bygone age.

"I am sorry to learn that your book, 'Iowa in War Times,' has not proven more profitable. Your case is not *exceptional*, as I have good reason to know. So many expect me to present copies of my 'Memoirs,' ignorant of the fact that the publisher gets nine-tenths, the author one-tenth, so that when I present a copy it amounts to my buying it at 80 cents less than the common purchaser. My annual receipts from Sherman's Memoirs don't pay one-quarter of traveling expenses *demanded* at the Army Reunion each year. The same is true of Sheridan's and other war books. Grant's case is exceptional, because purchasers believe they contribute to the support of his family.

"Of course I know nothing of your prospects for a mission or consulate. I infer the present administration, like all others, must use offices to pay for active political work.

"Present me kindly to Mrs. Byers. Lizzie is now absent on a visit to her sister, Mrs. Thackera, at Cape May. Rachel is at home, and we generally have visitors.

"Sincerely your friend,
W. T. SHERMAN."

Senator James F. Wilson, who had been a true friend in all the years that I had been in Europe, took me to the Executive Mansion one day, to introduce me to the President. It was a curious meeting that morning. I had never seen Mr. Harrison, and we waited with interest in the anteroom of his private office. The place was full of grave looking Senators. It might have been a funeral.

Mr. W. and I stood half an hour waiting among the rest. I wondered why the President's door did not open. All the time there was a little low buzzing going on among some of the waiting ones, and I noticed a few slip up and whisper to a very sober looking little man, in a corner by the window. I supposed him to be a Senator. There would be some low talk with him, a stiff bow, and then some other Senator would slip up and go through the same performance. At last I whispered to Mr. Wilson, "Who is that man by the window?" "Why, that is the President," he answered, to my complete astonishment. We had been in his presence all the time, and I had not known it. Now my attention was doubly fixed on him. Here was a quiet little man in the corner, ruling seventy millions of people. He seemed to indicate, by an extra glance, who might approach him next. I thought the Senators were all afraid of him, judging from the humble way in which they walked to the corner, and the very prompt manner in which they went away. There was not a smile on anybody's face, and all was silence. Had they all been stepping up to take a last look at somebody's corpse, the scene could not have been very different. If he actually promised some Senator something, there was no sign of the promise on his face.

After a while, he glanced over to Senator Wilson. We were but a few feet away. Mr. W. went up and spoke in a low voice, telling him, as I now know, something of the propriety of appointing men of experience to the service, and suggesting my name. Not a muscle moved on the President's face. It is no go for me, I said to myself. Then Mr. Wilson said, a little louder: "Now, Mr. President, let me present Mr. Byers." I heard him and stepped forward. I expressed the honor done me, and he mechanically took my hand; but, as if taking a second thought on the matter, he looked over my shoulder at somebody else, and, without saying a word, simply let go. My interview with the President of the United States was over. I laugh about it yet. "It did not promise much, did it?" I said to the Senator, as we went out. "Well, no, nothing extremely definite, or to count on," replied Mr. Wilson. "But he never says much, and means much more than he says. He is icy with everybody, you saw that?" Yes, I *thought I did*. A year went by and I did not try it again. A place was offered me in South America, but I did not care for it. Then one morning Mr. Wilson said, "We will go and see Mr. Blaine." The interview was absolutely the opposite of the one at the White House. Secretary Blaine had great esteem for the Iowa Senator, as did every one who knew him. He invited us both to come and visit him the next morning, at his private house. It was at the corner of Lafayette Square, opposite the Treasury. While we waited in the drawing-room I forgot for the moment what I had come for. I was only thinking of the singular history of that house.

Upstairs was the room where the attempt on Secretary Seward's life was made, the night Lincoln was assassinated. Out there in front of the door, Key was killed by General Sickles. At this moment, the house was the home of the most noted living American statesman.

Shortly Mr. Blaine entered, all cheer and sunshine. He was a handsome man, with his fine erect form, his intellectual face, his genial smile, his great, big heart. He did not need the Presidency to make him great. Though able for very hard work still, he was looking very white in the face, his hair was quite gray. He talked to us for a time about the need of keeping well. Did he have premonitions then? "Never sleep in a room without a window raised, be it ever so little," he said, "and don't go to late night banquets in crowded rooms. Secretary Windom," he went on, "has been murdered by trying to please crowds, speaking to them when he ought to have been in bed. I am done letting people make an exhibition of me. I will never, never sit in a room full of smokers again, and sacrifice health for others' curiosity. That's all they want of public men in such places, and one can die at it just as Windom has done."[11]

After a while I wondered if the Secretary had forgotten the object of our call. Senator Wilson hinted at it at last, and Mr. Blaine got up, walked about the room and said: "Really, now, I have been too busy to keep my promise." He asked us to come to him again, and fixed the morning. "Bring with you the consular list and we will go all over it together." He also spoke of a kind letter on file in my interests from General Sherman, who was then very ill in New York.

That afternoon, while on a street car going over to the Capitol, I heard the conductor tell a passenger that General Sherman was dead. I was greatly moved and pained. A thousand instances of his friendship for me rushed through my mind. In a few minutes I heard, from a seat in the Senate Gallery, the eulogiums pronounced by Senators Evarts, Hawley and Manderson. Hawley almost broke down in tears. The Senate adjourned, and probably every loyal heart in America was in sorrow. The Southerners in the Senate that afternoon, sat still, and heard the eulogies on Sherman in perfect silence. I wondered that not one of them had the nobility to rise in his seat and speak of the great dead.

I went to New York and on the morning of the funeral was with the family at the Sherman home. In the little back parlor, in the full uniform of his highest rank, lay the commander of the March to the Sea. Candles burned around his coffin in the darkened chamber. While I was standing there, looking at his face, his son, Father Thomas E. Sherman, who had that moment reached home from Europe, came into the room. He embraced me, for we had many mutual memories.

A short Catholic service was held by the children that morning over all that was left of their illustrious father. They were all sincere Catholics. The mother, devoted to the same church, had died in the room upstairs. The father had been reconciled to his children's kind of religion. He was not a professor of any creed himself, and for his children to have this farewell ceremony, conducted by his own son, seemed in every way appropriate.

That afternoon, New York City and the people of America buried General Sherman. A more imposing funeral was never seen in the United States, not even at the death of Washington.

Shortly, Senator Wilson and I, on invitation, went to Secretary Blaine's home again. There was a bright "Good morning, Mr. Wilson," as the Secretary again entered the drawing-room. Seeing me, he walked across the room, took me by the hand and congratulated me on my reappointment. "Your name goes to the Senate this afternoon for St. Gall," he continued, "the post shall shortly be increased in rank, and you will be made Consul General for Switzerland." He offered me my old post at Zurich, however, if I preferred it. I never saw Mr. Blaine again.

CHAPTER XXX
1891

GO TO SWITZERLAND AS CONSUL GENERAL--AN OCEAN VOYAGE THEN AND NOW--A GLIMPSE OF BURNS' HOME--THE HIGHEST CITY IN EUROPE--A NOVEL REPUBLIC--LIFE IN THE HIGHER ALPS--HEADQUARTERS FOR EMBROIDERY--PRINCESS SALM SALM--AN OPEN AIR PARLIAMENT--THE UPPER RHINE--AT HAMBURG--A SUMMER ON THE BALTIC--INTERVIEW WITH PRINCE BISMARCK.

In a few weeks I was again in Switzerland; this time away up among the Alps, for St. Gall is the highest city of any importance in the world.

The sea voyage had been uneventful. The only lion among the passengers on the "City of New York" was Henry M. Stanley. His wife, a distinguished looking English lady, was with him.

April 10, 1891.--This is my fourteenth sea voyage on the Atlantic. What changes in ships since 1869! First-class steamers of that time are now all off on second-class lines to South America; or else they are at the bottom of the sea. Three that I crossed on have since gone down--"City of London," "Anglia," "Deutschland."

Yet aside from the added speed, the changes in ocean ships are not so favorable as we try to think them. True, the vessels are more palatial, but one can be just as seasick on a floating palace as on board a schooner. Besides, speed and a palace are poor recompense for the crowds that pack a modern ocean greyhound. Twenty years ago everybody knew everybody on shipboard, and many of the ship acquaintances became friends for life. Then, too, few of one's fellow passengers had ever been to Europe. There was all the joy of expectation that made the little crowd happy. Those who fly often across the Atlantic have small pleasure compared with the delight of those who long ago saw land for the first time after a long voyage.

The crowds, the blasé character of half the passengers, have robbed a sea voyage of most of its delights.

April 20.--We came straight from Liverpool to Scotland, and staid a week in Ayrshire at the old home of my wife's father.

- 263 -

"Clerkland," their old farm place, is there as good as it was centuries since, when presented by Mary Queen of Scots to Mary Livingstone, one of her maids of honor. It seems strange to read in the town register the name of every owner of the Gilmour home for three or four hundred years down to the present time. We do things differently in America, where we hardly know where our own fathers were born.

The old-fashioned graveyard back of the kirk at Stewarton, with its big brown granite slabs, confirms the town register. They are all there, save an occasional one who wandered beyond the sea and died among strangers. A pretty memorial window in the same kirk tells of John Gilmour, my wife's uncle, a young poet, called the Kirk White of Ayrshire, who took all the Glasgow University prizes, won fame, and died at nineteen.

We went to every spot near Ayr, made illustrious by the name of Burns--Bonny Doon, Kilmarnock, Ellisland, everywhere, and held in our hands the very Bible the poet gave to Highland Mary as they bade farewell forever, standing with hands clasped across a little brook.

Our friend and guide was Mr. McKee, the old Burns scholar and historian, who in his youth had known many of Burns' friends. He is a last link with the poet's day. He gave me a souvenir, his own book on Burns. I have kept it with one given me later at Edinburgh by a friend of Walter Scott, who had been an apprentice in the printing house where Walter Scott was a member. As a messenger for the poet, he carried his manuscripts from Abbotsford to Edinburgh, and the money for them back to Scott. He wrote his name in an early edition of "Marmion," and gave it to us.

St. Gall.

St. Gall, Switzerland, May Day, 1891.--The Consulate and our home is at 41 Museum Strasse. The duties here are five times what they were at Rome. The district sends forty million francs worth of laces and embroideries to New York in a single year, and a hundred million francs worth of goods are sent from the country at large. These are all invoiced and samples examined at the consulates, while to avoid frauds, copies of the sworn invoices are sent to the shipper, to the Custom House, and to the Treasury.

There is not another city situated like St. Gall in all the world. It has 40,000 people, and they live like a little kingdom to themselves, up here among the Alps. The customs of the people differ from everything else in Switzerland. The families are as clannish as the old Scots, and their ways of doing things almost as old as their mountains.

This land of St. Gall was once a Republic by itself, like Venice. Its history is half forgotten. Napoleon put an end to it after it had endured five hundred years.

It was modeled on the plan of some of the Greek states. Its founders had been readers of history, not politicians trying experiments. They had a good chance to govern wholly for themselves, and to be let alone. They were isolated in the heart of the beautiful Alps, and their valleys were three or four thousand feet above sea level. Mountain scenery of the finest description surrounded them everywhere, just as it does the land of their children to-day. A thousand feet below them, lay a beautiful and historic lake.

They had Burgomasters for Presidents, and it was purely a people's government. Its type exists in neighboring Appenzell even to-day. There the parliament meets in meadows, and the people pass laws by the showing of hands.

Wegelin, the famous historian of Frederick the Great, speaking of this forgotten government of St. Gall, says: "It is a Republic where a handful of virtuous citizens accomplish what the greatest monarchs fail in. They guard their state from disorder and revolution by the simple grace of homely virtues. An habitual honor prevails there as a happy instinct."

To the honor of the modern dwellers in the land of the old Republic, let it be said, the virtues of their ancestors have not been forgotten.

A great Italian traveler visited the little old Republic once, and I translate from a letter he wrote home. It is a novel letter: "The people of the St. Gall Republic are great traders and manufacturers, and are noted for their integrity. Weaving linen is their great industry. There are few failures in business, and cheating is a crime. The merchants and traders are mostly nobles. They travel when young and learn all languages. Flax is spun here to the fineness of a hair. The bleaching is wonderful, owing to the pure water of the Alps. The rich own many estates in the Rhine valley near by, and beautiful gardens are about the town. The taxes are small, but more than support the economical government. The surplus in the city treasury is loaned to citizens at low interest, to insure factories, house building, etc. Officers are held to terribly strict account. The blessings of heaven rest on the Republic as a reward for its charities, which are unbelievably great. No citizen is permitted to live in bitter distress. The people are extremely pious and the men appear in church (close by) several times a day, in white collars and black mantles, while women serve God only in black dresses."12

With some modifications as to taxes, church-going, etc., this Italian's letter would be a fair description of the people here to-day. The manufacturing industry of their fathers, in changed form, continues, and St. Gall is the first embroidery-making city of the world.

In its neighborhood, 30,000 people work at hand looms in their pleasant homes, making curtains, lace edgings, handkerchiefs--the delight of mankind. Great factories, working steam machines, are also filling the world's market with the same articles. Designing these beautiful articles has become a St. Gall fine art. Nature helps the artist here, for after a moist day and a cold night in winter, the pines of the forest, the hedge rows, the lawn trees and the vines put on a magnificence of frost work absolutely indescribable. Millions of forest pines, drooping with icicles, snow and frost, resemble an ocean of Christmas trees glinting in the sunlit gates of paradise.

The people of St. Gall, surrounded as they are, could not help but make things beautiful. That many have grown rich at it, and live in beautiful villas on the heights about the city, is not to be wondered at.

Sometimes, though, a high American tariff, or bitter competition elsewhere, make hard times for the common embroiderer whose wages are never high. This very winter starvation stares many of the makers of the beautiful things in the face, and a franc a day is the poor pittance for twelve hours' work. In better times even six francs are earned. Then the great shippers, who furnish the linen and cotton and silk to the peasants, and buy their embroideries from them, grow rich. St. Gall is full of rich people, and it is full of scholars and culture.

Once a year the city itself, at its own expense, gives all the schools a great festival and banquet on some high, green meadow. The sight of from five to ten thousand happy boys and girls, all in pretty costumes, bearing garlands and marching with banners and music, is not to be forgotten.

*****

The Sirocco or Foehn winds have been blowing for a week. Sunday, the fine town of Meyringen was burned up, seven hotels and three hundred houses. Nothing can save a town, once on fire, when this dry scorching wind blast is in the mountains. It is no longer believed to be a Sirocco, however, coming from the African desert, but a thing born of the changeful temperatures in the mountains. It is a disagreeable freak of nature, and half the people are ill when the Foehn wind blows. But it brings the mountains out in added grandeur, everything seems nearer, snow fields and lofty mountains forty miles away seem but five miles off. Their distinctness then is marvelous, their beauty tenfold.

*****

The scenery everywhere about St. Gall is purely Alpine. The "Rosenberg," a long, low mountain close by, is lined with magnificent villas; nothing like it elsewhere in the world. Back of these villas, far below them, but still in view, is the Lake of Constance. In front of them, deep in the valley, sits the city, while beyond the valley rise the glorious mountains. Nature and man have combined here to make everything beautiful. The people are kind and hospitable, more so than elsewhere in Switzerland. Evenings, we are often invited out to homes where the characteristic St. Gall life is enjoyable.

Many a time we have climbed up the Apfelberg to the homes of Swiss friends. Sylvester evenings, Christmas evenings, and the like, are celebrated by family reunions, sparkling Christmas trees and great dinners. Wine flows like water and the fatted Nüremberg goose takes the place of the American turkey. A circle is formed around the Christmas tree and all join hands and dance, father, mother, sister, brother, friends and servants. As at the country houses in England, for once, servants and master are on a footing. Everybody taking part gets his present.

On summer evenings the young ladies of the house sometimes place by our plates at supper wild Alpine roses that grew in their own garden. Possibly not another spot in the world, where fine modern homes and Alpine roses are side by side.

The view of the illuminated city at night from these high villas, is grand beyond any fireworks ever conceived. On festive occasions, fires are built on the sides of the opposite mountains, or Bengal lights burn on villa lawns high up beyond the valley, when the scene reveals all our imagined pictures of fairyland.

The Americans, together with the Minister and Consuls in Switzerland, celebrated the Fourth of July at the hotel "Baur au Lac" in Zurich. Minister Washburn presided. Many were present. The day before, I had sent cowboys into the higher Alps about St. Gall, to gather Alpine roses for the occasion. They brought me bushels of them, and the chief decoration of the table at the banquet was a solid pyramid of Alpine roses ten feet high.

Few American tourists visit St. Gall, but many New York importers have agents and factories here. There is a constant business rivalry between them and the Swiss.

One of the interesting people who came to us this summer was Princess Salm Salm. She has her home at Bonn on the Rhine. She is one of the most beautiful women to be met anywhere. A kind heart has kept her young. She is one of the few Americans who married foreign titles and were happy. It was a love match--not a buying of a bride. Her life has been one of extraordinary interest. Her husband, a German Prince on General Bleeker's staff in our Civil War, fell in love with the young beauty at Washington, married her, and when the war was done took her with him to Mexico, where he was a high officer on the staff of the Emperor Maximilian. Like the Emperor, he was sentenced to be shot. His young wife, by extraordinary cleverness and great exertion, saved his life. History now relates how the Emperor's life would have been saved also, had he followed this clever woman's plans. All was arranged for his escape. The Emperor hesitated and was lost. The Prince and Princess went to Germany, where her beauty, talents and rank, brought her friends among the great people of the country. She and her husband were favorites of the King of Prussia. When the war with France broke out the Prince was an officer in the Fourth Guards, or the Queen's Own regiment. His wife was one of the titled women of Germany who labored in the army hospitals. The Prince was shot dead while leading his command at Gravelotte. The Princess remained, helping the wounded to the end of the war. A more fascinating book than her story of her life in three wars, I have not read. Many novels have this interesting woman for their heroine.

*****

Mer de Glace, Chamouny.

Last week, five of us, including my son, started to climb up the Saentis, the highest mountain in the vicinity. We began the ascent late. Storm and darkness coming on, we lost our way. Half the night was spent up there, creeping about on ice and stones. At last we stood still and yelled all together. We were heard at the little weather hut on top of the mountain at last, and the guides came down with dogs and lanterns and helped us out of our dilemma. We were all well used up, and as for myself, I received an injury that I may never get rid of. We got home next day, and were off the mountains just in time to escape a great snowfall that will bury the path till next year.

*****

General Sherman's daughter, Mrs. Thackera, paid us a long visit, as did our old friends, the Edmundsons and Frankels.

Together we made excursions, notably to *"The Little Land of Appenzell,"* described so beautifully by Bayard Taylor. We went to the meeting of the people's parliament--a strange spectacle. All the peasants came, wearing swords as signs of their right to vote. It was a mass meeting in the open air. Ten to fifteen thousand voters stood and voted on the laws of the canton. These laws, proposed by the outgoing officials, had been printed and distributed in the farmhouses weeks before. These officials in old-time garb now stood before the people on a raised platform. There was no discussion at the mass meeting. "Do you want this law--yes or no?" said the President, and that was all there was to it. In two hours' time new laws had been adopted. The canton officials went through the ceremony of transferring their state mantles to the shoulders of the newly elected officers. Then the vast crowd were asked to bare their heads, hold up their right hands and swear new allegiance to the Republic. When that packed mass of humanity turned their faces to the sun, and held up ten thousand brown hands, it was the most impressive scene one can imagine. They meant it. The vast mountains stood around and looked on in silence. Far below we could see the broad lake shining like a sea of silver. When the oath was over, the bands played, and the peasant lawmakers returned in silence to their homes. There had not been a single disturbance, not a rude, loud word.

For hundreds of years this simple people of Appenzell have met and made their laws in this way, and, as a historian said of the old Republic of St. Gall, "They guard their state from disorder and revolution by the simple grace of homely virtues."

*****

September, 1891.--The six hundredth anniversary of the founding of the Swiss Republic has now been celebrated--the most unique celebration possibly the world ever saw. Three million people took part in it. Every man, woman and child in Switzerland understood the significance of the festival, and contributed to its glory. On every mountain top joy fires burned, in every valley the bells rang paeans of liberty. On top of the mighty peak of the Mythen, in sight of the spot where independence was declared, stood a flaming cross of fire, fifty feet across and a hundred feet high. It shone like a beacon light to a million witnesses, who saw it from the heights near and far, over all the Alps. Illuminations shone in every hamlet, even to the edges of the snow fields and glaciers. For days Te Deums sounded, masses were said, and a whole people gave thanks for five hundred years of liberty. The usual vocations of men in the Republic came to a standstill, so that employer and employed, high and low, rich and poor, could participate in the dramatic rehearsal of the country's history. Near the town of Schwyz, where Swiss liberty was born, a vast stage and amphitheater were erected, where amid the applause of multitudes the whole panorama of Swiss history was reenacted with all the splendor of costume and scenic effect of past ages. Once more William Tell, Arnold Winkelried and Stauffacher with all the old Swiss heroes, walked among the people, in sight of the very lakes and mountains that had witnessed their heroic deeds. The great museums were emptied of their historic arms and banners, and Morgarten and Sempach were fought over again with the same hellebards, morgensterns and battle axes that had been used in the dreadful encounters of centuries ago. The blood stains of the ancient heroes were still upon their blades, and the descendants of the Swiss martyrs for liberty, counting the cost, stood as ready to die for their country as did ever the men who founded freedom among the Alps.

*****

The river Rhine is close by us here, flowing through Lake Constance. Every day in summer sees crowds of the St. Gallese rushing down to the lake by train, to bathe in its waters. The ride down there, with its glimpses of mountain valleys, blooming orchards, and shining waterfalls, is one of the most picturesque in Europe. Down by the water side are villages and walls old as the time of the Romans.

The little valleys and the plains between St. Gall and the lake, are planted with hundreds of pear orchards. In the spring, when this ocean of pear trees is in full white blossom, the ride down to the lake is truly wonderful.

*****

Spelterini is here with his big balloon, to take people traveling above the mountain tops. Some of our friends went up for a few hours, repeatedly, and pronounce the view of the lake, mountain and valley as seen from the sky, something wonderful. He charges 200 francs for a few hours' ride among the mist and clouds. He passed close above our house yesterday morning at a great rate. He has made a thousand ascents and never had an accident. Riding with his balloon at a height of 15,000 feet, and at an express speed is safer than riding on American railroads.

May 13, 1893.--News has come of the appointment of a new Consul General for Switzerland. The rotating machine has been put to work. I scarcely dare to complain.

A new administration at Washington can remove me from office, but it cannot take away from me the pleasure of the past years. Still I have lived so long among the delightful scenes of Switzerland I leave them with a pang.

"*Aufwiedersehen*," our friends call out as they throw us their roses, the train moves, we are looking for the last time possibly on the mountains.

Part of this summer of 1893 we spent with our friends, the Witts, at Hamburg, and then together we went to the Island of Rügen in the Baltic Sea, where many delightful weeks among novel scenes were ending our stay in Europe.

Later, our friends offered to take us to see Prince Bismarck, at his home at "Friedrichsruhe."

A couple of hours' ride from Hamburg through an uninteresting country of sand and pine trees, brought us to the little station not far from the ex-Chancellor's house. It seemed like a villa stuck away in the woods of North Carolina, yet delegations find this hidden spot from every corner of Germany, and come here by trainfuls, to do homage to the man who made the empire. He is a greater man here on his farm than the Emperor is in Berlin on his throne. There is not much about the rather ill-kept looking estate to attract attention. There are a thousand handsomer estates all over Germany.

We wait, as directed, under the trees behind the castle (though it is no castle at all) for pretty soon the great man will come down the garden walk. Miss Witt, who has an enormous bouquet of flowers for him (she has given him flowers before), will approach him first, and then the rest of us. There come his two big Danish dogs down the path now. In a moment they are followed by a powerful looking old man who carries a big club of a cane, and wears a great slouch hat of felt. He knows what the young lady and the flowers mean very quickly, and his strong, marked face is soon in smiles. We are all presented. I speak to him in English, but he says, "Please speak German. There was a time when I spoke English, but that is almost gone." I looked at him closely, when others were talking. His great, wrinkled, seamed face looked as powerful as his herculean frame. I could not help thinking to myself, here stands the man who overthrew Louis Napoleon, and here is he who once ruefully said, "The lives of eighty thousand human beings would have been saved were it not for me."

He had a few kind words for all of us, and Madame Semper he remembered well. But he was getting old, and seemed on the point of feebleness; his great race was done. His dogs rubbed against his legs and looked at us as if they wanted us to stay away from their master. Shortly he lifted his great broad hat, saying: "My wife is waiting for me at breakfast. I bid you good-day." Then he turned and walked back to the castle. We had seen Bismarck.

FOOTNOTES

1 "Switzerland and the Swiss."

2 A detailed description of the incidents of the adventure within the lines of the enemy appeared in the Atlantic Monthly, May, 1880, and is repeated in Mr. Byers' "Last Man of the Regiment."

3 Note.--The second edition of this book was printed under my own name. It is the volume from which Boyd Winchester, in his "Swiss Republic," borrowed so astoundingly, later, forgetting both my name, and the common use all but literary burglars make of quotation marks. Hepworth Dixon, though dead, and un-named, lives on in the book of Mr. Winchester in the same manner.

4 Details of this incident are related in Mr. Byers' "Last Man of the Regiment."

5 It was almost his last public performance.

6 This boy, Hamilton Fish, grew to manhood, and was the first American soldier killed for his country on Cuban soil.

7 The State Department also sent me a letter later, thanking me for my zeal. The publicity I gave to the outrages going on, has also led the Swiss Parliament to change its regulations as to immigration, while our own Congress has adopted severe measures against the traffic in paupers and criminals.

8 At last Mr. Sargent, tired and disgusted with the situation, resigned his post.

9 Harper's Magazine No. 477.

10 This refers to the Century Co.'s "Battles and Leaders of the Civil War," for which Mr. Byers was also invited to contribute his article describing Sherman's Assault at Missionary Ridge, in which he was a participant.

11 A few evenings before, Secretary Windom had dropped dead while addressing a company of banqueters in New York.

> 12 A detailed sketch by me of this remarkable little Republic, appeared in Magazine of American History, December, 1891.

Milton Keynes UK
Ingram Content Group UK Ltd.
UKHW030903151124
451262UK00006B/1050